450

Below: An amtrac tows a disabled DUKW ashore on Iwo beach. (USMC)

ACROSS THE REEF

The Amphibious Tracked Vehicle at War

VICTOR J. CROIZAT
Colonel, U.S. Marine Corps, (ret.)

BLANDFORD

Jacket: *Landing exercises being conducted at Camp Pendleton.*

Back of Jacket, Top: *Amtracs jammed with the initial assault force of 4th Division Marines churn towards Iwo Jima at H-Hour. (USMC)*

Bottom: *Authorized fraternization with the enemy. Marine Staff Sergeant Federico Claveria passes candy to a child through the barbed wire fence of a Tinian internment camp. (USMC)*

Published in Great Britain
in 1989 by Arms and Armour Press, Artillery House,
Artillery Row, London SW1P 1RT.

Distributed in the USA by Sterling Publishing Co. Inc.,
2 Park Avenue, New York, NY 10016.

Distributed in Australia by
Capricorn Link (Australia) Pty. Ltd, P.O. Box 665,
Lane Cove, New South Wales 2066, Australia.

British Library Cataloguing in Publication Data:
Croizat, Victor J.
Across the reef
1. United States. Military forces. Amphibious
combat vehicles, 1941–1986
I. Title
623.74'75
ISBN 0-7137-1894-3

Designed and edited by DAG Publications Ltd.
Edited by Michael Boxall; designed by David Gibbons;
layout by Anthony A. Evans; typesetting by Typesetters
(Birmingham) Ltd; camerawork by M&E Reproductions, North
Fambridge, Essex; printed and bound in Great Britain
by Mackays of Chatham PLC, Letchworth

Contents

Preface

THE amphibious assaults that swept over the reef-bound islands of the central Pacific in World War II represented the culmination of five decades of reflection, planning, and experimentation that made the United States Marine Corps masters of amphibious warfare.

America's opponent in the near four-year conflict was Japan. Until the mid-nineteenth century Japan had been a backward, feudal island nation. During the fifty years that followed it had become the strongest country in Asia. Then, through its participation in World War I, it had extended its domain deep into the central Pacific to gain a place among the world's five great powers.

The vigor with which Japan modernized was admirable. The aggressiveness that accompanied the effort, however, alarmed the United States and introduced the possibility of eventual war. This alarm encouraged the Marine Corps, already at grips with the problem of securing and defending advanced naval bases, to broaden its interests in the more general field of amphibious warfare. In so doing, it worked closely with the Navy to develop the techniques of ship-to-shore operations and acquire the resources needed for that purpose.

Most significant in this effort, was the appearance of the reef-crossing amphibian tractor without which, in the words of Marine General Holland M. (Howling Mad) Smith, "our amphibious offensive in the Pacific would have been impossible".[1] These sentiments were reinforced by the British military historian, Major-General J. F. C. Fuller, who added his view that the tracked landing vehicle was ". . . the most far-reaching innovation of the [second world] war".[2]

Across The Reef tells the story of this strange vehicle as it makes its way out of the swamps of Florida to the islands of the Pacific. There, at the beginning of World War II, the amphibian tractor first features in minor logistic roles at Guadalcanal and gains in importance as the Allies make their way up the New Guinea coast and the Solomon Islands chain. Then, at the end of 1943, the vehicle appears at Tarawa in the central Pacific in a new tactical role which establishes the amphibian tractor as an indispensable complement to the amphibious assault operation.

The principal perspective of *Across The Reef*, is that of the Marine Corps. However, reference also is made to major related U.S. Army operations and to the much more limited utilization of amphibian tractors in the European Theater of Operations. This is followed by brief commentaries on the employment of these vehicles in the Korean, Indochinese and Vietnamese Wars. The story concludes its fifty-year span with a summary report of the amphibious operation today and of the principal landing ships and craft involved – including the latest model amphibian assault vehicle and its continuing development.

Acknowledgements

A CROSS THE REEF is the story of the Pacific War as seen by the Marines of the amphibian tractor units. An effort is also made to note the role of LVTs in the European area during World War II, touch on the activities of Marine amtrac units in later wars and end with a status report on where the amphibian vehicle stands today. With such a broad scope, it is inevitable that much of the story is left untold. That is certainly not the fault of the many persons who facilitated my work and added from their own experience information which helped fill blank places in the record.

I wish first to acknowledge the assistance of those who served in the amtrac units of World War II and were the innovators who helped develop the techniques for the employment of these vehicles. At the head of the list is Lieutenant General Louis Metzger who commanded the first LVT(A)1 unit in combat in the Marshalls and was largely responsible for the eventual employment of the gun-mounting amtracs as self-propelled artillery. Then there are a number of Marine Colonels who commanded different amtrac battalions in the difficult campaigns of the central and western Pacific. These include John I. Fitzgerald, Victor J. Harwick, John T. O'Neill, Daniel J. Regan, Albert F. Reutlinger and Eugene A. Seigel. The list must also include the senior non-commissioned officers, notably Master Sergeant John J. Morgan and Sergeant Major Ralph J. Fletcher who kept the young enthusiastic officers from going too far astray, and such lower ranks as Jack F. Tracy who took off for Yap and ended at Leyte and John F. Sullivan who didn't get ashore at Guadalcanal but had some adventures on other islands.

Particular thanks are also due to Brigadier General Edwin H. Simmons, Director of the Marine Corps Historical Center; Colonel F. Brooke Nihart, Director of Marine Corps Museums; and Henry I. Shaw, Chief Historian, who gave of their time and made staff and facilities available to pursue research of documents, maps and photographs. Assistance in photo search was also provided by John G. Miller, Managing Editor and Patty M. Maddocks, librarian of the Naval Institute Proceedings and of John E. Greenwood, editor of the *Marine Corps Gazette*.

Most pleasant was to renew acquaintance with Clarence G. Taylor, one of the engineers of the Food Machinery Corporation, who became involved with the LVT program in its earliest days, and through him get to meet James L. Carter, Manager of FMC Marketing Services, and be put in contact with Albert H. Campbell, the present FMC historian.

The Marines at the Boat Basin in Camp Pendleton were most kind in making data available on current activities and trends. In this regard Lieutenant Colonel Donald A. Gressly and Lieutenant Colonel Richard E. Dietmeier were most helpful as was Lieutenant Colonel Don Head. John Wilson in the U.S. Army

Center of Military History provided information on the Army's amphibian tractor units, as did Mr. Thomas F. Edwards. and Mr. Edward Kitchens. Dr. Eugene Alvarez and retired Marine Colonel Hollis Dunn added useful material on Korea and Vietnam. Note also must be taken of a thesis entitled *Alligators, Buffaloes and Bushmasters*, prepared by Major Alfred D. Bailey USMC (retired), published as an "occasional paper" by the Marine Corps Historical Center, which contains a most interesting narrative of the history of the amphibian tractor and its employment in the Pacific campaigns. The map sketches are based upon materials included in official files and publications available at the Marine Corps Historical Center.

Finally, the contribution of Meda Fletcher Croizat as advisor, editor and partner is noted with sincere appreciation.

Below: U.S.S. Colorado, *Flagship of the U.S. Asiatic Fleet, 1871. Captain McLane Tilton (right), U.S. Marine Corps, with Corporal Brown and Private Purvis seen alongside the Korean Headquarters flag captured during the attacks on Salee River Forts, Korea, on 10 and 11 June 1871. Captain Tilton and his Marines led the advances and the assault on the forts during which Brown and Purvis won the Medal of Honor. (USMC)*

1. Globe, Anchor and Rising Sun

Japan in the Pacific; the Marines and amphibious war

T O the American aviators serving in the Lafayette Escadrille during World War I, the idyllic islands of the Pacific represented the ultimate contrast to the brutality of the war on the Western Front.[1] Regrettably, within less than a generation the new world war which again engulfed Europe extended its savagery to the far Pacific.

The romantic view of the great ocean that prevailed early in this century was compounded of myth and legend fostered by remoteness. It could not endure beyond the war between America and Japan. The U.S. Marine Corps, whose own history reaches into the realm of legend, began to uncover the reality of the Pacific in the last century and went on to gain its greatest renown when that vast ocean area became a theater of war in the early 1940s.

The myths and legends of the Pacific began some 20,000 years ago with the migrations that peopled its islands. Reality for the western world began in 1520 when Magellan first entered upon those waters and went on to meet an untimely death in the Philippines. The period of exploration which began with the Portuguese navigator ended with the Englishman, James Cook, who in three voyages beginning in 1769 mapped what remained unknown of Oceania. Thenceforth, the way was open for traders, missionaries and settlers.[2]

As these invaders spread over the islands, they engendered conflicts which, most often, ended in annexation. The pattern began in 1842 when the French established themselves in the Marquesas and Tahiti. It ended in 1900, by which time the whole of Oceania had been fragmented into territories ruled by the United States, British Commonwealth and European powers, among which imperial Germany was notably enterprising. The Germans had moved into Samoa in 1857, acquired New Guinea in 1873, and occupied the Marshall Islands in 1899. Soon after they purchased the Palaus, Marianas and Carolines from Spain. But, with the outbreak of World War I, Australia took German New Guinea, New Zealand assumed control of German Samoa, and Japan came into possession of Germany's remaining holdings.

The course followed by Japan to the coral islands of the central Pacific was long and tortuous. It began in the middle of the troubled sixteenth century when a storm-driven Portuguese ship appeared in Japanese waters. The incident led to the opening of trade with Europe and the arrival of Jesuit missionaries. The presence of these aliens at first brought a welcome vision of a wondrous western world, but, in time, the intrusion became an irritant. Missionary activity was curtailed in 1612; by 1635 no Japanese were allowed to go abroad, and in 1637

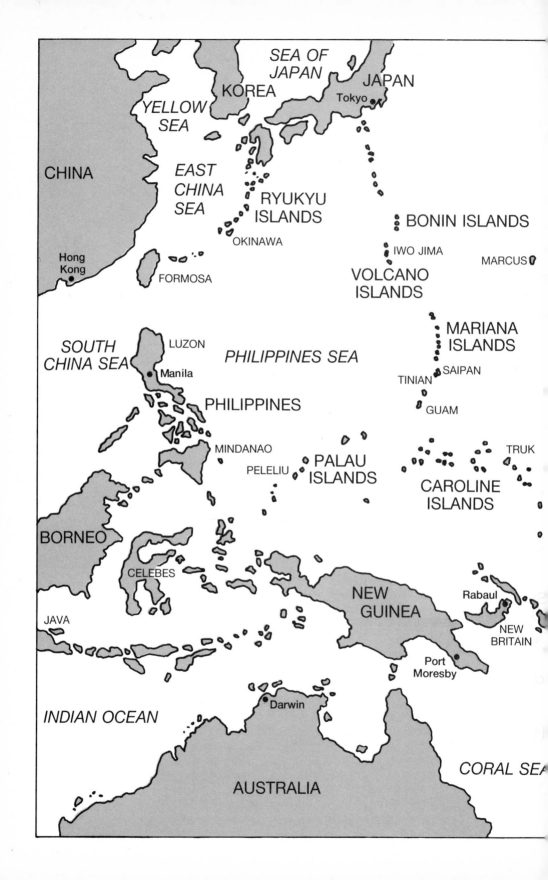

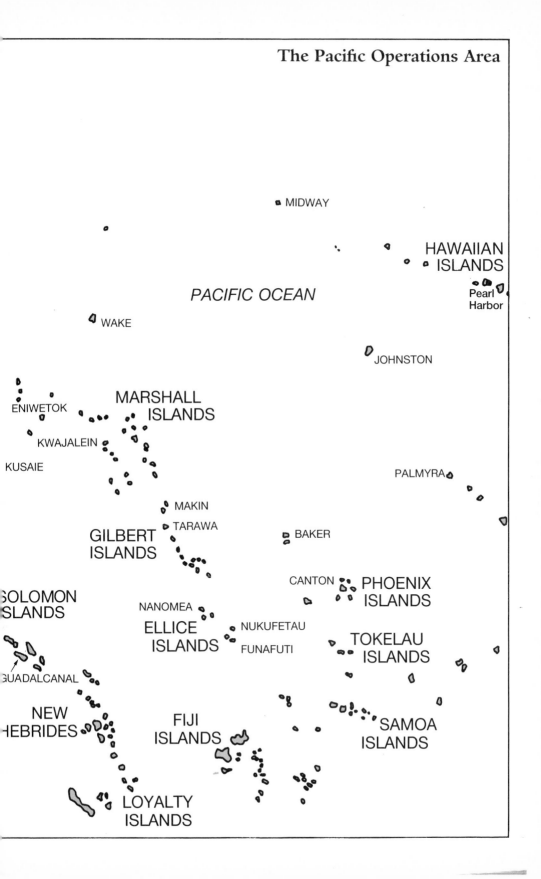

The Pacific Operations Area

MIDWAY

HAWAIIAN
ISLANDS

Pearl
Harbor

PACIFIC OCEAN

WAKE

JOHNSTON

MARSHALL
ISLANDS

ENIWETOK

KWAJALEIN

KUSAIE

PALMYRA

MAKIN

TARAWA

BAKER

GILBERT
ISLANDS

CANTON

PHOENIX
ISLANDS

SOLOMON
ISLANDS

NANOMEA

ELLICE
ISLANDS

NUKUFETAU

FUNAFUTI

TOKELAU
ISLANDS

GUADALCANAL

NEW
HEBRIDES

FIJI
ISLANDS

SAMOA
ISLANDS

LOYALTY
ISLANDS

the country was closed to all foreigners. Only the Chinese and the Dutch were allowed to maintain a discreet presence in Nagasaki. Japan remained isolated from the rest of the world for the next two centuries.[3]

That situation continued until 8 July 1853 when the American Commodore Matthew C. Perry arrived in Tokyo Bay bearing a letter from President Fillmore. When Perry returned for a reply in 1854 he obtained a treaty opening two Japanese ports to American ships. The British, French and Russians quickly followed so that by 1859 Yokohama, Nagasaki and Hakodate were opened to foreign commerce. A year later a Japanese mission visited the United States. Soon after, the Meiji government came to power and the modernization of Japan began in earnest.

The effort required to convert a divided feudal country into a modern industrial state was monumental. It began in 1867 with the dispatch of young Japanese to study abroad and the invitation of qualified westerners to come to Japan and help in its development. This was accompanied by a reorganization of the government, the promulgation of the Constitution of 1889, and the creation of a military establishment to support Japan's rapidly growing international interests. These last were manifested first in 1874, when Japan sent a punitive expedition to Formosa. Five years later the Ryukyus were incorporated into Japan. Then, in 1894, Japan was strong enough to challenge China in a war in which it gained control over Formosa and the Pescadore Islands and of the Liaotung Peninsula on the mainland.

The Europeans, busy consolidating their positions in China, were not willing to allow Japan to share in the process and forced Japan to relinquish its hold over the Liaotung Peninsula. Soon after, the rebellious Boxers went on a rampage in China. Bent on ending all foreign presence in their country, the Boxers stormed across north China as the century ended. By mid-1900 they had swept to within sight of the foreign settlements in Peking and Tientsin. Urgent calls went out for help. While beleaguered detachments, including a handful of American Marines and sailors, held fast in those two cities, an international relief force was hastily assembled. The force of 17,000 men from eight nations, including the 1st Marine Regiment and the 9th U.S. Infantry together with a well-disciplined Japanese contingent, eventually prevailed over the Boxers and Chinese imperial forces. The American reinforcements soon departed, but the Russians, who had used the occasion to move into Manchuria, remained. The British, concerned over this move and appreciative of Japan's exemplary conduct during the uprising, agreed to an alliance with Japan. This, formalized in 1902, gave the Japanese a free hand to deal with the Russians, whose presence in Manchuria was seen by Japan as a threat to its interests in Korea.

When the Russians failed to leave Manchuria as agreed, the Japanese at first sought to encourage their departure by diplomatic means. When these failed, the Japanese attacked Russian fleet units. In the war that followed, Japan defeated Russia and in 1905 gained control over all Russian concessions in China and the southern half of Sakhalin Island. The way was thus paved for Japan's annexation of Korea four years later. In this manner, by the end of the Meiji period in 1912, Japan had become the foremost military power in Asia.[4]

While Japan was establishing its primacy in the Far East, the United States fought a brief war with Spain in which it freed Cuba and acquired Puerto Rico,

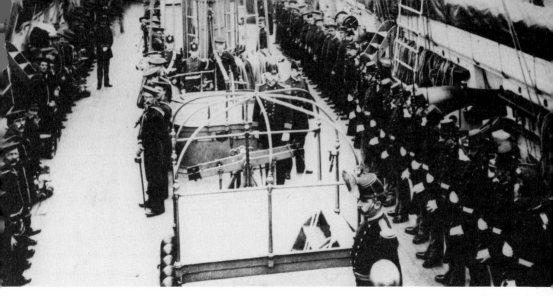

Above: *All hands to muster!*
U.S.S. Enterprise. *(USMC)*

Right: *Marine detachment on
the U.S.S.* Portsmouth, *1885.
(USMC)*

Right: *U.S. Marines and
Seamen in the ruins of Fort
Monocacy, Korea, which they
captured on 10–11 June 1871
after heavy fighting. (USMC)*

Above: *In March 1899 tribal war broke out in Samoa and on 1 April twenty U.S. Marines under First Lieutenant Constantine M. Perkins joined 36 U.S. Sailors and 62 British Marines in a landing. The column was promptly attacked on its flanks and rear as it moved inland. The Americans took nine casualties in the withdrawal and three Marines received the Medal of Honor covering the action. This photograph shows the Marine detachment from the U.S.S.* Philadelphia, *which participated in the operation; Lieutenant Perkins is in the white uniform and the civilians are the wife and son of the American consul at Apia. (USMC)*

Guam and the Philippines. The United States had already annexed the Hawaiian Islands and would soon occupy Wake Island. This new status as a Pacific power magnified existing American interests in Far East markets, notably those of China. But these were rapidly being closed as Japan and the Europeans established their spheres of interest there. To offset these restrictive actions, the United States proposed and gained acceptance of an "open door" policy wherein the interested powers accorded equal rights and investment opportunities to all nationals in their respective spheres.

Japan entered World War I as an ally and promptly occupied Germany's holdings in China and its islands in Micronesia. These and other actions extended Japan's presence abroad while, at home, Japanese industry and commerce enjoyed unprecedented prosperity. By the end of the war, Japan had gained a place among the world's five great powers and a permanent seat on the Council of the League of Nations. President Wilson, disturbed at Japan's stature and presence in China, sought a means to lessen that aggressive country's influence.

This was accomplished at the Washington Conference of 1921 in which Japan agreed to return the territory it held in China and replace its treaty with Britain by a Four Power Treaty which included France and the United States and called for consultation on problems of concern arising in the Far East and the Pacific. Japan also accepted a Five Power Treaty in which the ratio of capital ships was set at 10:10:6:3:3 for the United States, Great Britain, Japan, France and Italy respectively. The United States and Great Britain, in turn, agreed not to improve their naval facilities in the Philippines and Hong Kong.

By the mid-1920s Japan, as a recognized world power, appeared disposed to co-operate with the west, but this situation changed abruptly with the economic disasters that ended the decade. The Japanese, whose well-being depended largely on international trade, suffered heavily in the worldwide depression. This made them increasingly receptive to advocates of military conquest as the only road to economic solvency. Japanese expansionism, already a matter of long-standing concern was thus given fresh impetus.

The United States Marine Corps had been witness to much of Japan's modern history. Six officers and 200 men of the Corps, under Major Jacob Zeilin, were aboard the four ships of Commodore Perry's squadron that visited Japan in 1853. In the years that followed, Marines from American ships in Far Eastern waters participated in a host of actions. In 1856, they joined in the attack of four forts covering the river approaches to Canton. In 1867, a ship's detachment with 43 Marines went ashore on Formosa to punish the murderers of a shipwrecked American crew. One year later, Marines went ashore at Osaka and Yokohama to protect foreigners menaced by local Japanese. Then, in 1871, after another shipwrecked crew had been massacred by Koreans, a punitive landing force of 650 sailors and Marines went ashore and reduced a major fort on the Han River. The Marines were back in Korea in 1894, this time to guard the American legation in Seoul from possible incidents arising from the Sino-Japanese War.[5]

These actions though often bloody, were brief forays carried out by ships' detachments. This pattern of small unit actions continued. But, with the new century, situations arose in which substantial Marine Corps forces were committed in operations for extended periods of time. One of the earliest of these occurred in the Philippines. The decision to annex these islands, confirmed in 1899, precipitated a revolt which opposed 40,000 insurgents to 14,000 U.S. soldiers. Despite the contrary odds, the Americans succeeded in gaining control over the urban centers. However, they failed to destroy the rebels who faded into the countryside whence they began a guerrilla war. Soon after, Marines were sent to the Philippines. By the end of 1899 there were three battalions of Marines deployed there and other units were being prepared to follow.

Shortly before the New Year, however, the Boxer Rebellion was approaching its climax and all plans for the Philippines had to be set aside to make forces available to help protect the foreign settlements in Peking and Tientsin. By early fall the situation in China had been restored and the 1st Marine Regiment was moved to the Philippines. There it brought the Marines' strength to 1,600 men and enabled the formation of a brigade to provide security for the naval bases at Subic Bay and Cavite. After March 1901, when the Filipino leader Aguinaldo was

Above: Marines of the 1st Brigade on long-range patrol in the Olangapo area of the Philippines in 1903. (USMC)

Left: Marines manning outposts in the Shanghai area in 1937. (USMC)

captured, the rebellion wound down. The Marine contingents were gradually reduced and by 1914, the brigade was disbanded.

On the Asian mainland, meanwhile, the defeat of the Boxers had not brought peace. Turmoil continued and even intensified towards 1911, when a revolution brought down the Manchu dynasty. This prompted the landing of Marine detachments at Hankow and Shanghai and the dispatch of a battalion to Peking. These reinforcements were progressively withdrawn as the unrest lessened with the accession of Sun Yat Sen as president in 1921. But, Sun Yat Sen died in 1925 and a new period of strife began when Chiang Kai Shek assumed command of the Nationalist Army.

The 1920s was a decade of uncertainty and unrest during which warlords, revolutionaries, nationalists and communists struggled for power. The chaos, accompanied by anti-foreign sentiment, sorely tried the Marine detachments dispatched from one trouble spot to another. The most important of these moves occurred in 1927 when Chiang moved against Shanghai and four companies of Marines from Guam were landed in that city to safeguard the International Settlement. These troops were followed by the 4th Marine Regiment destined to remain in Shanghai for the next fourteen years, during which it seasoned seven young officers who were to become Commandants of the Corps.

The years that followed were the good years for the China Marines. Those were the times when privates had servants, the Horse Marines added color to the ceremonial routine, and the Far East appeared at its most exotic. But, in September 1931 the Japanese took over Manchuria and a new period of troubles began. The remaining years of the decade only intensified the unrest. The contest between Chiang Kai Shek's Nationalist Army and the Chinese Communists, whose party had been formed in 1921, facilitated Japanese expansion. By 1936, two years after the Communists had broken through the Nationalists and begun their Long March to the remote northwest, Chiang was forced to end his domestic struggle to allow China to unite and direct its efforts against the Japanese invader who was about to renew hostilities. In 1937 the Japanese were again on the march. They pursued their war against the Chinese with vigor and little concern for the interests of the other powers in China. They sank the U.S.S. *Panay* on the Yangtze River and repeatedly fired on American facilities. For the Marines, the stage was being set for a repeat of the events of 1932 when the Japanese had first approached Shanghai. Now, five years later, the Japanese were back, and the Marines again set up defenses on Soochow creek to deny access to the International Settlement.

In October the Japanese landed north of the city and forced the Chinese to retreat. They did not, however, approach the International Settlement but went on to take Nanking, Hankow and Canton. The Nationalist government, forced to fall back, finally sought refuge in far-away Chungking. The Chinese armies, now isolated from the coast, could only be supplied over long land routes from Indochina and Burma.

The war which erupted in Europe in 1939 was soon to make the Marines' situation in China even more precarious than it had been. The collapse of France in 1940 gave the Japanese the opportunity to force France to allow them entry into Vietnam and the British to close the port of Rangoon to military supplies for China. This would serve to seal off China from external sources of supply. But, the United States, exasperated by years of Japanese aggression, was determined to oppose such a situation. It froze Japanese assets in the United States and placed an embargo on shipments of metal scrap and petroleum to Japan. This confronted the Japanese militarists with the alternative of withdrawal or war. By 1941, the course to Pearl Harbor had been set.

In China, despite the evident deterioration of relations between the United States and Japan, the decision to withdraw the 4th Marines was not made until 10 November 1941. It was the Corps' 166th anniversary, but scarcely an occasion for celebration. The embarkation, completed on 28 November, brought to an end the epic story of the China Marines.

Until its war with Spain, the United States had had limited interest in the Far East and even less concern over any possible threat from that remote region. When that war had ended, the United States found itself a Pacific power with responsibility for the Philippines, some 7,000 miles from its west coast, and a growing concern over Japanese designs in Asia.

This expanded role led the United States to establish the Joint Army and Navy Board in 1903 to undertake, among other duties, the preparation of war plans identified by a country color code. Priority attention in this effort was given to a war with Japan, which had continued to demonstrate a disturbing aggressiveness after its victory over Russia in 1904. The development of Plan Orange, however, proved more difficult than anticipated because of differences between the Army and Navy over the defense of the Philippines. As a result, little was accomplished until after the reorganization of the Board in 1919. By that time the strategic problem had been further complicated by the establishment of Japan in the central Pacific. This ensured that in the event of war the Japanese

Left: *Marines manning 3in guns aboard U.S.S. Pennsylvania in 1919. It had become the custom during the Civil War for Marine gun crews to man certain shipboard guns. This has continued into modern times. (USMC)*

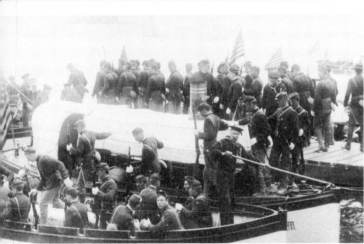

Left: *Marines embarking in boats for landing exercises off Hampton Roads, Virginia, 1890. (USMC)*

Below: *Gunboats in the background bombard San Fabian in the Philippines while Marines in whale boats form up behind steam launches for towing to the beach. (USMC)*

would be able to concentrate forces in the Philippines area more rapidly than the Americans, but this evidence was unacceptable to the planners since it would force the United States to acknowledge that the Philippines could not be held. Accordingly, this critical issue was not addressed in the Orange Plan finally approved on 16 July 1924. The Plan subsequently underwent modification but remained of questionable value. It lessened further in importance as Europe moved towards war and the United States shifted to the preparation of "Rainbow Plans" concerned with coalition warfare.[6]

The war with Spain also had far-reaching consequences for the Marine Corps. The transition from sail to steam had made the Navy dependent on coaling stations, which, as long as ships remained in home waters, could be readily provided. However, when at the turn of the century the interests of the United States became increasingly international, the acquisition of overseas bases became essential. This involved not only such permanent bases as Hawaii, but also advance naval bases such as would be required for the support of combat operations overseas. Neither the Army nor the Navy had forces available to commit to this task. As for the Marines, they were a small organization with little relevant experience and even fewer resources.

The matter was settled in the four-month long "splendid little war" when a Marine battalion under Lieutenant Colonel Robert W. Huntington went ashore in whaleboats and cutters towed by steam launches at Guantanamo Bay, Cuba to establish an advance naval base there. That was a relatively minor affair, but it was carried out in a professional manner and was well attended by the press. Added recognition came later when Admiral Dewey declared that had he had such a force he could have seized Manila and prevented the insurrection that would occupy the United States for three years. Whatever the merits of these considerations, after the Spanish-American War the Marines were charged with the advance base mission. This led to the establishment of the Advance Base Force which later became the Expeditionary Force and finally evolved into the Fleet Marine Force with which the Marines went on to meet the Japanese.[7]

Right: Officers of the Marine Battalion which landed at Guantanano Bay, Cuba on 10 April 1898. This was the initial introduction of the Corps to what would become its most enduring accomplishment . . . the amphibious assault operation. Left to right: First Lieutenant Herbert L. Draper; Colonel Robert W. Huntington; Captain Charles L. McCawley. (USMC)

The advance base mission formally proposed for the Marine Corps by the Navy General Board in October 1900 was not a charter for the Marines to develop the techniques of amphibious war. At the time the establishment of an advance naval base was not envisaged as requiring offensive action but rather as an occupation followed by the organization of a suitable defense. But, even so, there was little need to labor the issue for the Marines were heavily involved in expeditionary duties in the Far East and the Caribbean and had few resources for anything else. Thus, it was not until 1913 that the Marines could form a permanent Advance Base Force. Even then, the Force had little opportunity to work on its principal mission. The Marines, already in Nicaragua in 1912, were sent to Haiti in 1915 and to Santo Domingo in 1916. Then, in 1917, the Corps, grown to 75,000 men, sent 30,000 Marines to fight in France. And, when the Great War ended, there were still the "banana wars" to fight.

From a precarious beginning in 1775 the Marines had survived as a Corps by maintaining close ties with the Navy. During the Civil War they were used mainly in traditional seagoing roles and only rarely as landing forces. But that war brought many changes to the Navy and, as the influence of technology intensified, the Navy came to question the need for Marine detachments afloat. As a consequence, Navy support for the Marines lessened and the future of the Corps became uncertain until the war with Spain reversed the process.

The expeditionary duties performed by the Marine Corps in the Far East, Europe and the Caribbean were rewarding and important, but these were ground force operations which could not long remain unchallenged. To ensure the continuity of the Corps, it appeared desirable for it to support the Navy and its requirement for an Advance Base Force, while avoiding further intrusion into the Army's domain. This need was not universally appreciated but it was recognized by a number of perceptive Marine officers, among whom were three commandants: George Barnett, John LeJeune and John Russell. Under their impetus, the Marines undertook to address the problem of seizing as well as holding advance naval bases. The issues involved in such operations were most ably defined by a career Marine officer named Earl H. (Pete) Ellis who clearly foresaw the nature of the war against Japan.

Pete Ellis was a neurotic, hard-drinking visionary and gifted planner. He was not the first to foresee that a war with Japan would entail seizure of the islands of the central Pacific. He was, however, the first to detail how the islands were to be assaulted. Enlisted in 1900 and commissioned in 1901, Ellis served ashore in the Philippines for two tours of duty before joining the staff of the Naval War College. There, from 1911 to 1913, he evolved his views on amphibious war and wrote on advance base operations. He went on to Headquarters, Marine Corps and then to France where he served under General LeJeune, whom he had first met in the Philippines. On his return to Headquarters, Ellis drafted an operation plan entitled *Advance Base Operations in Micronesia*, which was approved as Marine Corps Operation Plan 712 on 23 July 1921 by General LeJeune; it was three years before the first Plan Orange would be issued. Ellis, meanwhile, was hospitalized for long-standing disorders. Upon his discharge he was granted leave to visit Europe. His actual destination, however, was the Japanese mandated islands of

Top: *France, 1918: Marines of the 4th Brigade stop for a meal provided by field kitchens. (USMC)*

Centre: *A unit of the 4th Marine Brigade standing in formation shortly before going into action at Belleau Wood in June 1918. (USMC)*

Right: *Lieutenant Colonel Earl Ellis. (USMC)*

Top: Landing exercises being conducted along the Potomac River near the Quantico Marine Base in Virginia. The landing boat is a standard 50-foot motor launch. (USMC)

Centre: An experimental "Beetle Boat" unloading a 75mm gun on maneuvers in Culebra during 1923. (USMC)

Left: Experimental Troop Barge "A" undergoing field tests off Culebra Island in 1923. The boat was 55 feet long, made of wood and fitted with an armoured cover; tests revealed it as unsatisfactory. (USMC)

the central Pacific, from which he never returned. Ellis died in the Palaus on 12 May 1923.[8]

Ellis's intelligence mission does not appear to have been fruitful. His plan for the reduction of Micronesia, however, well defined the techniques of the amphibious assault. He saw the Marine Corps, then only 20,000 men strong, as "an independent fighting force on land and in the air"[9] which was "to be prepared to accompany [the] fleet and reduce enemy resistance in the Marshall Islands . . . Caroline and Mariana Islands . . . and recapture Guam . . ."[10] He suggested that the enemy would have to "focus the defense on or near the beaches and provide the attackers with the possibility of effecting superiority at any given point".[11] Ellis also emphasized the need for surprise and rapidity of execution and called for landings to be made in daylight "to permit the fullest use of all weapons and give the landing force a full day in which to pursue its operations ashore".[12] He also identified the several types of air support required and called for "a battle chart . . . designating fire zones and special fire targets . . ." to help ships assigned gunfire support missions.[13]

Ellis's plan, read today, oversimplified the amphibious assault and attributed capabilities to landing craft that did not exist. Indeed, many of the resources needed to implement his plan were not available and some of the techniques he prescribed were untried or unknown. This adds merit to his vision, already remarkable, during this period when the amphibious operation had been discredited by the disaster of Gallipoli in 1915. Equally significant is that the Marine Corps at that time had just returned from fighting in France and was heavily engaged in the Caribbean. The circumstances were such that there could not have been many Marines able to write with the conviction that Ellis did . . . or another commandant like General LeJeune to give official recognition to his effort.

In February 1922, General LeJeune addressed a proposal to the Navy General Board for "a mobile Marine Corps adequate to conduct offensive land operations against naval bases."[14] This shifted the focus away from base defense to the offensive aspects of amphibious operations . . . the amphibious assault. But, while at the time the Marines had a newly formed Expeditionary Force of two infantry and one artillery regiments based at Quantico, Virginia, there were few funds for the training exercises and landing craft development that would have given substance to the Commandant's declaration. Only small-scale embarkation and debarkation exercises could be included in the fleet maneuvers until 1924, when 1,700 Marines of the Expeditionary Force assaulted Culebra Island organized as an enemy-held base. The results revealed that the attack force was too small to overcome the defenses, the simulated naval bombardment totally ineffective, and control of the ship-to-shore movement hopelessly inadequate. Even the single transport available had been improperly loaded! The exercise, though disastrous, had the merit of demonstrating the urgent need for a doctrine on amphibious operations. It also highlighted the value of regularly scheduled exercises and the opportunity they provided to test such items as a 55-foot troop barge and the Christie amphibious tank, neither of which had proven satisfactory.

Despite multiple distractions and difficulties, the Marines continued to work on improving their amphibious capabilities. In 1927 further recognition was given to the effort when the Joint Board made the Marine Corps responsible "for land operations in support of the Fleet for the seizure and defense of advance naval bases and such limited auxiliary land operations as are essential to the prosecution of a naval campaign."[15] Six years later, General John H. Russell, the Assistant Commandant, proposed that the Marines provide a Fleet Marine Force under the operational control of the Fleet Commander. The Navy agreed and on 7 December 1933 Navy Department General Order 241 was published stating " . . . The force of Marines maintained by the Major General Commandant in a state of readiness for operations with the Fleet is hereby designated as the Fleet Marine Force (FMF) and, as such, shall constitute part of the organization of the United States Fleet."[16] One day later, Marine Corps Order 66 designated Quantico, Virginia as the headquarters for the FMF, whose units were deployed on both the east and west coasts.

The Marines now had a mission and an organization that enabled it to serve with the Fleet and effectively extend its capabilities ashore. But while these administrative decisions set the route of advance for the Corps, its wide-ranging commitments allowed only 3,000 men for the Fleet Marine Force in 1934. Meanwhile progress was being made in an important related area, that of doctrine. Soon after publication of Navy General Order 241, the curriculum at the Marine Corps Schools was changed "to cover the entire field of naval landing operations."[17] At the same time the entire staff and student body were assigned to the task of writing what became the Tentative Manual for Landing Operations, 1934.[6] Subsequently approved by the Navy, the contents of the Marines' manual became Navy doctrine in 1938 under the title of Fleet Tactical Publication 167.[7] The Army issued the text in 1941 as Field Manual 31–5.[8]

In preparation of their 1934 Manual, the Marines had consulted many references. Among these was a publication prepared by the Joint Board entitled *Joint Overseas Expeditions* which defined an opposed landing as ". . . the assault of an organized defensive position modified by substituting naval gunfire for divisional, corps and [field] army artillery and, generally Navy aircraft support for Army aircraft support."[18] This revealed the close parallel between a ground attack and an amphibious assault. In both circumstances, the object is to gain control over a geographical feature such as a port, town, road junction or commanding terrain. In ground combat this is generally accomplished by infantry transported in compact formation to an assembly area. From there, forward movement is made in dispersed order to a designated control line which is crossed in open formation at a specified time for the final assault. The sequence of events is carefully timed and co-ordinated with the employment of aviation, artillery, armor and other support units. The amphibious assault follows this same general pattern with the singular difference that the landing force is powerless when afloat and gains its strength progressively as it lands.

The dependence of the landing force and the accomplishment of the complex sea-based deployment is addressed in seven chapters in the Marines' Manual which detail both the planning and conduct of an assault landing to seize an advance naval base against opposition and the complementary task of base defense. Most striking is that the Manual, like Ellis's plan for the seizure of the islands of the central Pacific, reveals thinking that was ahead of its time. For example, the Manual directs that ". . . the landing force . . . should be embarked on transports . . . as self-contained detachments . . . capable of independent combat action . . ." Further, ". . . organizations [are] to have their equipment and supplies available to them on debarkation in the order required by the tactical situation . . ."[19] These most important calls for maintaining the tactical integrity of units in embarkation and for the combat loading of ships came at a time when the Navy had only two transports; a deplorable situation which would continue until just before the start of the Pacific War when the Navy's transport inventory had grown to only six ships equally divided between the Atlantic and Pacific. In another entry, the Marines' Manual states ". . . it is highly desirable that sufficient boats be available to land all combat troops without the need for any of these troops having to wait a second boat trip . . ."[20] But, as late as 1940, the Navy still had only thirty-five 30-foot personnel landing boats and eleven tank/artillery lighters. In 1934 the Marines might have added a doctrine to their mission and organization, but much remained to be done to develop and acquire the resources needed to make it all real.

Marine Corps commitments in the late 1920s and early 1930s made it impossible to engage in significant amphibious training. Then in 1935 the conduct of regularly scheduled amphibious exercises was resumed. But even then, the Navy's annual budget had a bare $40,000 allocated to the development and procurement of landing boats.[21] That was a sum little calculated to inspire much confidence in the future. Fortunately, as the Navy and Marine Corps went on with their modest efforts to test and improve their new amphibious doctrine, two civilians working separately addressed the problem of moving men and materials in marginal terrain and restricted waters.

Andrew Higgins, looking for a means of navigating the difficult bayou country of Louisiana, found his solution in a shallow-draft boat with reinforced bow and tunnel stern which allowed it to ground and retract without damage or great difficulty. Donald Roebling, concerned with rescue operations in the Florida Everglades, devised a track-propelled flotation hull to meet his needs. It would have been difficult to predict at that time the critical impact these parallel developments were to have on America's military capabilities in the war to follow.

In 1933 the Marine Corps established its Equipment Board which added leverage to the Corps' efforts to have the Navy give higher priority to landing craft development.[22] At that time Marines still came ashore in ships' boats whose performance and utility were little related to a landing attack. In 1934 the Navy, aware of the requirement and sympathetic to the Marines' needs, turned to industry with a request for landing craft proposals. Meanwhile, during Fleet Exercise 1 (FLEX-1) in 1935, the Navy tested a non self-propelled artillery lighter originally introduced in 1926 and now fitted with a bow ramp and designated Type "B". Also tested was a standard 50-foot motor launch fitted with removable ramps identified as Boat Rig "A". The first proved difficult to handle and the latter was top-heavy and unsafe in a seaway. The exercise, a modest affair, was also marked by the use of twelve Marine observation aircraft from the 1st Marine Air Group for spotting naval gunfire. The naval gunfire exercises were unrealistic, but did allow for the testing of several types of projectiles. In addition, three battalions of Marines learned something of the problems of making a landing.[23]

FLEX-2, held in 1936 in the same Culebra Island area used for FLEX-1, was on a grander scale. The Marines brought the 1st Brigade and the whole of Air Group 1, but there was still only one transport available and it was not combat loaded. There were other artificialities to detract from desired realism, yet the exercise permitted further testing of bombardment projectiles. The Marines made eight landings and acquired added experience in the process. Five boats provided by industry were also tested, some across coral. None was found satisfactory, and landing across coral proved impracticable. Further tests were conducted with the artillery lighter and the 50-foot motor launch without significant difference from the earlier findings. FLEX-2, while not spectacular, was considered a success although it revealed yet again the urgent need for troop transports and suitable landing craft.

The 1937 Fleet exercise, FLEX-3, was held on the west coast and included two Marine brigades plus an Army regiment. Once again it was made clear that warships were poor substitutes for troop transports and ships' boats were not landing craft. Also revealed was the need for reliable means to get tanks ashore early in a landing assault. Beyond that the year was made notable by the creation of the Navy's Continuing Board for the Development of Landing Boats and the award of a contract to Andrew Higgins for one 36-foot "Eureka" type boat for test. The boat was tested during FLEX-4 in 1938 and found sufficiently good for a further contract to be issued calling for five more boats to be delivered for testing during FLEX-5 in 1939. The Marines had a hand in these latter trials and concluded that the Higgins boat was superior to all others. The Navy agreed and the 36-foot boat was adopted as the standard personnel landing boat in 1940 . . . but one problem remained.

The Eureka with its blunt bow was ill suited to offloading troops or supplies when beached. In April 1941, Major Linsert, Secretary of the Equipment Board, showed Higgins a picture of a Japanese Dai-Hatsu 14 M Type landing craft. The photograph, originally enclosed in a report entitled Japanese Landing Operations prepared by young Lieutenant Victor H. Krulak in Shanghai in 1937, revealed a boat with a ramp bow. Higgins was asked if he could put such a ramp on his boat.[24] Higgins replied "Can do!" and had a ramp boat ready for testing in a matter of weeks. The tests were conducted at Higgins' facilities in New Orleans where the boat proved most satisfactory. Soon afterwards, the boat was adopted as the Landing Craft Vehicle and Personnel (LCVP) and went on to serve in Europe, the Pacific and the Far East.[25]

That same year Higgins also solved the requirement for a tank/artillery lighter. The search went back to 1926 when the towed lighter first appeared, and continued until 1935 when ramps were fitted on a 50-foot motor launch. When these expedients proved of marginal use, the Navy took on the task of designing a lighter related to the size of the Marines' tank. The first of these was a 38-foot boat capable of landing the 9,500-pound Marmon-Harrington light tank. This was satisfactorily tested during FLEX-5. Soon afterwards, the Marines adopted the Army's 15-ton tank and the Navy returned to the drawing-board. The result was a 45-foot lighter tested during FLEX-6 in 1940 together with three other lighters and 25 various types of landing craft. The Navy lighter was found slow but

LANDING BOAT

Top: *A Japanese Dai-Hatsu 14-metre Ramp-Bow Landing Craft off Shanghai in 1937. This photograph was shown to Andrew Higgins when he was asked if he could fit a similar ramp on his landing boat. (USMC)*

Right: *Five weeks after being shown the photograph of a Japanese landing boat with bow-ramp Higgins produced an experimental ramp-type landing boat. This design became the basis for the 36-foot LCVP (Landing Craft, Vehicle & Personnel). (USN)*

Right: *A Navy 38-foot tank lighter offloads a Marmon-Harrington light tank during Fleet Exercise Five (FLEX-5) in 1939. (USMC)*

Above: *In order to carry the medium tank as well as a greater troop and cargo capacity, the original LCM was modified into the LCM6. The French added armour and armament to their LCMS for service in Indochina. (French Navy)*

Below: *Marines take cover in a steel hull Higgins landing boat, Eureka model, testing during FLEX-5 in 1939. It was designed to carry eighteen fully equipped troops, but could take as many as thirty men. (USMC)*

Above: *Units from the 1st Battalion, 5th Marines landing on Culebra Island in 1936 during Fleet Exercise 2 (FLEX-2). Although the occasion was used to test a variety of experimental landing boats, the Marines normally landed from Standard U.S. Navy motor launches as shown. (USMC)*

Below: *The initial procurement 36-foot LCVP which became the standard landing boat used throughout World War II. (USN)*

Left: A Marine Amtrac Detachment poses in front of the Dunedin Hotel, Florida in June 1941. The Hotel served as headquarters, mess and barracks for the initial 37-strong group of Marines to serve in the Detachment.

Left: An LVT(1) emerges from a bay near Dunedin during a driver training session. Second Lieutenant Harry Taylor wears the "tank" driver's helmet. (USMC)

Below: The first amphibian tractor procured by the Marines undergoing tests at Culebra Island in 1941 during Fleet Exercise Seven (FLEX-7). (USMC)

adequate, but when used again during FLEX-7 the lighter with tank aboard sank.

The Navy turned to Higgins who agreed to put a ramp on a 45-foot boat he was building for the Colombian customs service. The boat tested well during large-scale landing exercises held off the recently acquired Marine base at New River, North Carolina in the summer of 1941. Although the Higgins lighter had performed satisfactorily, the Army decided to adopt the 30-ton Sherman medium tank which the 45-foot lighter could not accommodate. Higgins was asked to design a larger version of his boat. The result became the 50-foot Landing Craft Mechanized (LCM) which joined with the LCVP to comprise the two most widely used landing boats of World War II.[26]

The attainment of an acceptable amphibious assault capability depends upon being able to land infantry promptly together with the supporting weapons, vehicles, other heavy equipment and supplies needed to sustain combat ashore. When, at first, landings were made from ships' boats, little more than infantry could be put ashore initially. As a result, the Marines became interested in amphibian tanks. However, the matter was not pursued with vigor because the requirements for fire support of troops ashore were being addressed by naval gunfire and aircraft whose employment, while not perfected, remained promising. Then, too, the search for landing craft capable of putting tanks ashore was being pursued vigorously, which made interest in amphibian tanks less compelling. There was, none the less, a tantalizing vision of an amphibious vehicle organic to the Marine Corps and able to come ashore with the infantry to give it support during its most vulnerable first moments ashore.

The realization of this vision had its origins in a hurricane which struck Florida in 1932 and caused extensive damage. John Roebling, son of the builder of the Brooklyn bridge, was appalled by the disaster and asked his son, Donald, to build a vehicle able to travel the swamps and assist in rescue operations in the event of other such cataclysms. Two years later, young Donald had a seven-ton aluminum amphibian powered by a 92-horsepower engine. When tested, the vehicle proved underpowered and the straight cleats on the tracks were inefficient as paddles for movement afloat. None the less, the concept of a buoyant hull fitted with tracks for propulsion afloat and ashore appeared feasible.[27]

In 1936, Donald Roebling built a lighter vehicle with diagonal cleats which gave it a water speed of five miles per hour. Then, in 1937, a four-ton version of this same basic vehicle demonstrated a water speed of eight miles per hour. By that time, Roebling's activities had attracted public notice and his latest vehicle was featured in an article appearing in *Life* magazine on 4 October 1937. That same month, General Louis M. Little, commanding the Fleet Marine Force, visited Admiral Kalbfus in reference to Hawaiian area maneuvers scheduled to take place early the following year. At dinner the Admiral mentioned the *Life* magazine article as describing an item of possible interest to the Marine Corps. General Little agreed the matter was worth looking into and sent a copy of the magazine to the Commandant. In due time, the Equipment Board was directed to contact Roebling and investigate. When the Secretary of the Board went to see Roebling, the first model had been dismantled and the second was being modified. Moreover, Roebling was not interested in a military application of his rescue vehicle. Still, the Secretary was impressed by what he saw and recommended a follow-on visit. This was agreed and the Secretary went back in January 1939 where he saw the third model in operation. Following a favorable report from the Secretary, the President of the Equipment Board, General Moses, visited Roebling in September 1939. There he saw the fourth model in operation and was able to persuade Roebling to work with the military. By January 1940, agreement had been reached on the general characteristics of a military machine and Roebling had even sketched an amphibian tractor fitted with a turret.

Roebling had spent $68,000 of his own money in developing his vehicle. He agreed to build one for the Marine Corps for $20,000. But the Equipment Board did not have such funds available and turned to the Bureau of Ships. Fortunately the Bureau had the needed money and in March 1940 Roebling began work. The first vehicle for the Marine Corps, actually Roebling's fifth model, was delivered later in the year. Of note is the fact that Roebling had spent only $16,000 on his effort and sought to return the $4,000 balance. But this was an unheard of precedent and took sometime to get sorted out.[28] Meanwhile, the amphibian had been taken to Culebra by Sergeants Raper and Gibson, where it was put through its paces under the supervision of Captain Victor H. Krulak, then serving as Assistant G-4 of the 1st Marine Brigade.[29]

Captain Krulak and the two sergeants ran the vehicle in mangrove, over coral and through surf. They found it to be underpowered and its track unreliable. They also concluded it should have a compartmented hull of sheet steel. But, on balance, the vehicle performed "reasonably well".[30] The findings were duly reported and the vehicle was shipped to Quantico. Soon after its arrival it was put through its paces for the Commandant of the Marine Corps and a high-level entourage that included Admiral King and General Marshall. The demonstration went well, several of the senior officers went for rides, and, within a week Donald Roebling had a Letter of Intent from the Navy for 100 machines. These, to be made of sheet metal and incorporating other recommendations based on Captain Krulak's tests, were to be built at the Food Machinery Corporation plant in Dunedin, conveniently located near Roebling's Clearwater home.

The first production model of the Landing Vehicle, Tracked LVT(1) was completed in July 1941. It was delivered to Major William W. Davies who, six weeks earlier, had arrived in Dunedin with four officers and 37 men to organize a training facility.[31] The headquarters of the Amphibian Tractor Detachment was established at the Dunedin Hotel, which also served as a barracks for the men and as a messhall for the whole detachment. The officers found housing in nearby communities.

The initial production amtracs delivered to the Dunedin detachment were put to hard use as training vehicles. This experience confirmed the weakness of the track system as had first been reported by Captain Krulak. Food Machinery Corporation and the Navy closely followed the operational experience being acquired and James M. Hait, the chief engineer for FMC at Dunedin, moved ahead with studies to improve the vehicle. In October 1941 the Navy invited the Borg-Warner Company to contribute its expertise in the matter. The company agreed that a redesign was needed and set about doing so. Meanwhile, Hait and his team had completed their designs and were busy building the prototype of the LVT(2).

Above: Sergeants Clarence H. Raper (right) and Walter L. Gibson pictured with the original amphibian tractor procured from Donald Roebling in 1940; the vehicle was aluminium and was powered by a Lincoln-Zephyr engine. (USMC)

Right: The 1937 Roebling Amphibious Tractor was made of aluminium and weighed 4 tons. It was the first model with the track running on roller bearings in a channel which gave it a water speed of six knots. (USMC)

Right: A "Christie" amphibious tank emerges from the sea during Marine Corps tests off Culebra in 1924. The vehicle was found to be unseaworthy and was rejected. However six of these vehicles were procured and used in China in 1927. (USMC)

Left: Donald Roebling pictured after receiving the Medal for Merit in Washington on 18 December 1946.

This modest beginning was followed by a veritable flood. More than 18,000 amtracs were built during World War II. Twelve hundred of these were LVT(1)s and 3,000 were Borg-Warner designed LVT(3)s, first used in the invasion of Okinawa in April 1945. All others were based on the Food Machinery Corporation LVT(2) design which was produced in six variants. The Food Machinery Corporation had started as a manufacturer of pressure pumps for agricultural purposes in 1884; the amtrac made it a major defense contractor, a status it continues to enjoy today. But all these events were in the future . . . war seemed a remote prospect from the vantage point of a quiet, friendly Florida community in 1941 preparing to enter the year end holiday period.

The even tempo of the passing days at the amtrac training facility in Dunedin changed just before Thanksgiving when a small group of Marines were selected to serve as the nucleus of the first amphibian tractor unit to join the Fleet Marine Force. The 1st Marine Division, recently established at New River, North Carolina, was organizing its support units. Included among these was the 1st Amphibian Tractor Battalion whose first unit, Company "A", would be formed around a detachment of Dunedin Marines scheduled to leave by train on 8 December 1941. Captain William K. Enright, the company commander designate, had elected to drive his personal vehicle to New River and had directed his executive officer, Second Lieutenant Victor J. Croizat, to take charge of the detachment moving by train. Thus it was that the morning after the Japanese attack on Pearl Harbor, 45 Marines in field equipment marched from the Dunedin Hotel to the railroad station. There they were greeted by most of the population of the area which had gathered to cheer them off. It was a memorable occasion whose recollection later compensated for the miserably cold winter of North Carolina and continued to linger as the campaigns in the Pacific followed one upon another.

2. Fall Back and Regroup

The Japanese advance; the Battles of Midway and Guadalcanal

T HE war in the Pacific exploded in a series of surprise attacks launched in early December 1941. Vice-Admiral Chuichi Nagumo's Pearl Harbor Strike Force hit military installations in the Hawaiian islands. Guam and Wake were the targets of Vice-Admiral Shigeyoshi Inouye's Fourth Fleet based at Truk. Hong Kong was invaded by three divisions under Lieutenant-General Sakai Takashi. Lieutenant-General Masaharu Homma's Fourteenth Army struck at the Philippines from Formosa. French Indochina, which Japan had already occupied, served as the springboard for the invasion of Malaya by General Yamashita's Twenty-fifth Army and for the advance of the Imperial Guards Division through Thailand to prepare the way for the entry of General Iida's Fifteenth Army into Burma. Other forces were systematically reducing the islands of the Dutch East Indies, acquiring the Bismarcks, and seizing outposts as far as the Gilberts.

On 10 January 1942, the hard-pressed Allies activated a joint command under the British General, Sir Archibald Wavell, to direct operations in the southern Pacific area. Within a month, only Java remained under Allied control, and after only six weeks of precarious existence, the Allied command was dissolved.[1] Thereafter, General Douglas MacArthur exercised command over the Southwest Pacific Area comprising the Dutch East Indies (less Sumatra), the Bismarck Archipelago, the Philippines, the Solomons and Australia. Admiral Nimitz received command of the Pacific Ocean Area (POA), which included everything else.[2]

In the span of ten weeks Japan had gained access to the oil, rubber and other raw materials of southeast Asia and the East Indies and its initial war objective was accomplished. The Imperial Army then was prepared to return to the war on the Asian mainland, where China remained to be finished off and Russia threatened. The Imperial Navy, however, argued that the "Southern Resources Area" remained vulnerable unless the defense perimeter was expanded. The Imperial Army was not convinced until two American task forces under Rear Admirals William F. Halsey and Frank J. Fletcher, lent credence to the Imperial Navy's arguments by striking Japanese positions in the Marshalls and Gilberts on 1 February 1942.[3] Japanese plans for the occupation of the southern Solomons and eastern New Guinea were then pushed ahead. No sooner had these moves been initiated than the Imperial Navy proposed further advances against New Caledonia, the Fijis and Samoa. Control of these islands, the Japanese Navy affirmed, would sever communications between the United States and Australia and leave the latter continent open to invasion. The Imperial Army was not enthusiastic. Neither was it prepared to agree to the Navy's parallel proposal to attack Midway. Then, on 18 April 1942, the Doolittle raid on Tokyo by B-25s flown off the carrier *Hornet* shocked the Japanese and ended opposition to the Imperial Navy's plans.[4]

The Japanese soon secured positions on New Guinea's northern coast and prepared to advance on Port Moresby. In a preliminary action, they moved against Tulagi, the headquarters of the British Solomons Islands Protectorate, which they reached on 3 May. The landing of the 3rd Kure Special Landing Force, although unopposed, had been observed by Rear Admiral Fletcher's Task Force 17. The American force moved into position that night, and early the next morning the carriers *Yorktown* and *Hornet* launched aircraft for a strike against Tulagi. Four Japanese ships, including a destroyer, were sunk.[5] That same day the Port Moresby Invasion Group under Rear-Admiral Chuichi Hara left Rabaul. The opposing forces spent the next three days looking for each other. Finally, on 7 May, they met and the Battle of the Coral Sea was on. In a series of actions involving only carrier aircraft, the Americans lost the *Lexington*, a fleet oiler, a destroyer and 33 aircraft. The Japanese lost the light carrier *Soho*, had the battle carrier *Shokaku* damaged, and lost 43 aircraft, including half the air group of their other carrier, the *Zuikaku*. The battle was a draw until the afternoon of 8 May when the Japanese commander broke off the action and returned to Rabaul. This removed the threat to Port Moresby and, although not apparent at the time, gave the victory to the Americans.[6]

The retirement of the Port Moresby Invasion Group did not alter Japanese plans for their moves into the south Pacific and against Midway. On 18 May, the Imperial Navy ordered preparations for the advance on New Caledonia, the Fijis and Samoa. In compliance, the Army activated the Seventeenth Army under command of Lieutenant-General Harukichi Hyakutake, an officer who would find defeat on Guadalcanal instead of glory in the south Pacific. Elsewhere the stage was being set for the battle of Midway. The U.S. Navy and Marines on Midway became aware of the impending threat against them when Admiral Nimitz arrived for a visit on 2 May. The news he brought was not welcome, but the reinforcements that he arranged to send were. Equally welcome was the absence of the Japanese during the final weeks of the month, which allowed time to continue improving the defenses. The expected battle was joined at last on the morning of 3 June 1942 when nine B-17s from Midway responded to a PBY sighting and bombed a Japanese force of eleven ships. The strike was without effect. However, the action alerted the American naval forces with their three carriers which, instead of being in Hawaiian waters as the Japanese expected, were positioned 300 miles northeast of Midway.[7]

In the early hours of 4 June, the Japanese, unaware of the American ships in the area, launched their aircraft against Midway. The atoll's defending aircraft rose to the challenge but suffered serious losses. Revenge was swift. The *Enterprise* and *Hornet* launched their aircraft at 0700 and the *Yorktown* followed two hours later. By 1030, three Japanese battle carriers were out of action; that afternoon the remaining carrier of Vice-Admiral Nagumo's Carrier Strike Force was finished. At 0255 on 5 June, Admiral Yamamoto decided to end the battle and ordered a general withdrawal.[8]

The successful defense of Midway cost the Americans one carrier and 124 aircraft. The defeated Japanese lost four carriers and 322 aircraft; and they too had reached the limit of their expansion in the Pacific. Their plans for moving to New Caledonia, the Fijis and Samoa were postponed, never to be resurrected. Thenceforth, the only option remaining for the Japanese was to try and hold what they had gained.

Before the waters of the central Pacific had been cleansed of the oil and debris of the battle of Midway, the American Joint Chiefs of Staff (JCS) were considering how best to exploit the victory. Other than the loss of Wake Island just before Christmas, the outpost line securing the Hawaiian Islands had held; any remaining threat to the communications between the United States and its major Pacific base was minimal. The situation with regard to the other part of Admiral Nimitz' basic mission, protecting the communications between the United States and Australia, was much less reassuring.[9] That the Japanese had not initially planned to cut those communications was not known in 1942; neither was it known that the Imperial Navy's subsequent plan to advance to Samoa had been laid to rest at Midway.[10] What was known was that the Japanese seizure of Tulagi created a dangerous salient which could not be ignored.

At the time of the JCS deliberations, the situation in the Pacific and the availability of forces for offensive operations reflected decisions and actions that had started with the findings of the Hepburn Board in 1938, which had called for the development of a series of island bases to defend Hawaii.[11] The declaration of a Limited National Emergency on 8 September 1939, just five days after war broke out in Europe, had cleared the way for preliminary surveys to organize defenses on Wake, Midway, Palmyra, Johnston and Samoa. Then, in the spring of 1941, Rainbow Plan 5 had confirmed the need to develop those islands and conceded that Guam would fall to Japanese attack. At that time, the Marines had four Defense Battalions, the 1st, 3rd, 4th and 6th, moving into position in Hawaii and four outpost islands. The 7th Defense Battalion, in addition, was on its way to Samoa.[12]

American involvement in these and other defensive actions in the Pacific had been gradual. In 1939 there were only 20,000 Marines, 25 per cent of whom were serving in the Fleet Marine Force. When the Organized Reserve was called to active duty in November of the following year, the strength of the Corps had leapt upwards: by 1941 there were 66,000 Marines, nearly half of whom were in the FMF. Despite the tripling of its strength, the Marine Corps had been barely able to keep up with the ever-increasing demands made on it. The upgrading of the two Marine Brigades and two Marine Air Groups into the 1st and 2nd Marine Divisions and the 1st and 2nd Marine Air Wings in February 1941 had absorbed large numbers of men; so had the organization of nine defense battalions that same year. The defense build-up of Pacific bases and the increase in the numbers of ships and stations had added further requirements. Particularly distracting in this period of unprecedented growth was the transfer in mid-1941 of the 6th Marine Regiment from the west to the east coast of the United States in anticipation of possible operations against Martinique or the Azores. These operations did not take place. Instead, the 6th Marines and the 5th Defense Battalion had been formed into the 1st Provisional Marine Brigade and moved to Iceland in July to relieve the British occupation force there.[13]

The entry of the United States into World War II was followed by the deployment of 80,000 Army troops to Australia, Hawaii and other island bases. The Marines had not been excluded from these new demands. In January 1942, the 8th Marine Regiment and the 2nd Defense Battalion were formed into the 2nd Marine Brigade and deployed to Samoa. Two months later, the 7th Marine Regiment and the 8th Defense Battalion had been organized into the 3rd Marine Brigade and sent off to garrison Wallis Island and western Samoa. At this same time, the Marines in Iceland had been relieved by U.S. Army troops. Thus, when the opportunity for offensive action in the Pacific presented itself in mid-1942, the Army was spread thinly over a large area and the Marines were striving to bring their two divisions, each short of one infantry regiment, to a satisfactory state of combat readiness. The need to continue the organizational development of the Marine air wings was no less pressing.

The difficult organization and training tasks confronting the Marines extended beyond the infantry and artillery regiments to the combat and service support battalions, without which a division cannot function effectively. Among these support units were the tanks, engineers, motor transport and other specialized units, including the novel amphibian tractor formations. For the most part, all Fleet Marine Force units had defined missions and conformed to established organizational and operational precedents. Because of this the organization of the schools and training programs needed to develop professional proficiency could proceed with confidence. The amphibian tractor units, however, had nothing to fall back on. They had no manuals, no experience, no antecedents and only the vaguest of functions. It would take active combat to provide the answers to questions which were largely unformulated in 1941 and 1942.

The first indications of how the amphibian tractor units would fare had appeared in the detachment at Dunedin, Florida. Major Davies, a pleasant and understanding regular officer, commanded with a light rein. This was fortunate because his officers were a mix of Naval Academy graduates, recent graduates of civilian universities who had entered the Marine Corps through the Reserve Officers Training Program (ROTC) and the Marine Corps Reserve. Captain William K. Enright, who commanded the company, whose first contingent left Dunedin on 8 December 1941 for the 1st Marine Division at New River, North Carolina, was an Academy graduate. Captain Henry C. Drewes who followed one week later, heading for the 2nd Marine Division at Camp Elliott, California, was a reservist. Among the enlisted men the range extended from old China hands to fresh recruits. Arthur Noonan and Thomas Hunt were among the experienced men who first personalized the war for the new Marines: Noonan had left a wife in China and Hunt had a family in Guam. The diversity of these individuals lessened as the old-timers taught the youngsters to be Marines; it disappeared as all turned to the challenge of mastering the strange machines coming out of the Food Machinery Corporation plant. It is notable that the brotherhood among amphibian tractor personnel created at Dunedin and later extended to all who served in amphibian tractor units survives to this day, near two generations later.

From the beginning of its war planning activities, the United States Navy had looked upon war with Japan as requiring prompt offensive operations. Even when the Army had argued in the 1920s for a Pacific strategy based upon holding the line Alaska–Hawaii–Panama, the Navy had vehemently held it imperative to bring the war to Japan's home islands as soon as possible. These views had not changed when the ARCADIA Conference of 22 December 1941 confirmed that the main Allied military effort would be made in the European theater of operations.[14] As far as the Navy was concerned, the strategic defensive imposed in the Pacific theater did not preclude offensive action, and that was just what it contemplated. The Marines had always shared in these sentiments.

The succession of disasters which befell the Allies in the two months following Japan's strike at Pearl Harbor had done nothing to alter the Navy's views. The Army's stand, however, had been modified at the Navy's urging and by the force of events to the point where it began to occupy island bases as far west as its resources permitted.[15] By the end of January 1942, U.S. Army troops had garrisoned Fiji; by mid-March they were in New Caledonia and had moved into the New Hebrides, where the Marines were positioning their 4th Defense Battalion. In May, General MacArthur, also a firm believer in the offensive, had proposed a move against Rabaul, but the troops required had not been available. Moreover, the Navy had not been willing to risk its few remaining carriers in the restricted waters of the Solomons Sea.[16] Admiral Nimitz, the Pacific Ocean Area Commander, had been willing, however, to strike at Tulagi. At first, even this had appeared premature, but the subsequent actions of the American fleet units in the Coral Sea in May and in the defense of Midway in early June had altered this perception. On 25 June, Admiral Ernest J. King, the Navy's top commander, directed Admiral Nimitz to prepare an offensive against the lower Solomons.

This decision introduced the question of command responsibility since the lower Solomons were in General MacArthur's Southwest Pacific Area. The Joint Chiefs of Staff entered into the debate and on 2 July settled the issue by defining three tasks to attain the final objective; control of the New Guinea–New Britain–New Ireland area. The first task, the seizure of Santa Cruz, Tulagi and the adjacent islands would be the Navy's responsibility. For that purpose the boundary between Nimitz' and MacArthur's commands would be shifted to the west. General MacArthur then would be responsible for tasks two and three; i.e., the seizure of the central and northern Solomons and New Guinea, and the attacks against the Japanese on New Britain and New Ireland.[2] In this manner, the first offensive drive against the Japanese would take place in Nimitz' Pacific Ocean Area command and within its recently designated subordinate South Pacific Area under Vice Admiral Robert Ghormley.[17] The warning order for the seizure of Tulagi and the adjacent islands had not awaited JCS deliberations but had been sent to the commander of the 1st Marine Division, Major General Archer A. Vandegrift, on 26 June.[18]

The 1st Marine Division, although recently formed, had a lineage dating back to 1934 when the 1st Marine Brigade had become the cutting edge of the new Fleet Marine Force. Elements of the Brigade had participated in six fleet exercises from 1934 to 1941, during which time its personnel had helped develop amphibious doctrine and tested Higgins boats and the Roebling amphibian tractor. The Marine force that sailed for the Caribbean in early February 1941 to participate in

FLEX-7 as the 1st Brigade, had returned in May as the 1st Division. By that time, the division, while still seriously understrength, had grown to 7,000 men. It could no longer be accommodated in its original home at Quantico and part was sent to Parris Island, South Carolina. This was a temporary arrangement; in June the division was again engaged in extensive landing exercises. These were held off the just acquired 100,000-acre New River, North Carolina base. When the exercises ended in August, the Marines remained ashore there in "Tent City", their new permanent home. New River was located in a remote coastal area of North Carolina. This meant that liberty for the Marines, who already had spent most of the year in the field, was literally beyond reach. The miserable quality of life under canvas diminished further when summer yielded to a very cold and damp winter.

A rude environmental shock awaited Company "A" of the 1st Amphibian Tractor Battalion when it arrived at New River on 8 December 1941. The 45 Marines of that unit, formed at Dunedin on 24 October, had become accustomed to Florida's blue skies, white beaches and comfortable billets, and where going on liberty was a matter of stepping outside. They were poorly prepared for life in "Tent City" at New River. But, worse was to come. A few days after their arrival, the company was joined by a group of "surfmen" from the Coast Guard. A mixed detachment was formed to train division personnel to fire landing boat machine guns against beach targets during a landing approach. The detachment set up camp on Onslow beach where they could be close to their boats and the firing range, and could readily embark the training details arriving from "Tent City" each morning by truck. The beach area was far removed from any other facility, and the weather, though clear, was bitterly cold. Fortunately, the detachment's survival was assured when the enterprising Coastguardsmen discovered a source of moonshine at a place known as Fulcher's Landing. The only other break in the routine of coaxing reluctant diesels to life in the numbing cold of first light, of organizing bailing details to keep the antique landing boats afloat, and of clearing jams in the ancient Lewis guns used for boat armament, were the nightly fireworks at sea, where German submarines were sinking unarmed American coastal ships with deck guns in order to save torpedoes!

The Headquarters and Service Company of the 1st Amphibian Tractor Battalion was activated on 16 February 1942, and the remaining Companies "B" and "C" of the Battalion were organized at the same time. The LVT(1), whose design had been frozen at the outbreak of the war to facilitate mass production, also began to arrive in numbers. The forming battalion, eventually to consist of some 500 men and 100 LVT(1)s, was moved to Peterfield Point where ready access to New River inlet and the sea allowed serious training to begin. This stressed vehicle operation and maintenance; training in field employment still lay in the future. The 3rd Platoon of Company "C" under 2nd Lieutenant John Fitzgerald, had the added privilege of being the first unit to learn how to load ungainly amtracs into the hold of a transport. This occurred when the unit was attached to the Army's 9th Infantry Division for joint landing exercises in Chesapeake Bay in an area with the prophetic name of the Solomon Islands.[19] The initial and subsequent training of the amtrac units and the fact that their organization was based on the tables of organization for a motor transport battalion made it clear that amtracs were viewed as simple transportation rather than combat vehicles. Most grievous was the fact that the amtrac unit organization would adversely affect the maintenance capabilities of the cargo amtracs throughout the war. In contrast, the cannon-mounting armored amtracs that were still in the future, were organized on the basis of tank battalion tables of organization and fared much better.

The North Carolina winter was yielding to the promise of a welcome spring when Lieutenant Colonel Merritt A. Edson arrived to form the 1st Raider Battalion around a nucelus provided by the 5th Marines. This disruptive incident was duplicated on the west coast by Lieutenant Colonel Evans F. Carlson where he engaged in a similar task to form the 2nd Raiders. These units, and other specialized formations such as the parachute battalions, were a reflection of President Roosevelt's interest. Indeed, his son James, a reserve Marine officer, was to serve with Carlson in the raid on Makin Island in August 1942.

In this same early spring period, the 7th Marine Regiment was detached from the 1st Division for immediate deployment to Samoa as part of the 3rd Marine Brigade. It left shortly before 10 April when the Division itself was alerted for transfer to New Zealand. The move down under was to be made in two echelons. The Division headquarters with the 5th Regiment and its attached units, including Company "A" of the 1st Amphibian Tractor Battalion, were to sail first. The 1st Marine Regiment and the remainder of the Division were to follow. All ships were to be commercially loaded for maximum cargo space utilization; the first echelon troops were to be embarked principally in the USS *Wakefield*. The USS *Ericsson* was to embark most of the follow-on echelon; the remaining troops and the bulk of the equipment were to be loaded on nine other ships. It was

Below: Prisoners of war during a brief respite on the notorious Bataan Death March in April 1942. When Bataan fell, thousands of prisoners were marched 85 miles to Camp O'Donnell. Among these were 1,388 Marines of whom 490 died of wounds, mulnutrition, disease or the brutality of their captors. (USMC)

expected that the move from New River to Wellington via Norfolk, New Orleans and San Diego would take the better part of two months. This would be followed by up to six months in New Zealand during which the Division would complete the unit training it needed to be ready for combat.

The USS *Wakefield* with 5,000 Marines aboard left Norfolk on 20 May with a strong escort as far as the Panama Canal. Once the transit of the canal had been completed, the ship bent on 20 knots and sailed off alone for Wellington, where it arrived on 14 June 1942; it had been a brief spring and now the Marines were back in winter. But, that would not last long. Twelve days after arriving, General Vandegrift learned that his Division would conduct assault landings against Japanese-held islands in the lower Solomons beginning on 1 August – just 37 days away.[20]

In that last week of June, the 1st Marine Division was dispersed over thousands of miles of ocean. The 7th Marines were serving in Samoa, the 5th Marines had just arrived in Wellington, and the 1st Marines, with most of the Division's equipment, was still at sea and would not reach New Zealand until 11 July. Equally disturbing was that Vice Admiral Ghormley, in whose area the WATCHTOWER operation would take place, had a new command which lacked the operations planning and intelligence capabilities to prepare and direct the contemplated operation. To complicate the matter further, Rear Admiral Richmond K. Turner, who was to command the amphibious force that included the 1st Division, could not report to Ghormley's headquarters until 18 July – when basic operational decisions would already have been made. Then too, Admiral Fletcher, the designated Expeditionary Force commander, had voiced strong reservations over the possible success of the operation and had made it clear that his principal concern would be the protection of his carriers.[3]

Fletcher's views were particularly worrisome because his 250 carrier aircraft were the major air support available. Ghormley had 166 additional Navy and Marine aircraft, 95 U.S. Army aircraft and 30 aircraft from the New Zealand Air Force in Rear Admiral McCain's shore-based command. But most of these lacked the range for effective intervention in the proposed operations area and no wing tanks were on hand. Finally, Ghormley had no ground units to provide a reserve for the Marine landing force, and whatever garrison troops might eventually be required would have to be found among the forces already engaged in base defense missions in his South Pacific Area. There were no smiles on General Vandegrift's face when he assembled his commanders at his Cecil Hotel headquarters on 19 July to announce that the Division would shortly be landing against Japanese forces on Guadalcanal, Tulagi, Gavutu and Tanambogo. Those who were present on that rainy Sunday, recall the stunned silence that greeted the news, broken soon after by low voices asking "Where in hell is that?" In those days the only Solomon Islands that the 1st Division Marines knew were in Chesapeake Bay, and they certainly were not the objective area.[21]

Lieutenant Colonel Frank B. Goettge, the Division intelligence officer, tried to answer the question as well as he could. But, it was quickly evident that only a modest amount of information had been gathered on his hurried trip to Australia, where General MacArthur's staff had helped in the search of files and libraries, the location and interrogation of former Solomons residents, and in arranging reconnaissance flights. After the war, it was learned that maps prepared at General MacArthur's headquarters from aerial photos and intended for the Marines had been sent to Admiral Ghormley's headquarters where they had been misplaced in the confusion of setting up that organization![22]

The picture presented to the assembled officers by Goettge revealed Tulagi to be a hilly, wooded island some two and a quarter miles long, lying in a bay off the coast of Florida Island. Two small islets, Gavutu and Tanambogo, were immediately to the east and connected by a causeway. Guadalcanal, across the 20-mile wide Sealark Channel, was a massive 90-mile long island with a rugged mountain backbone paralleling its long axis and serving as the backdrop of its coastal plain. In the south, these plains were relatively narrow, but in the north where the Japanese were developing an airfield, the plains were wide, cut by several rivers and interspersed with heavy jungle, grasslands and cultivated coconut plantations. Most of the beaches of Tulagi and the nearby islets were fronted by coral formations. These also were to be found on Guadalcanal except that the beaches near the Lunga River, where the Marines were to go ashore, appeared accessible to landing boats.

This information was barely adequate for planning. Considering the uncertain sources from which most of the data came, it is not surprising that the stream on the right flank of the landing beach had been incorrectly identified and that the high ground to be seized by the 1st Marines upon landing was actually six to eight miles inland. The estimates of enemy forces were even less reliable. SOPAC headquarters thought in terms of more than 8,000 Japanese troops in the objective area. Admiral Turner estimated 2,000 in Tulagi and vicinity and 5,275 on Guadalcanal. (The actual numbers were 1,500 and 2,230 respectively, of which one third were laborers.) Equally serious was the absence of any reliable information on Japanese reinforcing capabilities. This deficiency had not escaped Admiral Nimitz who, on 17 July, had informed Admiral King that the Marine landing force had to be strong enough to hold against the certainty that the Japanese would not allow the Marines to remain ashore . . . unless convinced otherwise. This meant that the two-regiment Division had to be reinforced.

The difficulties of acquiring suitable intelligence and carrying out any orderly planning were more than matched by the nightmare of embarkation. The focus of this was Aotea Quay in Wellington harbor, where the Marines labored around the clock to unload arriving ships, sort out their cargoes, and combat load essential equipment and supplies . . . often on the same ships that were being unloaded! The stevedores who normally worked the docks, not knowing of the impending operation, had baulked at the Marines' request to forego their tea-breaks and work in the driving rain of the New Zealand winter. The matter was only settled when the exasperated Marines closed the area to non-military personnel and did the job themselves. In these most unpleasant circumstances, the Marines combat loaded 12,500 men and equipment plus sixty days of supplies and ten days of ammunition. Regrettably, only half the motor transport could be taken but all serviceable amtracs were embarked. Individual Marines were allowed only what they could put in their packs and officers had the added privilege of a seabag. It was an austere and exhausted force that sortied Wellington harbor on the morning of 22 July 1942.

Two days earlier, the Division Operation Order 7–42 had confirmed the task organization and initial plans. By that time Admiral King had agreed to move D-Day to 7 August and sail the 2nd Marine Regiment, reinforced from San Diego, for assignment as the landing force reserve. Orders also had been issued for all units to rendezvous in the Fijis for a rehearsal and final commanders' conference. The landing force as finally constituted included the Guadalcanal Assault Force (Group X-ray) under General Vandegrift which would land the 5th Marines (less its 2nd Battalion) over Red Beach with its two battalions abreast. The 1st Marines would follow at H+50 minutes in column of battalions, pass between the 5th Marines units guarding the flanks of the beachhead and advance south and west to seize Mount Austen (Grassy Knoll). The Division headquarters and supporting units would land on order. The Tulagi (Northern) Assault Force (Group Yoke) under Brigadier General William H. Rupertus, the assistant division commander, would land the 1st Raider Battalion, followed by the 2nd Battalion, 5th Marines over Blue Beach on the northwest corner of Tulagi. Four hours later, the 1st Parachute Battalion would land on Gavutu. When that island was secured a unit of the battalion would be sent to Tanambogo to clear that island. The flank of the Tulagi Assault Force would be covered by a company of the reserve regiment (2nd Marines) which would land on Florida Island, immediately across from Tulagi Island shortly before the Raiders were to come ashore over Blue Beach.

Amphibian tractor units were assigned according to the usual practice of fragmenting combat and service support organizations to reinforce the infantry units. Thus, Company "A" with thirty LVT(1)s remained with the 5th Marines which, minus its 2nd Battalion, was to land on Guadalcanal; the 2nd Battalion with a platoon of amtracs would go ashore on Tulagi. Company "B" under Lieutenant Warren H. Edwards was assigned to the 1st Marines. The remainder of the 1st Amphibian Tractor Battalion, under command of Major Walter W. Barr, remained with the Division's support group. The 2nd Marine Regiment, the landing force reserve, brought with it Company "A" of the 2nd Amphibian Tractor Battalion which had sailed from San Diego on 1 July under command of Lieutenant Robert E. Smithwick. Of particular note relating to the employment of LVTs is a map with a notation that the coral off Tulagi made "landing not practical except for amphibian tanks [sic]".[23] This suggests that planners knew of the problem but no one thought of using amtracs to land the assault units. Accordingly, the LVTs were to come ashore after the assault troops, follow them with heavy weapons and ammunition, and later help move supplies as required. That all serviceable amtracs were embarked, while half the motor transport was left behind, suggests that the logistic capability of the LVT(1), if not its tactical worth, was recognized.

There were, however, innovative Marines able to see beyond the amtrac's transport role. Colonel Hunt, commanding the 5th Marines, had observed that the missnamed Ilu River on the right flank of Red Beach, while a barrier to a possible Japanese counterattack, was also an obstacle to the Marine advance. He discussed the problem with his engineer and amtrac officers who agreed it would be feasible to build wooden platforms to fit over LVTs so they could be used as bridges. Three amtracs were so modified using wooden sheathing from the refrigerator rooms of the cargo transport *Bellatrix*.

Thus it happened that early on 7 August, Sergeant Ralph J. Fletcher with three "volunteer" tractor crews that included William Price, John Ronzo, Frank Nappi and Giovanni Risciutto, spearheaded the landing on Guadalcanal and drove their amtracs into the stream to form two bridges over which the infantry advanced. The services of Sergeant Harry Elliott, who had volunteered to go ashore and scout out suitable bridge sites which he was to mark with red target cloth to help the amtrac drivers, were found to be unnecessary. This might have been a useful precaution if the Japanese had decided to oppose the landing and force the amtracs to pace their advance to that of the infantry.[24]

The rendezvous at sea some 400 miles north of Fiji took place on 26 July. The commanders' planning conference, which began at 1400 on the carrier *Saratoga*, was the last such occasion and also the first time that all responsible commanders had been assembled. There, General Vandegrift came in for additional suprises he did not need. Where the Marines had assumed they would receive adequate air and naval gunfire support throughout the landing, Admiral Fletcher made it clear he intended only a hit-and-run operation. His plan, as yet unpublished, was to offload the troops the first day, dump the cargo as rapidly as possible, and depart with his carriers by the end of the second day. Admiral Turner's insistence that unloading would take at least five days did not move Fletcher. Then, Turner himself added to Vandegrift's distress by insisting that the landing force reserve, the 2nd Marine Regiment, take unoccupied Ndeni Island over 200 miles away in the Santa Cruz Islands, on which to build an airfield. The final bad news was that the limited number of shore-based aviation units and the few bases in the area made it uncertain when aircraft could be sent to Guadalcanal. The possibility of using Ndeni as an interim airbase was even more remote and uncertain.

The rehearsal that followed from 28 to 30 July off Koro Island did nothing to relieve tensions or restore optimism. In General Vandegrift's own words it was a "complete bust."[25] Finally, on the evening of 31 July 1942, the eighty-two ships of the WATCHTOWER expeditionary force left Fijian waters for the run to the objective area. On board the thirteen troop transports, six cargo ships and four converted destroyer transports were 19,000 Marines. The rollback of the Japanese in the Pacific was about to begin!

The good fortune so missed in July made its appearance with the new month. The task force made its way to the objective area undetected. Equally encouraging, the first air strikes and the naval bombardment, which began soon after 0600 on the morning of 7 August 1942, caught the enemy completely by surprise. By 0740 Northern Group elements of the 1st Battalion, 2nd Marines reached Florida Island. Forty minutes later they were in position to cover the flanks of the 1st Raider Battalion, which had begun landing on Tulagi at 0800. Luckily, the landing was unopposed since the coral grounded the boats thirty to one hundred yards offshore, requiring the assault troops to wade to the beach. Once ashore, the Raiders had turned southeast to sweep the long axis of the island. No resistance was encountered until shortly before noon on the approach to the former British Residency, in the main population center. The 2nd Battalion, 5th Marines had followed the Raiders ashore and then turned northwest to sweep that part of the island. That done, the battalion had come to the support of the Raiders, who were encountering ever-increasing resistance as they pressed forward. Two enemy counterattacks were thrown back during the night, the first with some difficulty. The Marine advance was resumed the next morning with both Marine battalions in action. Although bitterly resisted by the fanatical Japanese, the advance continued until Tulagi was restored to Allied control on the afternoon of 8 August.

Four hours after the Raiders had started landing on Tulagi, the 1st Parachute Battalion scrambled ashore on Gavutu. The cruiser *San Juan* had pumped 280 eight-inch shells on to the island in four minutes and dive-bombers had added their loads to the preparation of the landing site, but the fully-alerted enemy hit the Marines hard as they came ashore. Despite ten per cent losses, the Marine paratroopers kept driving and by 1430 they held all of Gavutu, except for a section covered by fire from Tanambogo which made further movement impossible. Brigadier General Rupertus reacted by ordering Company "B" of the 1st Battalion, 2nd Marines then on Florida to assist the paratroops. The company embarked in six landing boats at 1800 and moved toward Tanambogo. On the approach, soon after nightfall, one boat grounded on the coral but the following boat landed thirty men without incident. Then a sudden fire in a nearby fuel dump illuminated the remaining boats as they prepared to beach. The Japanese immediately opened a heavy fire and forced the boats to retire. The thirty Marines already ashore also came under heavy fire. Unable to advance, the survivors, with their wounded, made their way back to their boat and withdrew. The difficult situation was reported to General Vandegrift who obtained the release of the force reserve from Admiral Turner. The 3rd Battalion, 2nd Marines was landed at 0730 the morning of 8 August with orders to clear Gavutu and take Tanambogo. By evening of the next day the job had been done.

It was during this period that five amtracs from the 3rd Platoon, Company "A", 2nd Amphibian Tractor Battalion, under Lieutenant Ray D. "Hootie" Horner, were put over the side to run emergency supplies, water, and ammunition from the transport *President Adams* to the troops ashore and evacuate

wounded on their return. This service continued until the islands were secured on 9 August. Incident to one of these supply runs, one of the LVTs moved deep inland to engage an enemy strongpoint with its machine guns and pick up seven wounded Marines who were unable to move because of enemy fire. The reputation of the amtracs as "can-do" people was beginning.[26]

On the other side of Sealark Channel, the landing on Guadalcanal, set for 0910, proceeded as planned. The LVT bridge-site reconnaissance team landed with the assault infantry and moved inland to find and mark the river access positions for the bridging LVTs, which quickly followed. These were successfully emplaced and immediately proved most useful. The overall movement inland, however, was slow because the troops, expecting to find the enemy at any moment, advanced with care. Moreover the terrain of the coastal plain, particularly near the Tenaru River on the route of advance of the 1st Marines, was extremely difficult. Trucks could not tow artillery in position and amtracs had to be pressed into service to do the job. At 1430, Colonel Cates's 1st Marines were still passing through the 5th Marines and were a long way from Mount Austen; Colonel Cates had already concluded that his assigned objective had been incorrectly located and was well beyond the reach of his regiment.

By evening of D-Day, the Division had moved its troops ashore in a relatively smooth landing. In contrast, the supply situation on the beach was chaotic. There, the Pioneer Battalion had far too few hands to unload boats and set up supply dumps. This situation had arisen because no combat unit commander wanted to weaken his force to provide working parties while expecting a fight at any moment. The result was a worsening confusion that by 2230 had forced General Vandegrift to request Admiral Turner, although to suspend unloading until the beach could be cleared. Admiral Turner, under pressure to get all supplies ashore as quickly as possible, accepted the situation and reluctantly agreed.

The enemy reaction that first day had been relatively light. Eighteen bombers

Left: LVT(1)s of the 1st Amphibian Tractor Battalion bring supplies ashore during the Guadalcanal landing on 7 August 1942. Note the canvas cover used to protect the cargo compartment in high surf. The LVT(1)s were unarmored and armed with three World War 1 model water-cooled .30 caliber machine guns and one .50 caliber machine gun. (USMC)

had arrived at 1320, but had damaged only one destroyer. A second attack at 1500 had caused no damage at all. That night the forces afloat were undisturbed, but trigger-happy Marines ashore were busy shooting at shadows, noisy land crabs . . . and occasionally hitting fellow Marines. The next morning the order to take Mount Austen was cancelled and the Marines were directed to take the airfield and expand the beachhead in preparation for establishing a defense perimeter. By nightfall, the Marines had overrun the unfinished airfield and uncovered large stocks of food, supplies and ammunition left behind by the Japanese. These had been quickly secured . . . but not before Sergeant Cantrell of Company "A", 1st Amphibian Tractor Battalion, had liberated a generous load of Japanese Asahi beer. Cantrell assured the friends he invited to share his bounty that he, personally, had tested the beer for purity and that warnings given earlier that the Japanese might poison abandoned consumables were unfounded.

The day otherwise had been marked by a forty bomber raid at noon which damaged a destroyer and set the transport *George F. Elliott* on fire; both ships later sank. The dramatic night to follow began with Admiral Turner's invitation to General Vandegrift to a conference on the flagship. There, shortly before midnight, Vandegrift learned that Turner would pull all transports and cargo ships out the next morning. The reasons given were that a Japanese task force was reported to be moving south and that Admiral Fletcher, having lost twenty-one aircraft, had already left . . . taking with him all available air support.[27] Soon after this bad news was announced, the Japanese task force, which was thought to be some distance away, appeared and opened a devastating fire against the American screening group ships patrolling off Savo Island to cover the approaches to the transport area. In a short 32-minute engagement seven Japanese cruisers poured a hail of gunfire and torpedoes at four American and two Australian cruisers that left four sinking and a fifth damaged. Then, inexplicably, the Japanese force withdrew. After the war it was learned that a salvo from the *Quincey* had struck the Japanese flagship's operations center, destroying communications and navigation facilities. Vice-Admiral Gunichi Mikawa, finding his command capabilities impaired and his forces scattered, decided he should retire rather than run the risk of being attacked after daylight by American carrier aircraft.

Not until dawn did the Marines ashore discover the magnitude of the losses sustained in the Battle of Savo Island: Navy personnel killed in this battle exceeded the total number of Marines who would die throughout the Guadalcanal campaign. The only consolation was that the departure of the Japanese and the need for repair and rescue operations caused Turner to delay his departure. This allowed the unloading of the transports to resume at the beginning of the day. Unfortunately when he departed in the late afternoon, he took with him 1,390 Marines from working parties, headquarters detachments and support elements, including Company "A" of the 2nd Amphibian Tractor Battalion. Also included among the Marines who had been unable to get ashore was the headquarters of the 2nd Marine Regiment whose battalions had been committed individually in the Gavutu and Tanambogo battles.

Throughout the first three days the amtracs on Guadalcanal joined in the round-the-clock effort to supply the infantry, position artillery and clear the beach. When Turner left on the afternoon of 9 August, these tasks were far from

Right: *Amtracs used as pontoons over which wooden bridges have been built. Speed is of the essence during the initial landing hence the use of field expedients to span waterways. (USMC)*

Right, centre and bottom: *The success of the LVT bridges in Guadalcanal led Marines in New Zealand to test various types of bridges using LVTs for flotation; here are crossings with a truck and a light tank, whilst the latter shows a hinged platform bridge. (USMC)*

complete. The general situation, however, appeared stable . . . if only for the moment. The Tulagi area had been secured and the lack of enemy resistance on Guadalcanal had facilitated the seizure of the airfield and the organization of beachhead defenses. The difficulty was that without the U.S. Navy, the nearby waters and skies were open to the Japanese. This made it unacceptably hazardous to shift Marine units from Tulagi to Guadalcanal where they were sorely needed to strengthen the thin defense perimeter. The problem was evidenced by the frequent appearance of Japanese aircraft and occasional submarines. These last were particularly annoying, not because of the harassing fire of their deck guns, but because their crews came out on deck to do their laundry! Strangely enough, the Japanese made little effort to hit the congested beach where one well-directed bomb or shell would have created havoc. It was during these same early days, when the amtrac battalion had moved to the Tenaru River, that an enterprising amtrac officer, Captain Horace "Hod" Fuller, with the help of Joseph "Hoboken" Burns, put the Japanese power-house, which had been damaged by naval gunfire, back into operation.

Initially, the Japanese had not looked upon the American intrusion into the lower Solomons as serious. This confident attitude was due to the priority attention they were giving to extending their hold on New Guinea and to their gross underestimation of the strength of the American lodgement. Then too, the Imperial Navy had kept quiet about its defeat at Midway, but had been loud in proclaiming its victory at Savo Island. Thus, when Lieutenant-General Hyaku-take, commanding Japan's Seventeenth Army, was ordered to retake the southern Solomons, neither he nor any other Japanese thought it would be difficult. Under the confidence that prevailed, the dispersal and fragmentation of Seventeenth Army units was not seen as a problem. However, the piecemeal commitment of that Army which followed proved disastrous.

The first to suffer was Colonel Kiyono Ichiki whose 28th Infantry Regiment had been turned back at Midway. The Colonel, returning with his unit to Japan, was halted en route and ordered to Truk where an initial echelon comprising a reinforced infantry battalion was loaded on six destroyers for movement to Guadalcanal. The force arrived without incident late on the night of 18 August. The next day, Ichiki sent out a strong patrol which was wiped out by a Marine force from Company "A" of the 1st Marines under Captain Charles H. Brush. Despite this loss, and without awaiting the arrival of the rest of his regiment, Ichiki advanced along the beach towards the Marine positions on the east flank of the perimeter held by the 2nd Battalion, 1st Marines under Lieutenant Colonel Edwin A. Pollock. By midnight, 20 August, Marine outposts began reporting the presence of a large Japanese force. This was soon confirmed by Sergeant Major Vouza of the Native Constabulary who, the day before, had been captured by the Japanese, tortured, and left for dead. Vouza, with multiple wounds, had chewed through his bindings, escaped, and made his way through the Japanese forces to the Marine lines to report. Decorated by the American and British governments, Sergeant Major Vouza survived to live a long and respected life.

Shortly after 0300 on the 21st, Ichiki struck at the Marine positions with a company-size force. An initial penetration was promptly thrown back. Ichiki then reorganized and, under covering fire from supporting weapons, launched his whole force into a frontal assault. Meanwhile, the 1st Battalion, 1st Marines under Lieutenant Colonel Leonard B. Cresswell, had worked its way around the Japanese formation and at 0900 struck its flank and rear. The Japanese crumbled under these hammer and anvil tactics. The action was climaxed by the arrival of several light Marine tanks which soon finished the job. By late afternoon there were 800 Japanese dead on the beach and fifteen dazed prisoners under Marine guard. A handful of stragglers had managed to disappear into the nearby jungle. The Battle of the Tenaru was over![29]

Although the Marines had never accepted the myth of Japanese invincibility which grew out of the spectacular initial victories of Japanese arms, the abrupt departure of the U.S. Navy had left them uneasy. This feeling had not been helped by the encounters of the first Marine patrols. One in particular, launched on 12 August, had been a terrible tragedy. It had involved an ill-conceived landing in the vicinity of the Matanikau River under the leadership of Lieutenant Colonel Goettge. Included among the 24 others in the ill-fated patrol had been Lieutenant Commander Malcom L. Pratt, the 5th Marines' surgeon, Captain William Ringer, the 5th Marines' intelligence officer, and Lieutenant Ralph Cory, a Japanese language officer with an exceptional understanding and appreciation of Japanese history and culture. Goettge had expected to find a disorganized group of enemy survivors. His patrol, instead, ran into a well-armed ambushing force which promptly killed all but three of the Americans.[30] These were able to make their way back to friendly lines and report on the disaster. The shocking news, which quickly spread to all the troops in the perimeter, was offset in part by word that a destroyer transport had arrived with aviation ground personnel, supplies and fuel . . . the newly named Henderson Field, it appeared, would soon be occupied. Four days later a battalion strength operation in the same Matanikau River area battered Japanese forces. Then, on 20 August, Major John L. Smith brought in

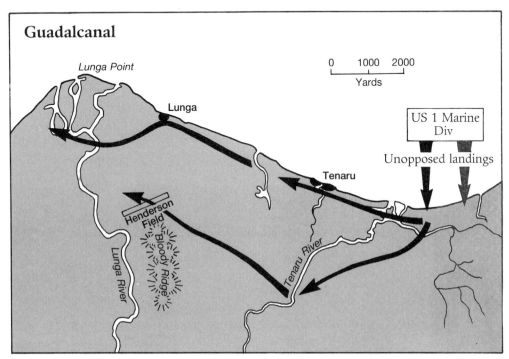

Guadalcanal

Above: *A Japanese officer of Colonel Ichiki's 28th Infantry, killed while leading his unit, during the Battle of Tenaru on 21 August 1942, against defences manned by the 1st Marines on the east flank of the American beachhead. (USMC)*

Right: *Native scouts lead a Raider unit into a ridge complex overlooking Henderson Field a few days before the attack by the Kawaguchi Brigade. Note the open nature of the ridges and the proximity of the jungle, providing excellent concealment for all movement even in daylight. (USMC)*

nineteen fighters from VMF 223 and Lieutenant Colonel Richard Mangrum landed with twelve dive-bombers from VMSB 232.

The arrival of Marine air units was an electrifying event which made it possible for the Americans to gain some measure of control over Guadalcanal's airspace and coastal waters, at least during the day. Thereafter, the Japanese were encouraged to conduct their supply, troop reinforcement and harassing operations at night . . . which gave rise to the Tokyo Express for logistic runs, to "Washing Machine Charlie" for nocturnal anti-personnel bomb drops, and to the use of destroyers for frequent night gunnery exercises targetting the Marines' positions. Everyone on Guadalcanal, ground troops, aviation personnel, officers and men, lived in foxholes or near dugouts where they shared in sleepless nights. It was a difficult period, particularly for the pilots who had to maintain demanding operational schedules each day. But with Marine aircraft now based ashore and with the first Japanese counter-thrust defeated, the Marines began to think that they might have a future after all!

The pattern of what was to follow was well set within two weeks of the Marine landings. Thenceforth each side sought to build up its forces on Guadalcanal to the point where it could drive the opponent out. The contest lasted six months and resulted in a succession of encounters at sea and ashore. Among the lesser of these were two incidents which involved Lieutenant Drew Barrett, a machine gun platoon commander in Company "M" of the 5th Marines. Barrett had found a Japanese 3-inch dual-purpose gun on the beach sector he was assigned to defend. He soon organized a gun crew and incorporated the weapon in his fire plan. The test came on 19 August when a Japanese light cruiser

slowly steamed by, well beyond the gun's maximum range. Undaunted, Barrett mustered his crew and opened fire. The cruiser disdainfully trained one turret and fired a single salvo which showered dirt over gun and crew and immediately convinced Barrett that the contest was unequal and should not continue. Five days later, a Japanese submarine fired a torpedo at a visiting American cargo ship standing off Barrett's platoon position. The torpedo missed the ship, ran up onto the beach and stopped directly in front of the 3-inch gun. Barrett regarded the torpedo attack as a personal affront and declared himself ready to fire again at the next opportunity. He was discouraged from doing so, however, by neighboring units who were not interested in being singled out as targets by Japanese gunners. The gun was never fired again.[31]

On 24 August, the day of Barrett's torpedoing, Admiral Fletcher with two carriers, encountered a strong Japanese force covering the movement of reinforcements to Guadalcanal. American carrier aircraft sank the Japanese light carrier *Ryujo*; the *Enterprise* was damaged in exchange. The contestants disengaged but later that night the Japanese reinforcement group reached Guadalcanal, unloaded its troops and shelled the Marine positions. The next morning Guadalcanal-based aircraft sank a Japanese destroyer. That ended the Battle of the Eastern Solomons, but not the Tokyo Express whose destroyers continued to ferry in men and supplies. In this fashion, General Kawaguchi's 35th Brigade and other elements making up a force of 6,000 men was assembled and readied for battle. The Americans, alerted to the imminent Japanese attack, strengthened their perimeter by bringing over troops from Tulagi and using support units, including the Pioneer and Amphibian Tractor Battalions, to occupy defensive positions. Included in these preparatory measures was the deployment of the raiders and paratroops under Lieutenant Colonel Edson on a commanding ridge one mile south of the airfield.

During this same period, the Cactus Air Force, so named after the code-name for Guadalcanal, continued to grow. The U.S. Army Air Corps contributed the 67th Fighter Squadron, equipped with limited capability P-40s. Soon after, other Marine fighter and dive-bomber squadrons were added. Then, on 30 August, the *Saratoga* was torpedoed and 24 of her fighters moved on to Guadalcanal. Less than two weeks later, on 12 September, a Japanese naval task force arrived to shell Marine positions while Japanese patrols probed Edson's force on the ridge. The next day was marked by sporadic fighting on the ground and in the air. That night, Kawaguchi threw in his main effort, which bent but did not overrun Edson's Marines. The precarious situation was stabilized by the arrival of the 2nd Battalion, 5th Marines which joined in the destruction of Kawaguchi's command. Colonel Edson's direction of the Battle of the Ridge, an exemplary example of personal leadership under the most demanding of combat conditions, earned him the Medal of Honor.

The days immediately following the defeat of the Kawaguchi Brigade were relatively calm. At sea, however, a task force bringing in the 7th Marines from Samoa together with badly needed aviation gasoline and other supplies was roughly handled. Japanese torpedoes sank the carrier *Wasp*, damaged the battleship *North Carolina*, and sank a destroyer, but the reinforcements arrived on 18 September and offloaded safely. The aircraft from the *Wasp* were added to the

Right: Guadalcanal, September 1942. A Japanese paymaster's safe has been converted to an oven by Marine cooks seeking to improve the two-meals per day routine imposed by shortage of rations. (USMC)

Cactus Air Force. The Marines now had eleven infantry battalions on Guadalcanal. Accordingly, General Vandegrift moved his infantry to the more vulnerable flank and inland defensive positions and entrusted the less threatened beaches to his support units, including the 1st Amphibian Tractor Battalion.

By now, most of the LVT(1)s had become inoperative. A few could still be used for special transport tasks such as the supply of the Marines at the Matanikau River in early October, where amtracs also were used to make noise at night to deceive the Japanese into believing the Marines were making a crossing. Other than for such infrequent assignments, the amtrac units settled into defensive positions whence they continued to assist aviation personnel in servicing aircraft armament and providing machine gun parts to infantry units . . . this being made possible by the generous allowance of three .30 caliber machine guns and one .50 caliber machine gun for each amtrac.

The Japanese themselves were not idle. As Marine patrols probed the Matanikau area it became apparent that strong new Japanese forces were being assembled there for yet another thrust at the perimeter. Most disturbing was the fact that the Japanese had now brought in several 150mm guns with the range to hit anything within the perimeter, including the airfield. The Marines decided to strike at the enemy and force his artillery beyond range of the airfield. By strange coincidence the Marine attack, launched on 7 October, came at the same time that Colonel Tadamasu Nakamura moved out with his 4th Infantry Regiment to bring the artillery closer to the Marine positions. In a confused and difficult three days of fighting, much of it in heavy rain, the Marines succeeded in killing 700 Japanese at a cost of 65 dead and 125 wounded. The action was broken off when the Marines learned that a massive new Japanese force was coming in against them; General Hyakutake himself had just landed and would take personal command of the decisive effort.

Even after the heavy losses they had sustained, the Japanese on Guadalcanal totalled some 20,000 men in mid-October. These included the 2nd Sendai Division, two battalions of the 38th Division, substantial artillery and combat support units, and the remnant of the Ichiki and Kawaguchi forces. The Marine strength was about the same. But, where the Japanese could continue to send in fresh units, the Americans had nothing in their rear areas to call forward. Moreover, battle attrition and disease were steadily weakening the Cactus defenders. These adverse circumstances caused Admiral Ghormley to relieve the Army's 164th Infantry Regiment from garrison duty in New Caledonia and send them to reinforce the hard-pressed Marines. The transports with the Army troops were protected by a task force built around four cruisers under command of Rear Admiral Norman Scott. Early on 10 October, Scott surprised a strong Japanese force near Guadalcanal and in a confused night action mortally damaged one Japanese cruiser, severely damaged another and sank a destroyer. The American cruiser *Boise* was damaged. The Battle of Cape Esperance was counted as an American victory not only because the losses favored the Americans, but also because the Japanese withdrew and left the way clear for the landing of the 164th Infantry two days later.

The newly arrived Army troops, former National Guardsmen from the Dakotas, received a rude welcome. On the day of their landing, the Japanese opened up with their long-range shore-based artillery. Then, that night, a task force including two battleships entered Sealark Channel, by then renamed Iron Bottom Bay, and in ninety minutes fired more than 900 fourteen-inch rounds into the airfield and vicinity. Half the American aircraft were destroyed and casualties, particularly among aviation personnel, were heavy. Daylight brought no relief; instead there were two heavy air raids. That night a cruiser force resumed the bombardment of the airfield; the same pattern was repeated the next day and the night that followed.

On the night of 14 October, while Japanese cruisers were delivering the first allotment of 750 eight-inch rounds to the groggy Marines, five transports arrived and started to disembark General Maruyama's 2nd Division. When daylight appeared, the Marines patched up whatever remaining aircraft appeared operational and launched a succession of strikes against the Japanese transports unloading within full view of the beleaguered Marines. Even the 1st Marine Air Wing commander's PBY was pressed into service for a spectacular torpedo run which earned Major Jack Cram, General Geiger's pilot, the Navy Cross. That evening the Japanese transports were beached and afire, but more than 3,000 troops with large quantities of equipment and supplies had been put ashore. These were quickly integrated into the Japanese commander's attack plan, which called for a major thrust against the Marine perimeter from the south and a diversionary attack across the Matanikau to the west. These attacks were scheduled for 18 October.

Heavy rains and difficult terrain hampered the movement of the Japanese main body and forced a delay in the main effort. However the diversion force near the Matanikau began to probe Marine lines with patrols on 20 October. All of these were thrown back by the vigilant Marines. Finally, on the evening of the 23rd, the Japanese spearheaded an attack with nine tanks. Marine 37mm guns stopped the Japanese armor cold; heavy artillery fire from the 11th Marines then decimated the Japanese infantry and ended the action.

The main attack, directed against the same ridge unsuccessfully assaulted by General Kawaguchi in September, began at 0300 on 25 October. This time the position was held by the 1st Battalion, 7th Marines under command of the legendary Lieutenant Colonel Lewis B. "Chesty" Puller; the 2nd Battalion, 164th Infantry was deployed on the left. The American line met the initial Japanese attack, but as the enemy continued to press, Puller called for reinforcements. The 3rd Battalion, 164th Infantry was ordered forward. Their move at night in heavy rain and into an area swept by enemy fire resulted in the Army battalion being fed piecemeal into the battle. Despite this unavoidable procedure, the Japanese attacks, which continued throughout the night, were all contained. At dawn the Japanese 150mm guns, which the Marines collectively called "Pistol Pete" opened a sustained fire. Soon after, Japanese aircraft began to parade overhead in a succession of raids which kept the Marines at "Condition Red" for the entire day. Finally, to ensure that this Sunday would not be forgotten, three Japanese destroyers dashed into Iron Bottom Bay, drove off two American destroyer transports, sank a tug, set two harbor patrol boats afire and bombarded beach positions.

That night the Japanese infantry again tried to pierce the American lines . . . and, again they failed. Then, after having lost a divisional commander, two regimental commanders and 3,500 officers and men, the Japanese broke contact and withdrew. The ground action was over. At sea, however, a large Japanese task force built around four carriers and four battleships appeared off the Santa Cruz islands. Rear Admiral Thomas C. Kincaid, who had relieved Fletcher, moved to the attack. In a violent exchange of air strikes on 26 October, three Japanese carriers and two destroyers were damaged. The Americans lost the *Hornet* and one destroyer, and had the *Enterprise, South Dakota, San Juan* and one destroyer damaged. The Americans also lost 74 aircraft. Far more crippling to the Japanese was the loss of one hundred of their carrier aircraft. The Battle of Santa Cruz was inconclusive, but when the Japanese commander heard of the failure of the ground forces' attack against the American perimeter, he withdrew. The round thus went to the Americans.

The tide appeared to be favoring the Americans. Already, on 18 October, the aggressive Vice Admiral William F. Halsey, Jr. had replaced the ill-served Ghormley and had immediately promised General Vandegrift all the support he could find. Then General Holcomb, the Marine Commandant who was visiting the area at the time, initiated action to place the landing force commander on the same command level as the naval task force commander for planning and grant the landing force commander unhampered authority over operations ashore following the assault phase. This would henceforth give the landing force commander a stronger voice in planning decisions and would help in keeping aggressive admirals from trying to direct combat operations on land. The final positive note of the month was sounded on 24 October when President

Roosevelt, confronted by the conflicting demands of the European and Pacific theaters, had directed the Joint Chiefs of Staff to ensure that Guadalcanal be rapidly reinforced.

The first unit affected was the 147th Infantry Regiment, standing ready to implement the long-waiting plan to occupy Ndeni. Halsey cancelled the plan and sent the regiment to Guadalcanal. The 8th Marine Regiment and the 2nd Raider Battalion followed, along with numerous Army and Marine support units. One of these, an Army 155mm gun battery which went into action on 2 November 1942, was equipped with French GPF guns manufactured at Le Creusot in 1917; a reminder that in World War I, a good portion of the artillery of the American Expeditionary Corps had been provided by our ally. This was not the only example of vintage armament used on Guadalcanal. The Marines went ashore with the 1903 bolt-action rifle and their 1917 water-cooled .30 caliber machine guns were carried on the same two-wheel hand-towed carts that had been used on the Western Front a generation earlier.

The Marine command on Guadalcanal moved quickly to exploit the defeat of General Hyakutake and make use of the arriving American air and ground units. Early on the morning of 1 November, the 5th Marines crossed the Matanikau River and advanced some 1,000 yards against light resistance, to the vicinity of Point Cruz where a strong Japanese force was encountered. The Japanese were encircled the next day and on 3 November the position was assaulted and overrun; more than 300 enemy dead were counted in the area and twelve 37mm anti-tank guns and thirty-four machine guns were also captured. At the news of this new disaster, General Hyakutake decided to forego a planned move against Port Moresby in favor of cleaning the Americans out of Guadalcanal once and for all. To that end, he called for his remaining reserves from Rabaul.

The first move in the Japanese plan was to assemble all units remaining on the island at Koli Point, some dozen miles to the east of the Marine perimeter; these forces would then be augmented with new arrivals. A Marine patrol had the area under observation on 2 November when six Japanese ships brought in 1,500 fresh troops. This began a month-long series of violent clashes scattered over a wide area, which succeeded in destroying most of the Japanese in the eastern part of the island. The action then shifted back to the area west of the perimeter, where additional fresh Japanese had landed. But, as the Americans began to move against these new intruders, word was received of a possible major Japanese offensive. The Marines pulled back to the Matanikau to prepare themselves. On 12 November the Japanese landed the remainder of their 38th Division without incident. The same day the Americans brought in the 182nd Infantry Regiment. That night a Japanese bombardment force with two battleships moved down to hit the airfield. Rear Admiral Daniel Callaghan with five cruisers took on the superior force and drove it off. The cost, however, was high. Admiral Callaghan was killed, as was Admiral Scott who had brought in the troop transports. In addition the Americans lost two cruisers and four destroyers and had two other cruisers and two destroyers damaged. The Japanese battleship *Hiei* received eighty hits and was finished off by the Cactus Air Force the next morning.

A second Japanese bombardment group moved in on the night of 14 November and worked over the Guadalcanal airfield for half an hour. Damage

Above: *A Marine patrol prepares to move out in captured Japanese Army trucks to an assembly point from where it will continue on foot into the interior. (USMC)*

was slight and the force withdrew. The next morning, Guadalcanal aircraft from Henderson Field were surprised to discover that a large Japanese force with transports carrying an estimated 10,000 men and large stocks of supplies was heading for Guadalcanal, despite the obvious failure of the two bombardment groups to put the airfield out of action. The Japanese task force was taken under attack by shore- and carrier-based aircraft throughout the day. By evening, nine transports had been hit and seven sunk; 5,000 troops, however, were rescued by Japanese destroyers. That night Admiral Kondo with one battleship and four cruisers made one more attempt at hitting the airfield. The Americans had two battleships waiting for him. When the Japanese arrived the Americans sank the battleship *Kirishima* and one destroyer at a cost of three destroyers and 42 hits on the American battleship *South Dakota*. The Japanese withdrew without striking at the airfield. At daybreak the last four Japanese transports, now unprotected, ran themselves up on the beach where they were able to disembark 2,000 troops before being destroyed by Cactus aircraft. The Battle of Guadalcanal was over; the last Japanese offensive had been stopped before it started, and although more fighting remained, the issue was no longer in doubt.

After the Battle of Guadalcanal, the Imperial Navy was ready to abandon the island. But in a reversal of earlier roles, the Imperial Army objected. Thus, one more attempt was made to uphold a lost cause. On 30 November, Rear-Admiral Taizo Tanaka with eight destroyers, six of which were crammed with troops, arrived off Tassafaronga where he encountered a strong American force under Rear Admiral Carleton H. Wright. The Americans detected the Japanese but waited too long to launch torpedoes. When they did, they hit nothing. The twenty Japanese torpedoes fired in reply sank one American cruiser and damaged three others. The Battle of Tassafaronga was a costly affair for the Americans, but it denied the Japanese access to Guadalcanal and cost them one destroyer.

Most importantly, it demonstrated to the Japanese that entry into Guadalcanal waters would henceforth be difficult if not impossible.

Whatever the news, nothing could depress the Marines of the 1st Division, who had just learned they were to be relieved. On 9 December 1942, General Vandegrift passed command of the Guadalcanal area to Major General Alexander M. Patch, commanding the Army's Americal Division. The 5th Marines were embarking on their transports even as the change-of-command ceremony was taking place. The remainder of the Division soon followed and by Christmas most of the troops were in Australia and under General MacArthur's command.

The Japanese retained some 25,000 troops on Guadalcanal. These were scattered, short of supplies and physically spent. But, 50,000 fresh troops had arrived in Rabaul waiting to move into battle. The difficulty, as demonstrated in December, was that runs to Guadalcanal were now prohibitively costly; three such attempts had cost the Japanese ten destroyers damaged and one submarine sunk. Thus, with the New Year, the Japanese decided to abandon Guadalcanal to the Americans. During the following six weeks some 11,000 Japanese were evacuated. At that same time, the Americans brought in the 8th Marines, the last element needed to complete the 2nd Marine Division, and the Army's 25th Infantry Division. This gave General Patch a three division force which, on 2 January 1943, was designated XIV Corps. The Army and Marine units supported by more than 200 Army, Navy and Marine aircraft, based at the newly designated Marine Corps Air Base, Guadalcanal, moved off against the remaining Japanese and, in a succession of sharp actions, cleared the island. On 9 February 1943, General Patch reported "The Tokyo Express no longer has a terminus on Guadalcanal!"[32]

Guadalcanal cost the Marines 4,000 battle casualties and twice that number were incapacitated by malaria and other tropical diseases. The price, though painful, was relatively low in terms of what had been accomplished. In General Vandegrift's own words written five years later:

> "We struck at Guadalcanal to halt the advance of the Japanese. We did not know how strong he was, nor did we know his plans. We knew only that he was moving down the island chain and that he had to be stopped.
>
> We were as well trained and as well armed as time and our peacetime experience allowed us to be. We needed combat to tell us how effective our training, our doctrines and our weapons had been.
>
> We tested then against the enemy, and we found that they worked. From that moment in 1942, the tide turned and the Japanese never again advanced."[33]

The amphibian tractor units had shared in the hardships of the campaign and had demonstrated the versatility of their vehicles in a host of logistic tasks. There also had been a few incidents where individual amtracs had served as tactical vehicles. The other lesson learned was that the LVT(1) was not mechanically reliable. Thus, as time went on most of the amtracs became inoperable and the troops were used for perimeter defense. Under the circumstances there was no reason to suggest changes in organization or function of amphibian tractor units. The 1st Battalion left its few remaining serviceable vehicles on Guadalcanal, and went on to Australia to be rested and re-equipped with new LVT(1)s in preparation for the campaign to follow.

3. From Service Troops to Shock Troops

The Southwest Pacific jungles to Tarawa Atoll, 1943

THE gloom cast over the western Pacific by the Japanese victories of early 1942 was dispelled by the success of American arms in the Guadalcanal campaign and the equally decisive battles that ended the year. While the Army, Navy, Air Corps and Marines had irreversibly stopped the Japanese advance, the American home front had been mobilized for production of the resources needed to force the Japanese back to their home islands and ultimate defeat. The outpourings of farm, mill, shipyard and factory increased progressively in 1943, even as the armed forces multiplied.

Included in the shipbuilding effort were several novel amphibious seagoing ships able to unload troops, vehicles and other cargoes directly on to a beach. The most important of these was the 300-foot Landing Ship, Tank (LST). Among other smaller landing ships were the Landing Ship, Mechanized (LSM) and the Landing Craft, Infantry (LCI). A host of other landing craft also were

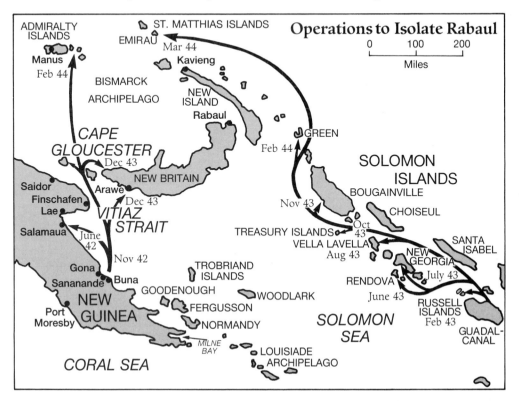

Operations to Isolate Rabaul

Above: *The LVT(1) made its first appearance in 1941 and first saw battle action at Guadalcanal in August 1942. The LVT(1), 1,225 of which were built, was 21 feet 6 inches long, 9 feet 10 inches wide and 8 feet 2 inches high. It weighed 18,500 pounds and had a cargo capacity of 4,500 pounds. Power came from a 150hp Hercules gas engine which provided a land speed of 12mph and a water speed of 6mph with ranges of 120 miles on land and 50 miles on water. The vehicle was unarmored and normally armed with three .30 and one .50 caliber machine guns. Note the pipe-guards on this model which prevented vegetation or other debris from damaging the forward idler sprocket – this was a local modification never adopted generally. (USMC)*

Below: *The LVT(3), produced by the Borg-Warner Company in 1944, was first used in the Okinawa operation; a total of 2,962 were produced. The LVT(3) had a cargo capacity of some 12,000 pounds and a weight of 26,600 pounds. Its power was provided by two 220 hp Cadillac V-8 engines which gave a land speed of 17mph and a water speed of 6mph; land range 150 miles, water range 75 miles. (USMC)*

being built; these included the Landing Craft, Utility (LCU) and the LCVP and LCM encountered earlier. In similar fashion, the amphibian tractor or Landing Vehicle, Tracked (LVT) was evolving and diversifying.

Earlier reference has been made to efforts to design a cargo amtrac superior to the LVT(1). This was accomplished in the latter half of 1941 by the LVT(2), a Food Machinery Corporation (FMC) design offering greater cargo capacity and a much improved track and suspension system. But, with the onset of the war, the design of the LVT(1) had been frozen to facilitate mass production. Hence, it was not until early 1943 that production of the LVT(2) could get under way; 2,963 of these vehicles were eventually built. Meanwhile, production of the LVT(1) continued throughout 1942 and into early 1943, by which time 1,225 of these first generation machines had been produced.

At the time LVT(1) production had started, the Commandant of the Marines Corps had recommended to the Chief of Naval Operations in a letter dated 27 June 1941, that an armored amtrac mounting a 37mm gun be made available to support infantry in the early hours of a landing.[1] The Navy invited Roebling and FMC to join in satisfying the requirement. The result was the design of the LVT(A)1, an LVT(2) built of light armor rather than sheet steel, and mounting the 37mm gun and turret currently used on the light tank. A pilot model of the LVT(A)1 was completed in June 1942, tested, and put into production in the summer of 1943; 509 of these armored amphibians were eventually built. Earlier that same year, production also began on an armored version of the cargo-carrying LVT(2), which the Army had requested. This amtrac, of which 450 were built, was designated LVT(A)2 and was the only cargo amtrac to carry the (A) designation.

While the Navy and FMC were moving ahead with their LVT(2) and LVT(A)1 designs, the Borg-Warner Corporation built a prototype amtrac with stern ramp in response to a Marine Corps request for an LVT from which troops could easily disembark and whose capacity was not limited to cargo that could be manhandled over the side. The prototype proved unacceptable, but the design was subsequently improved and modified and went into production in 1944 as the LVT(3); 2,962 of these were completed and went on to serve in the invasion of Okinawa, the post-war Marine Corps and throughout the Korean War.

FMC also had responded to the Marine request by moving the LVT(2) engine forward to a position immediately behind the cab, and fitting a ramp on the stern. This became the LVT(4) whose production began in December 1943 and was continued until 8,348 of the model had been built. The final innovation in LVT design to take place during World War II was the substitution of an open turret with a 75mm howitzer from the M8 motor-gun carriage for the 37mm gun turret on the LVT(A)1. This more powerful armored amtrac, the LVT(A)4, was put into production in early 1944 and 1,890 were eventually built. The next year a gyro-stabilized and power-traversed weapon turret was introduced in what became the LVT(A)5. A total of 269 of these were produced, but too late to see any action until the Korean War.

Of note is the fact that most of the improved amtracs were designed in the 1942–1943 period before the tactical value of the vehicle had been demonstrated. This makes it evident that the combat potential of the vehicles was appreciated before they were put to the test in active operations. No comparable innovation, however, was revealed when it came to the production of recovery, maintenance or command vehicles. No such specialized vehicles were factory-produced during World War II. Those that appeared were built by the using units who made do with parts from winch-trucks, machine-shop trailers and other maintenance equipment normally found in motorized units. In that regard, the cargo amtrac units had the greater difficulties because their organizational allowances were inferior to those of the armored amtrac units. In all cases, however, the multiple difficulties arising from the need to salvage vehicles on reefs, swamped in the surf, or inoperative on land taxed the ingenuity of amtrac battalion maintenance sections. No less demanding was the requirement to service and keep in operation the maximum number of machines for extended periods of time with limited spare parts and the most rudimentary of facilities.

The necessary emphasis on recovery and maintenance capabilities coupled with the constant demands from using units for "all the amtracs available" lessened the opportunity and resources to undertake other efforts to devise amtracs for such ancillary uses as command or engineer support. One command LVT was built but never used because the LST on which it was embarked broke down and could not offload it. The only recorded "engineer" adaptation was a yard-arm with hanging grapnels that was to be fitted at the end of a boom fixed to the forward end of an amtrac. The device, intended to detonate mines near or on a beach, could not be installed on an LVT afloat, and, if it had, it would have affected the vehicle's flotation and made it impossible to land through surf. This device, like the command LVT, did not see combat.

The increasing tempo of industrial production which characterized 1943 was complemented by an equally important growth of Marine Corps ground combat units. The year began with the reassembling of the long fragmented 2nd Marine Division whose regiments had been sent separately to Guadalcanal, and now had left for New Zealand. Then, on 15 February 1943, the 2nd Amphibian Tractor Battalion also found itself again complete when its Company "A" arrived from the New Hebrides where it had been sent after its withdrawal from Guadalcanal in mid-August 1942. By that time the 1st Division with the 1st Amphibian tractor Battalion attached, had settled down in the Melbourne area of Australia.

In May 1942, after the 1st Marine Division had left New River, its rear echelon had been used to form the 3rd Marine Infantry Regiment intended for eventual assignment to the new 3rd Marine Division. In August 1942 the 3rd Marines had been sent to San Diego whence, within a week, they sailed for Samoa. Meanwhile, the 9th Marine Infantry Regiment, which had been formed as part of the 2nd Marine Division in February of 1942, was left behind at Camp Elliott, California, later to be incorporated in the 3rd Marine Division. The last of the three infantry regiments of the Division, the 21st Marines, had been formed from elements of the 6th Marines left at New River and moved to Camp Elliott in November 1942.

The 3rd Amphibian Tractor Battalion had an equally incremental origin. Soon after the 3rd Marine Division was formed in September 1942, Captain Erwin F. Wann had organized the headquarters of the 3rd Amtrac Battalion in

Right: An LVT(4) of the 3rd Amphibious Tractor Battalion surrounded by Marine dead awaiting burial on Iwo Jima, February 1945. (USMC)

Right: The LVT(4) fitted with stern ramp and armed with four .30 caliber machine guns, could carry 8,000 pounds of cargo or 35 fully equipped combat troops. The most widely used amphibian of WWII, of which 8,348 were built, it first appeared in combat during the Saipan landing on 15 June 1944. (FMC)

Right: The LVT(A)1 with hull built of light armor was the first amphibious tank. It was fitted with a revolving turret mounting a 37mm cannon and two aft scarf ring machine guns. (FMC)

Above: First used in combat in Saipan in June 1944, some 1,890 LVT(A)4s were produced during the war. (USN)

Centre: The LVT(A)1 was first used during the invasion of Kwajalein atoll, Marshall Islands, beginning on 31 Jan 1944. Some 509 were produced during the war. (USMC)

Bottom: After WWII, LVT (3)s were fitted with an armored overhead cover and a single forward machine gun turret. The LVT(3)C became the standard post-war Marine amphibian vehicle, being used in the Inchon landing in 1950 and throughout the war in Korea. (USMC)

San Diego using stay-behind elements of the recently departed 2nd Amtrac Battalion. In the following three months, "B" and "C" Companies, formed earlier at New River, had moved west where the remaining units of the battalion had been organized, and the whole was brought up to strength. At the end of 1942, Major Sylvester "Pete" Stephen had come aboard as battalion commander, and "Bob" Wann had become his exec; the 3rd Amphibian Tractor Battalion was then moved to Camp Pendleton. There, its Company "A" was detached to reinforce the 9th Marines, and its "C" Company went on to Samoa to reinforce the 3rd Marines. In February 1943, the remainder of the battalion was sent to New Zealand where the 3rd Marine Division was later brought together. Four months later, the 3rd Division with its amtracs was deployed to an advanced base on Guadalcanal for final training and preparation for combat.

The organization of the 4th Marine Division had followed a similar sequence of events. Its oldest infantry regiment, the 23rd Marines, had been formed at New River as part of the 3rd Marine Division together with the 21st Marines. In February 1943 the 23rd Marines had been detached from the 3rd Division and earmarked for assignment to the new 4th Division. A part of the regiment was split off in May to form the 25th Marines; both regiments then moved to Camp Pendleton in the summer of 1943. The last infantry regiment of the 4th Division, the 24th Marines, was activated in August of that year. During the previous month, Major Louis Metzger had formed the 1st Armored Amphibian Battalion. This had been followed by the organization of the 4th Amphibian Tractor Battalion by Major Victor J. Croizat, who later passed command to Major Clovis B. Coffman.

This compressed summation of major unit activations in 1943 fails to convey any feel of the difficulties they engendered. For the men, most of whom were recruits, the strange but orderly life of boot camp was replaced by a confusing existence that mixed individual and unit training with incessant working parties to build facilities, receive, sort and prepare equipment and supplies for combat, and attend to a multitude of routine housekeeping details. Liberty ranged from most agreeable in Australia and New Zealand to non-existent on Guadalcanal. Even in the United States, neither Camp Pendleton nor New River offered many opportunities for "going ashore" because they were isolated and poorly served with any form of transportation. The officers shared in the uncertain existence of their men and had the added problem of sorting out a daily ration of conflicting requirements, all with the ultimate objective of getting the command ready for combat. Finally, for those who had already experienced the Japanese soldier on Guadalcanal, there was the knowledge that the enemy was a dedicated and resolute opponent who would do the utmost to ensure that the price of any encounter would always be high. The unusual demands of that year of accelerated growth reached a climax in the last month of 1943, shortly after the shock of the Tarawa operation reached home.

The assault landing on Betio Island in November 1943, as will be recounted later, moved the amphibian tractor from its logistical to a tactical role. The 4th Division observers who had survived Tarawa, had returned to report on the necessity of having adequate numbers of LVTs for the forthcoming landings in the Marshall Islands. At that time, each division had one amphibian tractor battalion which, when used in a tactical role, could land only the assault elements of two infantry battalions at one time. Thus, it was essential that the 4th Marine Division, due to land on the northern islands of the Kwajalein atoll in the Marshalls in a complicated amphibious assault operation, be given an additional amtrac battalion. To that end, the Commandant authorized the activation of the 10th Amphibian Tractor Battalion, reinforced by Company "A" of the 11th Amphibian Tractor Battalion. Major Croizat was given this command at the headquarters of the 4th Division at Camp Pendleton on 5 December 1943; the sailing date for the LSTs carrying the amtrac units to the invasion of the Marshalls was 6 January 1944, just thirty days away.[2]

The activation order authorized the use of elements of the 4th Amtrac Battalion as nuclei for the new units. That would help but, even so, within a brief month it would be necessary to erect a camp, integrate a flow of new personnel into cadre units, undertake such training as could be arranged, prepare the equipment and supplies needed for an assault landing, and participate in a rehearsal. It was also necessary to receive, service, arm, armor and install radios in new LVT(2)s located at naval facilities in San Diego, some fifty miles from the battalion's location at Camp Pendleton. Finally, for the 10th Amtrac Battalion, reinforced, there was the need to prepare the embarkation plans for units to sail on six LSTs, and co-ordinate landing plans with the Division artillery regiment and two infantry regiments whose battalions were to be landed by amtrac on D and D+1 days. For the 4th Amtrac Battalion, faced with comparable requirements but of a somewhat lesser magnitude, Christmas 1943 was a difficult and trying period; for the 10th Amtrac Battalion (reinforced), it was a blur of overlapping demands, fragmented decisions, and the passage of time in which days merged into nights without differentiation. Surcease did not come until early on 6 January 1944, when the laden ships cleared San Diego harbor and set course to the west. But, before those Marines can be followed to the central Pacific, the narrative must return to the clearing of the Solomans and Bismarcks.

When the Japanese decided to evacuate Guadalcanal in early 1943, they also conceded the Papuan peninsula to the Americans and Australians . . . who had paid for that decision with 8,500 casualties. The six-month struggle for that eastward extension of New Guinea had its origins in July 1942 when Allied intelligence learned of an imminent Japanese landing at Buna. Unfortunately, no response had been made to this information. The Japanese, thus, had been able to land 16,000 men and commit them in a drive over the Owen Stanley mountains towards Port Moresby. That effort had been marked by vicious fighting under exceptionally adverse climatic and terrain conditions. The determined Japanese had been worn down by a desperate delaying action that finally forced them to stop before they could break out of the mountains. It had then been the turn of the Americans and Australians to drive the Japanese back over the Kokoda Trail. The Allied offensive launched for that purpose began in October. A month later, Allied formations had reached the north coast of New Guinea. A final effort had then been mounted against the Buna–Sananda–Gona areas, where the decimated Japanese had concentrated. By January 1943 it was all over; the Japanese survivors had pulled out and regrouped in the Lae–

Above: *An LST with its top deck loaded with LVT(2)s heads in convoy for the Marshall Islands in January 1944.*

Below: *An LVT(2) with its hoisting cables still in position shortly after being lowered over the side – note the clutter and relatively small cargo space.*

Salamaua area of central New Guinea. Among the casualties of that little-remembered campaign had been the reputations of several senior Allied officers and the life of the Japanese commander, General Horii Tomitare, killed in action on the infamous Kokoda Trail.

The successful conclusion of the campaigns on Papua and Guadalcanal had opened the way for the next stage in the Allied advance towards Rabaul. This, as envisaged by General MacArthur in his CARTWHEEL plan, called for an advance up the Solomons by South Pacific forces and a parallel advance along the New Guinea coast by his South West Pacific forces. The Japanese, meanwhile, had sought to frustrate Allied moves by building an airfield at Munda Point on New Georgia Island, 170 miles west of Guadalcanal. No sooner had that field become operational in late 1942 than another had been started on nearby Kolombangara Island. Reports of the existence of these fields and of the deployment of forces for their defense had aroused Allied interest and caused the planners to urge that action be taken against them while it was still possible to do so with modest forces.

At that juncture the question of command once again appeared. The Solomons had originally been included in General MacArthur's South West Pacific Area (SWPA). Then, to accommodate the fact that the Guadalcanal campaign would initially be waged principally with naval forces, the Joint Chiefs of Staff had shifted the boundary of Admiral Ghormley's South Pacific Area (SOPAC) slightly to the west. Now, in early 1943, the Navy proposed a further boundary shift to enable the Navy to continue to move into the central and

Right: An LCI of General MacArthur's "Navy" lands a unit of the 1st Marine Division on Cape Gloucester, New Britain, Dec 1943. (USMC)

northern Solomons; the Army disagreed and no boundary change was made. Instead, Admiral Halsey, who by now had become the commander of SOPAC, was given responsibility for the advance up the Solomons chain, but under the "general directives" of General MacArthur.[3] Fortunately, the Admiral and General quickly established cordial relations and the command arrangement worked without friction.

With the command issue resolved, the Navy's attention turned to Munda, the obvious and immediate target. But the Japanese had earlier occupied the Russell Islands, 35 miles off Guadalcanal, for use as a staging area. Since these islands lay on the direct route between New Georgia and Guadalcanal, Admiral Halsey had to clear them before moving on to Munda. Approval for this preliminary operation was given by Admiral Nimitz on 23 January 1943. Soon after, the 43rd Infantry Division under Major General John H. Hester was designated as the landing force and directed to take Banika Island in the southern Russells; the 3rd Marine Raider Battalion under Lieutenant Colonel Harry B. Liversedge, would take Pavuvu Island in the north. The amphibious force under Admiral Turner sailed at midnight on 20 February and the landings began soon after first light on the 21st. By late morning both objectives had been secured and all supplies unloaded; the Japanese had decided not to contest the place and had cleared off before the Americans arrived. Strangely enough, no Japanese reaction took place for the next two weeks. Then the Russells were raided by determined Japanese air units almost daily for four months. The Americans, none the less, had pushed forward with their base development until on 15 April the first airfield became operational. It was not too much longer before the Russells became a major forward base and staging area.

Halsey had intended to begin his move against Munda on 15 May in conjunction with General MacArthur's advance in New Guinea and his seizure of the off-lying Trobriand Islands. In preparation, the Navy command launched a series of patrols into the New Georgia area to reconnoiter possible landing sites and report on Japanese activities. These patrols were continued until, at General MacArthur's request, the invasion date was delayed to 30 June. By late May, Admiral Turner, who would command the amphibious force, had prepared his plan. It envisaged a series of landings undertaken by two major task groups. The Western Force, built around General Hester's 43rd Infantry Division, Lieutenant Colonel William J. Scheyer's 9th Marine Defense Battalion with a platoon of twelve amtracs from the 3rd Amtrac Battalion headquarters and service company, and other reinforcing units, would land on Rendova Island. From there, shore-to-shore operations would be conducted against Munda and adjacent positions on New Georgia Island. The Eastern Force with the U.S. Army's 103rd Infantry Regiment under Colonel Daniel H. Hundley and the 4th Marine Raider Battalion commanded by Lieutenant Colonel Michael Currin, would take Segi Point, Wickham Anchorage and Viru Harbor on New Georgia.

Earlier, the Japanese had decided to strengthen their remaining positions in the Solomons and had ordered two divisions into central New Guinea. Incident to the implementation of those decisions, a convoy carrying 6,900 men of Japan's 51st Division embarked in eight transports and eight destroyers, had been spotted on 1 March and attacked by aircraft of the U.S. Army's Fifth Air Force on 2 and 3 March. The Battle of the Bismarck Sea, as the drama came to be known, cost the Japanese all eight of their transports and half of their destroyers. This disaster had so shocked the Japanese high command that it was moved to establish a system of small hidden staging bases to support the movement of troops and supplies by boats and barges operating along the chain of islands, rather than entrusting such cargoes to transports steaming across open waters. In this manner, the Japanese were enabled to continue their defense preparations.

By mid-1943, these had become sufficiently advanced to disturb Admiral Turner and cause him to move up the date for the landing at Segi Point to 21 June. This went off as planned and enabled the Americans to get an early start on the airfield planned for the area. Advancing the date for the landing of the Eastern Landing Force had upset the logistic support arrangements for the landing of the Western Force on Rendova. However, this adverse effect had been overcome and the main landings were able to proceed as originally scheduled on 30 June 1943.

Since the troops heading for the Rendova beaches expected to find friendly scouts awaiting them, the landing boats had raced towards the shore with little attention to formation or destination. But, to everyone's surprise, there were Japanese in the beach area who opened a brisk fire. This completely destroyed any semblance of order and organization in a landing already confused. Not until Colonel David N. M. Ross, commanding the 172 Infantry Regiment, got ashore was control restored, the beach cleared of the enemy, and the move inland started. Once that had been accomplished, things moved quickly and by early

Above: *A Bureau of Ships Tank Lighter, 1941 model, landing a truck on Guadalcanal in November 1942.*

Right: *LVT(3), recovery vehicle, with a winch, lifts a 105mm howitzer weighing 5,000 pounds. (USMC)*

Right: *LVT(1), modified into a recovery vehicle by the 2nd Amphibious Tractor Battalion in New Zealand, 1943. (USMC)*

Above: *The final campaign in the northern Solomons was the invasion of Empress Augusta Bay at Bougainville by the 3rd Marine Division in November 1943. The swampy terrain was exceptionally difficult and the 3rd Amphibian Tractor Battalion proved its worth. Here, an LVT(1) nicknamed "Swamp Angel" moves supplies through the mud on Bougainville. (USMC)*

afternoon the first echelon was ashore with fifty tons of supplies. By 4 July, Rendova was secured as were all other initial objectives assigned.

The shore-to-shore movement of units from Rendova to New Georgia for the move against Munda airfield had already started on 2 July. The build-up then continued until more than 30,000 troops, including the U.S. Army's 25th, 37th and 43rd Infantry Divisions, were engaged in the struggle for Munda. This action extended over a long month because of torrential rains, an able Japanese General, Noburu Sasaki, and 8,000 determined Japanese soldiers . . . more than half of whom had to be killed before the objective could be secured. The effort cost the Americans 5,000 casualties. While this bitter contest was unfolding, an equally vicious encounter, but on a lesser scale, was taking place to the northwest, where a mixed force of 2,200 soldiers and Marines under newly promoted Colonel Liversedge, was seeking to destroy Japanese detachments covering the Bairoko–Munda Trail in order to cut Munda supply lines from the north. Unfortunately, the American force lacked the heavy support weapons needed to overcome the stubborn Japanese defenders and its attack against Bairoko did not succeed.

With the fall of Munda on 5 August 1943, the campaign for the central Solomons had entered its final phase. General Sasaki, forced out of his positions in the south, sought to secure a beachhead in the northern part of New Georgia where he could receive reinforcements and prepare a counter-offensive. On 6 August, one such reinforcing group comprising 940 soldiers and 700 naval personnel embarked in four destroyers, entered Vella Gulf near Kolombangara Island. There, the Japanese force was surprised by Commander Frederic Mossburger with six destroyers. His American ships had promptly launched torpedoes and scored hits which sank three of the Japanese troop carriers; the fourth fled. That action, the Battle of Vella Gulf, ended Sasaki's hopes for a stand on New Georgia and forced him to withdraw the remnant of his command to Kolombangara. While the Japanese force was withdrawing, the Americans had undertaken mopping-up operations against scattered Japanese survivors, and landed on Arundel Island. On 15 August, landings were also made on Vella Lavella Island to isolate Kolombangara, where the Japanese were digging themselves in. The struggle for Vella Lavella continued until 9 October when the 3rd New Zealand Division finally liquidated the last pocket of enemy troops. By that time the Japanese had evacuated Kolombangara and the Allies found themselves masters of the central Solomons.

The U.S. Army, with its XIV Corps of three divisions, had well and fully carried the main burden of the three-month campaign. Still, the Marines, while engaging only 5,000 men, had taken 726 casualties . . . an earnest measure of their contribution. Of note is the fact that the 9th Defense Battalion had taken only three amtracs into its first action and had found these so useful it quickly called for the remainder of the platoon. Later, at Vella Lavella, the 4th Defense Battalion had also used LVTs for logistic purposes. The importance of these vehicles in difficult terrain with poor communications, first noted at Guadalcanal and confirmed in the central Solomons, would be even more appreciated in the move into the northern Solomons that was about to begin.

In the same month of June 1943 when Halsey had struck against New Georgia, MacArthur had moved beyond Goodenough Island to seize positions in the Trobriands. With his flank thus covered, the General had begun his move out of Papua, using the limited shipping in the Seventh Amphibious Force under Rear Admiral Daniel E. Barbey and the services of a novel organization, the 2nd Engineer Special Brigade under Colonel William F. Heavy. This latter unit, in the theater only since January, was equipped with sufficient landing craft, eventually to include amtracs, to lift an infantry division and move it from friendly to hostile shores over a distance of up to 100 miles.

On 4 September, Allied forces were landed at Lae; the next day Major General Kenney's Fifth Air Force dropped 1,700 paratroopers on Nadzab. Salamaua, next on the target list, fell on 11 September, and was followed by the capture of Finschafen on 2 October. This gave the Allies one side of the Vitiaz Strait, which separates New Guinea from New Britain. Seizure of western New Britain was all that was needed to isolate Rabaul from the south. But, before that move could be made, the six airfields on or near Bougainville in the northern Solomons had to be neutralized and Allied air power brought in to enable shore-based fighters to reach Rabaul.

Bougainville, the last enemy stronghold in the Solomons, was occupied by an estimated 40,000 Japanese. The immediate problem was to find suitable landing sites away from the enemy but within range of aircraft based at Munda and Vella Lavella. Empress Augusta Bay, mid-way on the 130-mile long island, appeared to meet the requirement. Another problem was the shortage of shipping caused by the diversions made to meet the needs of the central Pacific drive which was about to open with the assault on the Gilberts. Only eight troop transports and four cargo ships were available to lift the initial assault echelon to Bougainville. This meant that only two-thirds of the 3rd Marine Division could be accommodated; the remainder of the force, including the Army's 37th Infantry Division, would have to follow in turn-around shipping.

Lieutenant General Vandegrift, who had moved up to command the First Marine Amphibious Corps (I MAC), was responsible with Rear Admiral Theodore S. Wilkinson for the initial planning of the operation. These officers, working in close collaboration, agreed that a solution to the shipping shortage was to move a base depot into Vella Lavella and seize the Treasury Islands, southwest of Bougainville, as an intermediate advance base. Motor torpedo-boats from there could then harass the enemy on Bougainville, interfere with his barge traffic and, most importantly, cover the American communications between the rear depot and the Bougainville beachhead. As a further measure, it was agreed that the landings would be made on a wide front and that as much as forty per cent of the assault echelon would be used to work the ships and the beaches to ensure prompt offloading and early departure of the assault shipping. Finally, lest the enemy correctly assess the purpose of the landing in the Treasury Islands, the 2nd Parachute Battalion was ordered to land on Choiseul Island, southeast of Bougainville, to create a diversion.

As these problems were being addressed in mid-1943, the 3rd Marine Division under Major General Allen H. Turnage moved to Guadalcanal from New Zealand, where it had been occupying 22 separate campsites since its arrival in increments earlier in the year. In August, the Division undertook a vigorous training program to fine-tune the men for the battle to come. At the same time, the staffs went into the final detailed planning. In general, the assault would be made by the 3rd Marines and the 2nd Raider Battalion landing over six beaches on the right, while the 9th Marines with the 3rd Raiders were to land on six beaches on the left. One of these last was actually on Puruata Island, which was to be cleared by the 3rd Raiders of any defenders who might bring fire to bear over any of the beaches. The 21st Marines in reserve, together with the 3rd Amphibian Tractor Battalion and other Army and Marine units, were to move up in turn-around shipping as soon as possible. In short, the plan called for landing 14,000 men and 6,200 tons of supplies on D-Day and the prompt release of shipping to return to nearby bases for succeeding increments of troops, equipment and supplies.

The logistic aspects of the operation appeared to be well in hand; 29 amtracs were to accompany the initial force to work the beaches, the other 95 LVTs of the 3rd Battalion would join later. Tactically, however, there were two problems. The first was that detailed information on the landing beaches and enemy dispositions was lacking. A patrol sent in September had identified beaches for landing and had reported no enemy activity. However, aerial reconnaissance had revealed enemy forces in the Cape Torokina area and a second patrol dispatched to verify this latest information had failed to return. The landing force would have to cope with more than usual of the fog of battle. What added to the concern was that only four destroyers had been assigned to provide naval gunfire support, and these ships had no experience in this task.

The assault echelon of the 3rd Marine Division left Guadalcanal on 13 October for Efate where a week-long rehearsal was held. On 26 October, Brigadier Row's New Zealanders landed on the Treasury Islands and the next day Lieutenant Colonel Krulak's paratroopers came in over the beach at Choiseul. The landings on Bougainville began on schedule shortly after 0700 on 1 November 1943. The 9th Marine landed without opposition. The surf, however, was difficult and caused some 70 boat casualties. The 3rd Raider Battalion found a platoon of Japanese soldiers on Puruata Island. These were promptly engaged and soon dispatched, but not before they had interfered with the landings of the 3rd Marines. The greatest difficulty encountered by that regiment befell its 1st Battalion near Torokina Cape where 300 Japanese had organized a strong defense around 25 pill-boxes and one 75mm gun. The gun knocked out six boats during the landing and a strafing run by several Japanese Zeros at the same time did not help. Still, the Marines got ashore and in a bitter hand-to-hand fight which lasted for three hours accounted for 270 of the defenders. This was a highly commendable performance for green troops coming up against the first defended beach encountered in the war.

To support the operation, General Kenney had launched a series of air strikes against Rabaul beginning on 12 October. These, unfortunately, had been hampered by bad weather, with the result that the Japanese hit the Marine landings twice on D-Day with fighter and bomber units. The day after, a Japanese surface force with four cruisers and six destroyers came down from Rabaul to challenge the American Navy. The Japanese were received by Rear Admiral Aaron

S. Miller's Task Force 39 which, while inferior in strength, sent the Japanese back less one cruiser and one destroyer at negligible cost to itself. Admiral Halsey, perturbed by these shows of Japanese force, decided, with reluctance, to risk a carrier strike against Rabaul. This was accomplished on 5 November when Rear Admiral Frederick C. Sherman sent off 47 aircraft which damaged six cruisers and two destroyers and removed the surface threat to the Bougainville beachhead. On 11 November, additional carriers borrowed from the central Pacific joined Sherman in another strike against Rabaul in which 50 Japanese aircraft were shot out of the sky and shore facilities were heavily damaged. This greatly lessened the air threat against the Americans on Bougainville.

Meanwhile, the Marines ashore were extending their perimeter and developing strong defense positions. In so doing they encountered extensive swamp areas where, as the 3rd Division's report states:

> "The worth of the amphibian tractors soon became apparent as the problem of supply to the advancing units became more acute . . . Due to the swampy terrain and complete absence of roads, the LVTs were the only vehicles that could be used. In addition, displacement of three pack howitzer battalions was accomplished by amphibian tractors."[4]

In the execution of these varied duties, twelve amtracs from the headquarters of the 3rd Battalion had been assigned to support the 9th Defense Battalion. Support for the 3rd, 9th and 21st Marines was regularly provided by Companies "C", "A", and "B" of the 3rd Amtrac Battalion, respectively. The hard use to which all these amtracs were put is attested to by the fact that the battalion had 124 LVT(1) at the start of the Bougainville operation; three weeks later only 29 of these remained serviceable.

On 10 November, General Vandegrift turned over his I MAC command to Major General Roy S. Geiger and departed for Washington and new duties as Commandant of the Marine Corps. The 3rd Division went on to consolidate its defense perimeter, complete work on one airfield, start work on two more, and develop other facilities in Bougainville. Then, by December, the Army's XIV Corps had moved up and the Marines were relieved. The 3rd Marine Division was back on Guadalcanal by January 1944, having earned its first battle star.

Operations in the upper Solomons clearly demonstrated the interdependence of the military services. The multiple attacks launched by Allied forces threw the Japanese off balance and compounded their problem of adjusting plans to meet unexpected events. On the American side, the defense battalions had proven their worth. Initially intended for coast defense as well as anti-aircraft artillery roles, the defense battalions found themselves integrated into the Marine perimeter defenses at Guadalcanal and elsewhere. Because of this, tank platoons were assigned to these units as were amtracs to help in their local defense and general support. With the reduction in enemy capabilities, involvement with ground combat lessened and, eventually, the defense battalions were redesignated anti-aircraft units.

The raider battalions, as expected, proved to be excellent infantry, but their lack of heavy weapons severely limited their capability for sustained combat. This was demonstrated at Bairoko where the attack launched by Colonel Liversedge with the 1st and 4th Raider Battalions supported by the 3rd Battalion, 148th

Infantry had failed because the requested air support did not materialize and the 60mm mortars available were too light to have much effect.

During this same period, Major General Mulcahy, commanding the 2nd Marine Aircraft Wing, organized seven air support parties each with one officer and two communications technicians, to serve with ground units and direct air support missions. This was the beginning of an effort to formalize air-ground liaison procedures and develop the means of improving close air support for ground units. The Marines already had a reputation for excellence in aerial combat. Of the 2,500 enemy planes lost over the Solomons, 1,520 were shot down in aerial combat by Marine pilots. Marine aviation would soon gain added fame for the close air support it would provide. This, as it turned out, would primarily benefit the Army in its drive into the Philippines, since most of the air support for central Pacific operations would be provided by carrier-based Navy aircraft.

The stage was now set for the final act in the isolation of Rabaul, the seizure of western New Britain to mark the completion of CARTWHEEL. New Britain was perhaps the most forbidding of the islands of the southwest Pacific. Its exceptionally heavy rainfall makes for a dense jungle growth and discourages visitors; as a result, the island had been avoided for three centuries after its discovery. Then, in 1880, the Germans had moved in and built the orderly town of Rabaul on Simpson harbor at the eastern end of the island. The Australians had acquired the island after World War I but had done little to improve it. The economy of the island had deteriorated by the time the Japanese arrived in January 1942. Since then, the place had been developed into a major base complex with five airfields, an excellent fleet anchorage and, reportedly, the best brothel east of the Dutch Indies. When the war ended in 1945 the Imperial forces based at Rabaul numbered 100,000 men.

In June 1943, General MacArthur established the New Britain Force under Lieutenant General Walter Kreuger. This was the Sixth Army, also known as the Alamo Force. A month later, the Alamo Force issued its first directive on the New Britain operation. In response, the 1st Marine Division began moving into staging bases in New Guinea. In September, Division headquarters and the 1st Marines moved to Goodenough Island where the Sixth Army had its head-quarters. The 5th Marines, reinforced, arrived at Milne Bay and the 7th Marines, reinforced, set up at Oro Bay. This dispersal corresponded to the original plan proposed by Sixth Army for multiple landings. The Marines were unhappy with the concept because the Japanese had been developing western New Britain as a base area to support their forces in New Guinea. In the Marines' view the Cape Gloucester area with its airfield constituted the key objective and the fact that there were 10,000 Japanese defending it argued for a landing in force. In contrast, the Army plan for scattered small landings invited defeat in detail. The Marine view eventually prevailed and a plan was developed wherein the 7th Marines would land in assault over two Yellow Beaches followed by the 1st Marines, less the 2nd Battalion. The 5th Marines would be in reserve. The 2nd Battalion, 1st Marines would land around the tip of the Cape on Green Beach to cut the only known trail leading to the airfield from the west. The Army, reluctant to yield

Above: Marines wade in three feet of water as they leave their LST, heading for the beach at Cape Gloucester during the final phase of the Cartwheel *Plan for the isolation of Rabaul, December 1943.* (USMC)

entirely on the issue of multiple landings, added a provision for a preliminary landing at Arawe, on the southwestern coast of New Britain, ten days before the main landings, to seize "light naval facilities."[5]

The 1st Amphibian Tractor Battalion, now under command of Major Francis H. Cooper, received 15 LVT(A)2s from the Army to add to the 29 LVT(1)s of its Company "A" assigned to support the landing of the 112th Cavalry Regiment on Arawe. The remainder of the Amtrac Battalion was assigned in the usual manner; i.e., Company "B" with the 1st Marines, Company "C" with the 7th Marines, and the 2nd Platoon of Company "B" to the 2nd Battalion of the 1st Marines for its separate landing over Green Beach. The 5th Marines should have received Company "A" but that unit was assigned to the Arawe force. Thus, LVT support for the 5th Marines was provided by a composite unit made up of amtrac battalion headquarters and part of Company "A" which was sent to Finschafen after the Arawe operation had ended. Beyond the 15 LVT(A)2s provided by the Army, the amtrac battalion had received six LVT(2)s ten days before the landings at Cape Gloucester and would receive another 44 in short order. The introduction of a new type of amtrac with improved performance immediately before a major operation somewhat complicated plans already made difficult by the fragmentation of the battalion. This, however, was nothing new.

The Arawe landing took place on 15 December 1943. The landing plan called for two groups to land by rubber boats from destroyer transports (APD), while the main landing was made by troops embarked in LVTs able to ride over the reef obstructing the beach. Of the two groups in rubber boats, one got ashore without incident. The other came under heavy enemy fire, which destroyed twelve of the fifteen rubber boats and killed sixteen of the 152 men boated. The main force, launched far out at sea, required 90 minutes to reach the shore. In that time the different speeds of the LVT(1) and LVT(2) had resulted in the disruption of the formation. The confusion was aggravated when the LVT(A)2s were ordered to stop to avoid getting caught in the naval gunfire preparation.

Above left: Marines' half-track comes ashore from LST at Cape Gloucester, New Britain, December 1943. (USMC) *Above right:* Coast Guardsmen and Marines push a jeep ashore through the surf at Cape Gloucester, New Britain. (USMC)

Despite these difficulties, the force came ashore without opposition. The Army troops quickly pushed patrols out to the off-lying islands and set up defenses across the Arawe peninsula. The initial Japanese reaction to this lodgement was minimal on the ground. In the air, however, there followed a week of violent attacks by as many as 100 aircraft. Despite the magnitude of this effort, casualties were surprisingly light. Once Allied air had cleared the skies, ground action began to intensify, but the American force was never seriously threatened. The operation ended in late February 1944 when the Japanese survivors withdrew.

The Fifth Air Force flew 1,207 bomber sorties against targets in New Britain from 15 to 25 December 1943, to pave the way for the main landings scheduled to begin the day after Christmas. On D-5 a rehearsal was held at Oro Bay in New Guinea and at 0600 on 25 December the convoy moved out for the run to the objective. The assault force was embarked in ten destroyer transports (APD), sixteen Landing Craft Infantry (LCI) and 24 Landing Ship Tank (LST). The 2nd Battalion, 1st Marines heading for Green Beach was embarked in fourteen LCMs and twelve LCTs which also carried some rocket-equipped amphibious trucks (DUKW) from the Army's 2nd Engineer Special Brigade (ESB). The bombardment, planned to begin at 0600 on D-Day, was to be delivered by four cruisers, eight destroyers and two of the new rocket-firing LCIs. Aerial reconnaissance and three amphibious patrols had provided a reliable estimate of the enemy dispositions and strength in the area and had indicated unsuitable beaches. However, details on the beaches selected remained uncertain, as usual. This was typified by the identification of a "damp flat" to describe what actually was a quagmire lying between the two Yellow Beaches over which the main landings were to be made.[6] The only consolation for the Marines was that the Japanese thought the terrain too difficult for a landing to be made near it.

D-Day began on schedule with a 90-minute bombardment. Then the two LCIs moved out to mark the beach flanks and the APDs came in to discharge their troops into waiting LCVPs. An initial strike by B-24 bombers came at 0700.

That was followed by a flight of B-25s on another bomb run and a strafing attack by A-20s. The 7th Marines then hit the beach and immediately found themselves up against a wall of vegetation only a few feet from the water's edge and almost impossible to penetrate.[6] They finally hacked their way in only to encounter the misnamed "damp flat." Despite these severe difficulties, the Marines slowly made their way inland while the 1st Marines landed and headed for the airfield. The first enemy opposition was encountered by Company "K" of the 3rd Battalion, 1st Marines, which came upon a road-block on the coastal track. Enemy fire stopped the Marines and hit both the company commander and his executive officer. At that moment an LVT carrying ammunition appeared and opened fire on the Japanese. Unfortunately, the amtrac became wedged among several trees while maneuvering. Alert enemy troops quickly stormed out of their positions, swarmed over the amtrac and killed the two Marines manning machine guns. The driver, however, managed to extricate the machine and went on to crush the Japanese defenses. This allowed the infantry to close in, eliminate the road-block, and end the major opposition encountered on D-Day.

In the air the Japanese were more trying. At 1430, a flight of 88 enemy aircraft struck at the beachhead, causing little damage. The aircraft, however, also hit the first group of LSTs, which had discharged their cargoes and were on their way back to New Guinea for new loads. In a brief action, one escorting American destroyer was sunk and three others damaged; two LSTs also were hit. Then the rains began! This was the beginning of the northwest monsoon, which brought as much as nine inches of rain in one night. Many large trees weakened by the bombardment were toppled by the torrent of water; twenty Marines were killed in this fashion while three others died by lightning. The rain which kept everyone and everything soaked throughout that first night ashore, was even less kind to the Japanese, whose attempted attack against the 2nd Battalion, 7th Marines was literally rained out.

Despite the rain and the difficulties caused by the saturated terrain and dense vegetation, the landing on New Britain was carried off in a most professional manner. The logistics, in particular, worked well. The rotation of LSTs was accomplished as planned. Only the problem of finding solid ground for the supply dumps had proved frustrating. The work of the amtracs was acknow-ledged in the official Marine Corps history in these words:

> "The extraordinary capabilities of these versatile machines had certainly not entered the Japanese calculations regarding the invaders' ability to maintain a beachhead in that region, and the part played by the LVTs during this crucial phase would be difficult to estimate."[7]

Where nothing else could move, the LVTs had hauled supplies, deployed artillery, evacuated wounded and, on occasion, had supported advancing infantry with machine gun fire.

The 5th Marines, in reserve, were brought in on 29 December and, by the end of the year, the airfield had been captured. The landing of the 2nd Battalion, 1st Marines on Green Beach also had gone well, and its mission of cutting the communications to the south had been accomplished without great difficulty. Thereafter, the tasks of the 1st Division were to develop facilities, organize defenses, and undertake wide-ranging patrols to find and destroy any enemy

Right: An LSM has taken a direct hit from Japanese coast artillery on the approach to the beach during the assault landing on Iwo Jima, 19 February 1945. (USMC)

remaining in the western part of the island. On several occasions, this involved using the Boat Battalion of the Army's 2nd ESB, whose lift capabilities enabled the Marines to carry out amphibious envelopments without always calling on the Navy.

One such effort was the landing of the 5th Marines in the Talasea area in central New Britain on 6 March 1944. For that operation, the Marines used 38 LCMs and seventeen LCVPs from the Army engineers, plus five LCTs borrowed from the Navy. The Marines loaded five amtracs from "B" Company of the 1st Amtrac Battalion on each LCT to carry the first wave of troops over coral reefs. The operation was to be preceded by an air strike, which did not materialize. However, one lone Piper Cub flown by Captain Theodore A. Petras came up with Brigadier General David Ogden, commanding the newly arrived 3rd Engineer Special Brigade, who wanted to observe the Marine landing. Petras' aircraft was unarmed, but he had 30 grenades available, which he dropped on the Japanese in a succession of "bomb runs." The landing went well, as did the subsequent clearing of the area of Japanese.

By the beginning of April 1944, combat operations in the western part of New Britain had virtually ceased and the Japanese were bottled up in Rabaul where they remained for the rest of the war. On the 25th of that month, the 1st Marine Division was relieved and began its move to Pavuvu in the Russells from where it would later move into the central Pacific, where other Marine Divisions had already given new meaning to the term amphibious assault.

Left: In Mid-October 1943 Captain Fenlon A. Durand, commanding Company "C", 2nd Amphibian Tractor Battalion in New Zealand, took a detachment of LVT(1)s to the Fiji Islands to test their ability to cross fringing reefs. This photo shows the preliminary landings over rocky New Zealand beaches before sailing to Fiji for the more conclusive tests. (USMC)

Left: LVT(A)2. A total of 450 of these armored cargo LVT(2) were built for the U.S. Army; this was the only cargo vehicle with (A) designation. (FMC)

Left: The standard LVT(2), successor to Roebling's LVT(1), was the basic design for all amtrac models during WWII with the exception of LVT(3). The LVT(A)2 was an LVT(2) built of armor; the LVT(A)1 was an LVT(A)2 with 37mm gun turret; the LVT(A)4 was an LVT(A)2 with a 75mm howitzer and the LVT(4) was a (2) with engine moved forward and a ramp fitted aft.

Left: The LVT(A)(4), with its 75mm howitzer turret and two .30 caliber machine guns, spearheaded the landings in the Marianas and continued to serve throughout the remainder of the Pacific War and, later, in Korea. (FMC)

The Navy had insisted, early in 1942, on the imperative need to stop the Japanese at Guadalcanal. Later, it had agreed to the parallel drive up the Solomons and New Guinea to isolate Rabaul. These operations had removed the threat to the communications between the United States and New Zealand and Australia. Now a decision was needed on the course to be followed to bring the war to Japan. General MacArthur wanted to continue operations in the southwest Pacific and move into the Philippines from the south. The Navy, however, urged the exploitation of the newly formed carrier groups in a direct drive across the central Pacific as originally conceived in the Orange Plans. That strategy, the Navy claimed, should be pursued and timed to operations in the southwest to keep the enemy off-balance and prevent him from shifting forces to meet separate American thrusts. The issue, debated for months, was finally resolved at the Quadrant Conference held in Quebec in August 1943, where operations were authorized against the Gilberts, Marshalls, and Marianas. In anticipation of this authorization, the JCS had already directed Admiral Nimitz to plan the invasion of the Gilberts on 20 July.

Micronesia, the principal goal of the central Pacific offensive, which carried through 1944, comprises an ocean domain larger than the continental United States, with numerous island groups aggregating less than 2,000 square miles of dry land. The fifteen islands of the Marianas, some 1,300 miles south of Japan, are the largest land area. Below them lie the Carolines, a group of 500 volcanic islands which include the Palaus and the then major Japanese naval base at Truk. Northeast of the Carolines lie the 32 atolls of the Marshalls, one of which, Kwajalein, is the largest in the world. South of the Marshalls are the sixteen atolls of the Gilberts, which reach almost to the Equator. For the Americans, seizure of the British Gilberts would further distance the Japanese threat to Allied communications in the south Pacific and would provide a platform from which the little-known Marshalls could be observed in preparation for their penetration. Moreover, the Gilberts were close enough to the south Pacific to avoid an undesirable dispersal of naval resources.

GALVANIC, the code-name given to the operation against the Gilberts, was to be carried out by the new Fifth Fleet under Vice Admiral Raymond A. Spruance. The Fifth Amphibious Force under Rear Admiral Turner would conduct the landings. These were to be executed by forces assigned to Major General Holland M. Smith, commanding the recently created Fifth Marine Amphibious Corps (V MAC). The initial assaults were to be made by Major General Julian C. Smith's 2nd Marine Division landing on Betio Island in the Tarawa atoll, and by Major General Ralph C. Smith's 27th Infantry Division, landing on Butaritari Island in the Makin atoll. The island of Nauru, some 380 miles from Tarawa, had originally been targeted for attack, but Spruance, Turner and H. M. Smith had persuaded the high command to substitute Makin, which was closer to Tarawa, less heavily defended and better suited to development. Insofar as Tarawa was concerned, there had never been any question but that Betio held the key to control of the Gilberts. CINCPAC Operations Plan 13–43 issued on 5 October 1943 confirmed these final agreements and decisions.[8]

Japan had taken the Gilberts early in the war to use as observation points. A seaplane base and light defenses had been built on Butaritari Island. However, after Lieutenant Colonel Carlson with 221 Marines of the 2nd Raider Battalion had struck Makin in August 1942 and found only 70 Japanese defenders there, the Imperial government had decided to fortify the Gilberts. It had also adopted a strategy calling for island garrisons to hold firm in the event of attack until air and surface forces could be brought in to drive the attackers away. In compliance, powerful defenses had been built on the 18-mile long and 12-mile wide Tarawa atoll, notably on the 3 × 1-mile Betio Island, where an airfield had been completed and twenty coastal guns emplaced. The shoreline, already protected by a reef extending 500 or more yards to seaward, was further defended by 31 heavy automatic weapons, 25 field pieces, seven light tanks and an array of infantry weapons. In addition, barbed wire, tetrahedrons, mines, and a seawall made up a formidable succession of barriers to any movement inland. Finally, if any invader succeeded in penetrating inland, he would run foul of a series of bunkers housing communications centers, command posts, ammunition and supplies which could also serve as strong-points to disrupt any hostile attack. The formidable defenses on Betio were under command of Rear-Admiral Keiji Shibasaki and included 2,600 combat troops, supported by 2,200 construction personnel. On Butaritari Island in the Makin atoll, the defenses were much more modest and were manned by only 384 combat troops, supplemented by 400 construction personnel.

Aerial photographs enabled analysts to make remarkably close assessments of the Japanese strength on Betio. Most useful were the photos of the toilet facilities on the beach that provided the main clue as to the number of men present. Far less accurate was information on tides and the depth of water that could be expected over the reef. The island traders consulted in the matter agreed that a comfortable five feet of water would be available. However, New Zealand Major F. L. G. Holland, a long-time resident of Tarawa, voiced strong reservations over the traders' assertions. This raised serious doubts in General Julian Smith's mind and decided him to use amtracs to carry his assault troops ashore. Related to the issue was the direction of the landing approach; i.e., whether to come in from seaward where the surf was high but ship maneuver was easier, or approach from the lagoon side where sea conditions would be more favorable but navigation more restricted. On Betio the answer was simplified by the heavier defenses noted on the southern (seaward) beaches. On Butaritari, the defenses were relatively rudimentary, and the reef represented a less difficult obstacle. Thus, it was decided that the landings on Betio would be made from the north or lagoon side while those on Butaritari would be made on the west (seaward) side and on the north (lagoon) side.

The Marines' landing plan was simple. The Corps commander had decided to retain the 6th Marines as his reserve. This left Julian Smith with only two infantry regiments, the 2nd and 8th, with which to assault an island defended by nearly 5,000 men. With such unfavorable odds, the General believed it essential to land in maximum strength. Accordingly, he attached the 2nd Battalion, 8th Marines to Colonel David M. Shoup's 2nd Marines and gave him the assault task. Shoup decided to land three battalions abreast and hold the 1st Battalion, 2nd Marines as his reserve. The assault companies of the 2nd Battalion, 8th Marines and of the 2nd and 3rd Battalions, 2nd Marines would go ashore in amtracs which were to proceed from fifty to one hundred yards inland before unloading troops. The ability of amtracs to cross reefs had been demonstrated in May by Lieutenant Colonel Krulak, then commanding the 2nd Parachute Battalion based in Noumea. Krulak, who had run the tests of the early prototype LVT(1) in the Caribbean on the eve of the war, had been directed to handle the over-the-reef tests in New Caledonia. These had shown that the vehicle could make such landings. The finding was later confirmed by Captain Fenlon A. Durand, who took a detachment of amtracs from "C" Company, 2nd Amtrac Battalion, then in New Zealand, to Fiji in mid-October 1943 where he spent four days practicing landings across reefs. The vehicle, it appeared, could indeed do the job; the problem was to find enough of them to embark at least the first three waves of assault troops.

The 2nd Amphibian Tractor Battalion, like the 1st, had started with the nucleus of one company formed at Dunedin. Company "A" of the 2nd had been activated with 69 men on 3 December 1941 and moved to San Diego on 15 December. There, the unit had been brought up to strength and given time to train before shipping out to Guadalcanal in July as a reinforcing element of the 2nd Marine Regiment. Only the third platoon had gone ashore for an action-packed 24 hours on Gavutu and Tanambogo, after which the whole company had been withdrawn and sent to the New Hebrides. Soon after its arrival at Espiritu Santo and as a consequence of Admiral Turner's predilection for raider units, "A" Company had found itself reorganized as a provisional raider unit. One month later, it was back as an amtrac unit, but for the next six months it provided personnel and detachments for a wide variety of unrelated duties. Finally on 15 February 1943, Company "A" rejoined its parent battalion whose other companies had arrived separately in New Zealand in the final months of 1942.[9]

During the months that followed, the 2nd Amtrac Battalion operated 100 LVT(1)s in training. Many of these vehicles had already seen hard service in several operational areas. Thus, when the decision was made to use amtracs for the assault of Betio, there were only 75 LVT(1)s available for the purpose. Fortunately, there were fifty LVT(2)s in the United States assigned to the battalion as replacement vehicles. Arrangements were soon made to move these to Samoa. Meanwhile, the highly elastic Company "A" was pressed into service once again. Using amtrac, tank and other divisional personnel, Company "A" formed a provisional company, designated "A-1", which departed New Zealand under command of Captain "Hootie" Horner on 14 October 1943 for Pago Pago where it arrived on 21 October. One week later, Lieutenant Manuel Schneid-miller with 39 maintenance men and 50 LVT(2)s appeared. These last, it was discovered, were in poor mechanical condition due to long storage. In the hectic week remaining, Horner's men restored all LVTs to an acceptable operational condition. He also had all the vehicles armored with a 40in × 28in piece of boiler plate welded in front of the cab, and armed with one .50 caliber and two .30 caliber machine guns each. The 50 amtracs were loaded on three LSTs on 6 November. The day after, Major Henry C. Drewes, the Amtrac Battalion commander, arrived to brief the men on the forthcoming operation. The LSTs sailed from Samoa on 8 November and, in the twelve days that followed, the men familiarized themselves with their vehicles and held a practice landing on

Funafuti Island on 15 November. At 0330 on 20 November 1943, the LSTs took position in the transport area off Tarawa atoll where the LVTs were launched, troops transferred into them, and the formation was led to the line of departure in readiness for the final run to the beach.

While Company "A-1" was busy in Samoa, the remainder of the 2nd Amtrac Battalion under its executive officer, Major Henry G. Lawrence, Jr., had armored its 75 LVT(1)s with ½-inch plate, armed each with three machine guns and fitted several with stern grapnels to pull up wire entanglements. Fifty of these LVT(1)s intended to transport the first assault troop wave were loaded on the weather decks of ten transports. Of the remaining 25, seventeen went to the 2nd Marines and eight to the 6th Marines for supply. These were preloaded with ammunition, water and rations and were loaded in the holds of twelve transports. Lastly, because of the fragmentation of the Amtrac Battalion, one officer from the battalion was assigned to each group of six amtracs to maintain control in the execution of the landing. Thus loaded, the task force sortied from Wellington harbor on 1 November for Efate where a rehearsal was held from 7 to 9 November. The force then moved out and arrived off Betio Island in the early hours of 20 November to join the LSTs from Samoa.[10]

While this activity was taking place, air strikes were being flown against the objective area each day, beginning on 13 November. On 18 November, 115 tons of bombs were dropped; the next day only 68 tons fell, but 250 tons of 8in shells were fired from three heavy cruisers on selected targets. This did much to destroy the enemy's communications, but many installations remained intact as did most of the defenders. Earlier, Colonel David Shoup, commanding the 2nd Marines, had requested that the Seventh Air Force drop 2,000-pound anti-personnel bombs on the landing beaches to destroy buildings and personnel. This request, although approved by the 2nd Division, had not been fulfilled. Similarly, a feint against the southern beaches had been proposed by the Division, but this had been rejected by the Navy to avoid diverting destroyers from their assigned fire support tasks. The result was that the Japanese capabilities had not been seriously impaired by the time the invasion fleet appeared.[11]

Fortunately, the landings of the 3rd Marine Division at Bougainville on 1 November had absorbed Japanese air resources in Micronesia and surface units based at Truk. Also, these units had been severely mauled, leaving those remaining in the Marshalls too weak to interfere effectively in the Gilberts. As it happened, a Japanese submarine sank the escort carrier *Liscome Bay* off Makin with heavy loss of life on 24 November, but the real test of strength came with the assault on Betio.

Rear Admiral Harry Hill with the Southern Attack Force arrived off Betio at 0320 on 20 November. Soon after, the transports lowered their boats, which were quickly filled by troops scrambling down cargo nets. This gymnastic exercise, already tricky when carried out by heavily laden troops in the dark with a heavy sea running, was repeated under even more difficult conditions when the troops had to transfer from boats to amtracs at sea. This transfer, a confused affair at best, was carried out without untoward incident despite a rough sea and an occasional shell from alerted coastal batteries. The laden LVT(1)s, joined by the LVT(2)s from Samoa, were formed into three columns and slowly made their way towards the lagoon.

The naval gunfire which had started just after first light, was interrupted from 0542 to 0620 to allow for an air strike. A few minutes after sunrise at 0612, the minesweeper *Pursuit* began to sweep a channel into the lagoon. Two destroyers followed to deliver counter-battery fire. The columns of amtracs then entered the lagoon, took position at the line of departure, executed a right turn and headed for the shore.

The first wave of 42 LVT(1)s, each with eighteen Marines aboard, crossed the line of departure at 0824. Three hundred yards behind, 24 LVT(2)s with twenty troops each formed the second wave; another three hundred yards to the rear, the third wave made up of 21 LVT(2)s, also with twenty troops each, completed the assault formation. In addition, eight empty LVT(1)s followed the first wave, and five empty LVT(2)s followed the third wave to assist or replace any tractor that might break down on the way to the beach. If these spare amtracs were not needed, they would proceed to the beach to take out wire entanglements.

The area between the line of departure (6,000–7,000 yards offshore) and the beach had been receiving intermittent fire from several coastal guns, finally silenced by two destroyers. However, as the LVTs got to within 3,000 yards of the shore, Japanese artillery firing air burst projectiles opened up. This fire intensified and was supplemented by anti-boat guns, automatic weapons and infantry arms as the amtracs closed their assigned beaches. At 0910 the 3rd Battalion, 2nd Marines under Major John F. Schoettel reached Beach Red One on the right. All his LVTs had been hit on the way in but none had been knocked

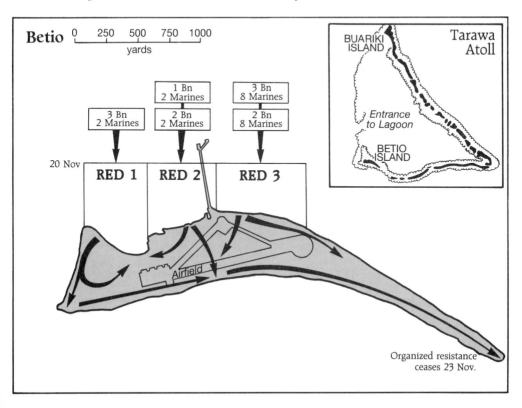

out. Casualties were light until the troops began to disembark in front of a log barricade. In the next two hours the battalion's two assault companies lost half of their men, while making only a slight advance on the right.

The next unit ashore, Major Henry P. Crowe's 2nd Battalion, 8th Marines, reached Beach Red 3 on the left at 0917. Of the 522 men in the unit only twenty-five had been hit on the way in. Then, two of Crowe's LVTs found a gap in the log barricade and made their way to the airfield where they disembarked their troops; the others offloaded at the barricade where five of the six officers of "E" Company were promptly hit. Despite the loss, the company worked its way to the airstrip. The relative success of Crowe's landing was probably due to the fire support from the two destroyers in the lagoon which had continued until just seven minutes before the troops reached the shore.

At 0922, the final assault unit, the 2nd Battalion, 2nd Marines under Lieutenant Colonel Herbert Amey came ashore on Beach Red 2. Six amtracs were lost before reaching shore, and the fire on the beach was so intense that only a narrow toehold could be established on the right; the troops that should have landed on the left actually landed on Beach Red 1. Altogether 1,698 men from three battalions had started for Betio in 87 amtracs. Eight LVTs were put out of action on the initial run in, fifteen more were lost after they retracted and reached deep water where the sea entered through bullet and shell holes. Still, more than 1,500 men had come ashore in under ten minutes and in good order, after crossing a reef swept by intense and direct enemy fire. The follow-on units that were to come in by boat were less fortunate.

The water over the reef, as Major Holland had warned, did not allow the boats to reach shore; the only boat channel available led to a pier which projected along the boundary between Beaches Red 2 and 3. The fourth wave, carrying the reserve companies, infantry support units and the battalion command groups, was in boats which had been grounded on the reef 500 or more yards from the shore. From there the Marines had to wade in or, if fortunate, find an LVT to take them in. Lieutenant Colonel Amey and his command group, in an LCM, was able to transfer to two LVTs returning from the beach. On the way ashore Amey's amtrac was stopped by a wire entanglement. Amey jumped over the side wtih intent to wade ashore; he was hit by a burst of machine gun fire which killed him instantly. That incident, repeated across the whole of the reef, soon resulted in the fragmentation of tactical units. Even so, individual Marines and small groups ignored the murderous fire and continued towards the shore, where they added their strength to the embattled units already there.

Colonel Shoup, like Amey, started ashore in a boat, transferred to an LVT at the reef, and, with better luck, reached the shelter of the pier at 1030, after having been shot at with every weapon the Japanese still had in action. By that time Shoup had already ordered Major Wood B. Kyle to land his 1st Battalion, 2nd Marines on Beach Red 2. Kyle mustered enough LVTs to take two of his companies ashore. These arrived at 1130 after a harrowing ride; the heavy fire that had followed them all the way ashore had continued as the troops left their LVTs and decimated their ranks. The remainder of the 1st Battalion came in at noon after sustaining heavy casualties while crossing the reef. Kyle's unit, the Regimental reserve, had been brutally handled even before it had a chance to fight.

Above: *Marines disembark from LVT(1) on Betio Island, November 1943 and come under heavy fire from strong enemy positions. (USMC)*

Below left: *A Marine infantryman at Tarawa, armed with an MI Carbine, runs forward with a belt of machine gun ammunition while another Marine prepares to throw* a grenade into an enemy emplacement just over the barricade. *(USMC)*

Below right: *Betio Island, Tarawa, November 1943. A Japanese soldier who chose suicide rather than surrender. (USMC)*

Left: Battle losses on Betio beach, November 1943. LVT(1) No. 27 appears to have suffered a gas tank explosion due to enemy fire; No. 39 is also disabled and only No. 33 remains serviceable. The low tide reveals the barbed wire defences on the reef.

Left: LVTs lie disabled off Betio, No. 49's boiler plate armor has been penetrated by machine gun fire. (USMC)

Left: Betio Island. Major Henry P "Jim" Crowe, commanding the 2nd Battalion, 8th Marines, attached to the 2nd Marine Regiment, shelters behind a disabled LVT(1) to issue instructions. (USMC)

While Kyle and his men were enduring their ordeal, General Julian Smith ordered the 3rd Battalion, 8th Marines, comprising half of the Division reserve, to land on Beach Red 3. Unfortunately for Major Robert H. Ruud's men, the amtracs had suffered heavily in their repeated runs over the reef during the long morning. Thus, Ruud's battalion had to come in by boats. Out of his first wave disembarking at the reef edge, only 100 men managed to wade ashore. Luckily, Colonel Shoup, still near the pier, witnessed the disaster and signalled the following waves to make their way to the pier and use it for protection on their way to the beach. The Division reserve that eventually got ashore was only slightly less battered than the Regimental reserve that had preceded it on the adjacent beach, and was far from being a coherent combat force.

Despite these staggering difficulties, the build-up ashore continued to a point where by nightfall several tanks and pack howitzers had been landed and were in action. The situation remained precarious, but when the Japanese failed to counter-attack that first night, the prospects of the Marines brightened. Credit for the lodgement on Betio belongs to all the Marines who made it ashore on that memorable first day. Among the more deserving were the LVTs that returned time and again to the beach with additional troops, urgently needed loads of ammunition, rations and water, and carried off wounded on each trip seaward. The seventeen pre-loaded amtracs of the 2nd Marines had come ashore soon after the initial assault, offloaded, and joined in the shuttle of troops and supplies from the reef to the beach. The performance of all concerned had been more than commendable.

The second day began with the landing of the remainder of the 8th Marines. This was followed by the landing of units of the 6th Marines, the Corps reserve, on nearby Bairiki Island and the western end of Betio. Six of the eight cargo-carrying amtracs assigned to the 6th Marines landed their supplies on Betio at that time; the other two amtracs never got off their ships and did not participate in the operation. By noon of the second day, the shore party had established a control point near the end of the pier where the 2nd Amtrac Battalion set up its command post. This enabled control to be regained over the remaining LVTs and the organization of a vehicle pool to support an orderly flow of ammunition and priority supplies to the combat weary troops whose work was not yet over. However, as the second day ended, the situation definitely began to favor the Marines.

On the morning of the third day, General Julian Smith decided to move his command group ashore. A tractor was found for the purpose, but this, like so many others, was hit on the way in and disabled. The general and his party had to transfer to another tractor before they were able eventually to reach Colonel Shoup's command post at 1335. That afternoon, the Marines launched a series of attacks which forced the Japanese into the eastern part of the island without, however, settling the issue. By then, the Marines had suffered cruel losses in officers and non-commissioned officers while the Japanese remained capable of organized resistance.

The Marines, candidly assessing the situation, estimated that it would take five days more to clear the island of its defenders. That night, however, the Japanese commander launched two probes and an all-out attack at 0400. The

Above left: *Marines of 2nd Division scramble down cargo nets into landing boats which will take them to the reef where they will transfer to LVTs. (USMC)*

Above right: *A Navy medical corpsman attends to a minor "embarrassing" wound caused by shell fragments. The*

LVT(1), disabled by enemy fire, provides the Marines with shelter. (USMC)

Below: *Marines land from LVT(2). The high drop required of troops laden with individual weapons and*

equipment was always difficult, as was cargo-handling over the side. (USMC)

Below: Marines assault a Japanese bomb-proof bunker on Betio Island, Tarawa. (USMC)

Above: Marine infantrymen slowly work their way inland on Betio Island, Tarawa Atoll. A two-man machine gun team prepares to fire on the Japanese defenses while Marines with carbines protect them. (USMC)

Marines, who had been waiting for just such an opportunity, settled the matter in just one violent hour. By 0500 on D+3, the Japanese on Tarawa were finished. The remainder of the morning was spent in mopping up and by 1330 the island was secured. By that time, the Amtrac Battalion had set up a maintenance facility ashore near Beach Red 2 and started to salvage and recover whatever amtracs appeared worthy of the effort.

Of the near 5,000 Japanese on Tarawa, all were killed except seventeen combat troops and 129 construction personnel. The Marines suffered 3,301 casualties of whom 1,070 were killed. Among these were 33 dead, 100 wounded and 47 missing Marines of the 2nd Amphibian Tractor Battalion. Included among the dead were Major Henry C. Drewes, the battalion commander, killed while approaching the beach in an LVT(2) at about 0930 on 20 November, and Captain Bonnie A. Little of Company "C", killed while landing a unit of the 2nd Battalion, 8th Marines on Beach Red 3. Of the 125 LVTs in the operation, only 35 remained operational and eighteen of these were left with the garrison force on the island when the battalion departed Tarawa for Hawaii on 5 December. Of the 90 vehicles lost, eight failed mechanically; all others were put out of action by the enemy. Among these last, two were blown up on mines, nine were set afire while crossing the reef, ten were hit and destroyed on the beach, 26 were hit and put out of action on the reef and 35 disappeared, presumably sunk as a result of bullet and shell holes having pierced the hull. Years later, in 1982, an

Left: Marines patrol struggles through the mud of Bougainville, November 1943. (USMC)

Right: Three LVTs knocked out on the beach of Betio Island by Japanese fire from 37mm guns, 75mm anti-boat guns, and 13mm machine guns.

Australian group working on Tarawa reported finding an LVT that apparently had been disabled and buried in a bomb crater. Near the vehicle were the remains of Private First Class Spurlock and 30 orientals. No more eloquent memorial could have been found to mark those four days of a distant November.[13]

Makin, 105 miles to the north of Tarawa, was the target for the Northern Attack Force. Its 6,470-man landing force comprised the 165th Infantry Regiment, detachments of the 105th Infantry and other combat and service support elements of the Army's 27th Infantry Division under Major General Ralph C. Smith. The main island in the Makin atoll is Butaritari, thirteen miles long, one-third of a mile wide, and shaped like a crutch lying on its side with its arm rest to the west. The island was occupied by less than a thousand Japanese only half of whom were combat troops. The principal defenses were contained between two tank barriers in the central part of the island. General Ralph Smith's plan was to land two battalions along the "arm rest" in the west. Two hours later, he would land one battalion on the inner side of the west tank barrier against a part of the main defenses. Like his Marine namesake, the Army General was concerned about getting boats over the off-lying reef. Although neither the reef nor the enemy defenses on Butaritari were as bad as those of Betio, the General hoped to get some LVTs to help him ashore. A shipment of 48 LVT(2)s reached Hawaii, the Division's base, on 29 October where they were quickly taken over by a provisional company of the 193rd Tank Battalion. This allowed little time for familiarization or training before the unit was loaded on three LSTs for the long cruise to the objective. Still, the Army found it possible to fit several of their amtracs with rocket-launchers. The 27th Infantry Division also had the time to acquire 1,850 pallets on which were stacked and lashed priority supplies. This technique of using wooden sleds to carry supplies had first been used by the Army's 7th Infantry Division in the Aleutians where it had greatly expedited cargo handling.

The Makin force arrived off its objective on 20 November at the same time as the Marines to the south. Troops were embarked in boats, and the assault units transferred to LVTs which then began their approach to the Red beaches on the west at 0815. Soon after, 32 LVTs with troops of the 105th Infantry reached the beach. These were quickly followed by two battalions of the 165th Infantry. The landing was unopposed and the reef, while an impediment, had little adverse effect. The experimental rocket-equipped amtracs proved useless when sea water soaked the firing circuits. Two hours later, the remaining sixteen LVTs hit Yellow Beach under heavy enemy fire. Rocket-equipped LVTs were able to get off their salvoes on that occasion, but their fire was too scattered to be effective. The troops none the less got ashore and were soon followed by the 3rd Battalion of the 165th Infantry. Within two and one half hours the troops on

Below: LVT(A)4s form the first wave in the landing assault on Iwo Jima in February 1945; note the gunner manning the .50 caliber machine gun while the howitzer is elevated to maximum range in order to begin firing as the vehicles approach the beach. (USMC)

Below right: Cargo LVT(A)2 at Eniwetok, February 1944; so designated because it was built of armor plate instead of sheet steel. The same hull fitted with the 37mm gun and turret from the light tank became the LVT(A)1, seen in the foreground. (USMC)

the west had advanced 1,300 yards, while those behind the west tank barrier had to fight their way to the opposite side of the island. By nightfall, the west side of Butaritari was in Army hands.

On the second day, the remaining enemy were mopped-up, while artillery paved the way for a co-ordinated tank–infantry attack against the eastern tank barrier. This proceeded in deliberate fashion and was suspended at nightfall within striking distance of the objective. The attack was continued on the third day when the eastern tank barrier was overrun. Six amtracs were used to land a company of the 165th Infantry in the rear of remaining Japanese defenders. An additional detachment of ten LVTs was used by the 105th Infantry to take Kuma Island, an extension of Butaritari. All of these operations were accomplished without difficulty and on the fourth and final day of the operation, 23 November 1943, Makin was secured and the troops re-embarked for their return to home base. All the Army amtracs were left behind for the garrison force. The seizure of Makin had cost the U.S. Army 66 dead and 187 wounded. The Navy, less fortunate, suffered 687 dead and many more wounded in the turret explosion aboard the battleship *Mississippi* and in the sinking of the escort carrier *Liscome Bay*.[14] The Japanese had 550 men killed and 105 taken prisoner in the four days of the fighting and lost 143 other personnel in subsequent mopping-up operations.

The entry of the Americans into the central Pacific had been dramatic. Casualties had been heavy but any remaining doubts as to the validity of the Marine doctrine for amphibious warfare were cast aside. The implementation of Ellis's plan for the penetration of Micronesia had been well and truly begun, albeit with some alterations in scale brought about by advances in techniques and resources. Among the latter, none had been more decisive than the amphibian tractor which, henceforth, would spearhead the many landings that still had to be made before the war could end.

Above: *Major Victor J. Croizat, commanding the 10th Amtrac Battalion, at his command-post on Ennubir Island during the invasion of the Marshalls.*

4. New Battalions, New Tactics

The Marshalls, Marianas, Palaus and Philippines, 1944

LANDINGS attempted against opposition before World War II most often failed. Yet, of the 70 opposed landings carried out during that war, only two were repulsed, one by a superior enemy and the other by an air attack launched in error. The reasons for this striking contrast between success and failure are many. However, there is little question that successful amphibious operations became possible only with mastery of the technique of deploying an assault force afloat and landing it ready to fight. This required the combat loading of transports, adequate air and naval gunfire support, a command and control organization with reliable communications, and sufficient numbers of specialized landing craft to permit the landing of organized units in proper tactical formations. This wisdom was acquired in the 1930s and early 1940s and battle tested in 1942 and 1943. It would be refined in 1944 and, in so doing, would confirm the exceptional utility of the amphibian tractor as a tactical as well as logistic vehicle.

The landings at Tarawa had demonstrated the capability of the amtrac to make its way from distant ship to reef-bordered shore and land troops and supplies under heavy fire with acceptable losses. The Tarawa landings had also given new meaning to the concept of courage. They had shown dramatically how inadequate that word was in identifying the quality that moved men to wade a fire-swept reef towards an even more dangerous shore . . . or urged amtrac drivers to repeatedly run up the odds against survival by providing critical shuttle services from sea to land during the 48 hours in which the contest was decided. Even more, beyond being a tribute to brave men, that landing also provided valued lessons that would greatly reduce the casualties in the Marshalls campaign to follow.

The American high command had agreed since mid-1943 on the invasion of the Marshalls, but the decision of where to strike among the 32 atolls, remained open for some months. Numerous proposals were advanced. Admiral Nimitz, almost alone, held for a strike directly at Kwajalein, the Japanese nerve-center located within the inner "sunset group" of islands. The Joint Chiefs, meanwhile, had made available to the Pacific Command the 4th Marine Division, which was then completing training in Camp Pendleton, the 7th Infantry Division, which had recently arrived in Hawaii after campaigning in the Aleutians, and the 22nd Marine Regiment, then guarding Samoa. Planning did not proceed further at that time since the naval headquarters that would direct FLINTLOCK, code-name for the Marshalls campaign, was occupied with the execution of GALVANIC, the landings on Tarawa and Makin. Thus, it was not until

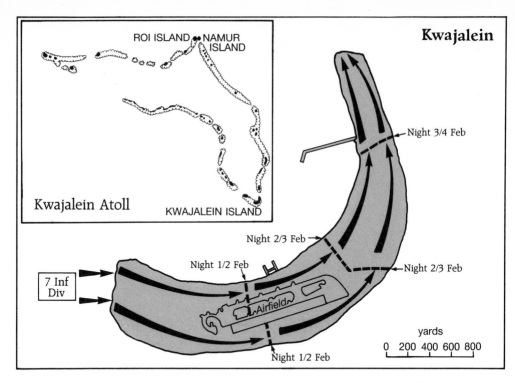

Kwajalein

ROI ISLAND • NAMUR ISLAND

Kwajalein Atoll

KWAJALEIN ISLAND

Night 3/4 Feb

Night 2/3 Feb

Night 1/2 Feb

Night 2/3 Feb

7 Inf Div

Airfield

Night 1/2 Feb

yards
0   200 400 600 800

mid-December 1943 that the decision to attack Kwajalein, together with Majuro, on 31 January 1944 was formalized. At that same time, the 106th Regimental Combat Team (RCT) of the 27th Infantry Division was added to the forces available. Soon after, Admiral Turner, the Joint Expeditionary Force commander, organized the 297 ships provided for FLINTLOCK into three attack groups. The Southern Attack Force, which he would retain under his own command, would land the 7th Infantry Division on Kwajalein Island. The Northern Attack Force, under Rear Admiral Richard L. Conolly, would land the 4th Marine Division on Roi-Namur and the Majuro Attack Group, under Rear Admiral Harry Hill, would use a battalion of the 106th RCT to take Majuro.[1]

In the detailed planning that followed, a serious effort was made to exploit the lessons just learned at Tarawa. New command ships (AGCs) were assigned to the two Attack Force commanders. This would eliminate any repetition of the communications failures that had occurred at Tarawa when the battleship *Maryland*, in which the senior command headquarters was embarked, fired its main battery. Another major improvement was in supporting fire. Naval gunfire was to be far heavier in the Marshalls than it had been at Tarawa and was to be delivered primarily for "destruction" rather than "neutralization". Further, air strikes to cover the assault landings were to be tied to the progress of the LVTs rather than to any time schedule. Additionally, rocket-firing LCI(G)s would complement the air strikes just before the landing, and the new LVT(A)1s with their 37mm guns would provide initial support for the troops on the beach. This imposing array of support means was to be augmented further by the landing of artillery on nearby islets to join in the support for the main effort against the principal islands. Finally, Landing Craft Control boats (LCC) would be used to help guide amtrac formations, Submarine Chasers (SC) would be provided for the control officers, and in the northern area, the destroyer *Phelps* would serve as the primary control vessel.

The 120-square mile Majuro atoll, some 220 miles southeast of Kwajalein, appeared to be lightly defended. Accordingly, Admiral Hill planned to use the Reconnaissance Company of the V Marine Amphibious Corps to take two islets covering the entrance to the lagoon. This would clear the way for the entry of the main force, the 2nd Battalion, 106th Infantry, under Lieutenant Colonel Frederick B. Sheldon, which was to seize Darrit and Majuro Islands. These plans were executed without difficulty since the Japanese had evacuated the atoll before the Americans arrived. The seizure of Kawjalein atoll, however, was quite a different matter.

The Japanese on Kwajalein were believed to number from eight to ten thousand men, concentrated on some twelve of the atoll's 93 islets and islands. The majority of the troops, some 1,800 strong, along with about 800 casuals and laborers, were located on Kwajalein Island in the south. On Roi-Namur in the north, there were some 3,000 Japanese but only one quarter of these were combat troops. The main defenses on these islands were oriented seaward. But, after Tarawa, the Japanese began to improve their defenses on the lagoon side. Even so, they had fewer heavy weapons emplaced in the Marshalls than they had had at Tarawa, and these had been subjected to early systematic attack. Two hundred and forty-six carrier aircraft had struck at Kwajalein on 4 December 1943. Four Japanese cargo ships had been sunk, two cruisers damaged and nineteen fighters shot down. That night, the Japanese had retaliated with torpedo-bombers which damaged the *Lexington*. Land-based U.S. Army and Navy aircraft had then taken over and continued frequent attacks until 29 January 1944 when the carriers returned to support the invasion.

As the softening of the Marshalls began in earnest, the landing force commanders completed the detailed plans for their operations. Major General Harry Schmidt, commanding the 4th Marine Division in the Northern Attack Force, planned to seize four islets, later increased to five, on D-Day with Colonel Samuel Cumming's 25th Marines. Artillery would then be landed to support the main landings the following day. On D+1, the 23rd Marines, under Colonel Louis Jones, would land on Roi Island while Colonel Franklin Hart's 24th Marines would take Namur Island. In the south, the 7th Infantry Division under Major General Charles H. Corlett, would use a similar pattern. The 17th Infantry and Division reconnaissance units would take four islets on D-Day, upon one of which artillery would be emplaced. The main landing on Kwajalein Island would be conducted by the 182nd and 32nd Infantry Regiments on D+1. Once the main islands in the north and south had been cleared, Army and Marine units would move along the atoll to mop-up any remaining Japanese.[2]

To carry out its plan, the 7th Infantry Division had a mix of 174 troop-carrying and gun-mounted LVTs. The 708th Amphibian Tank Battalion with 79 LVT(A)1s had joined the Division in mid-December. The troop-carrying amtracs, 49 LVT(2)s and 46 LVT(A)2s were manned by the Division's anti-tank companies, whose personnel had started training on LVTs on 25 November. All these LVTs were formed into the 708th Provisional Amphibian Tractor Battalion which was made up of four groups, each with fourteen LVT(A)1s and twenty troop-carrying LVT(2)s. Another seventeen LVT(A)1s were held for separate assignment. In addition, a reserve pool of fifteen cargo amtracs and six LVT(A)1s was created and embarked on an LSD. All other LVTs were embarked on LSTs, four of which were assigned as maintenance ships and fitted accordingly. An additional seven LSTs were loaded with priority supplies, including ammunition, water and rations, to be landed by LVT.

The islets of Ninni and Gea, controlling access to the deep-water Cecil Pass, were to be taken on D-Day by reconnaissance troops landed from destroyer transports (APD) in rubber boats approaching from seaward. The landings on Ennylabegan Islet (Carlos) adjacent to Gea was the responsibility of the 1st Battalion, 17th Infantry coming ashore in one of the 34 amtrac groups. The 2nd Battalion, 17th Infantry would come ashore in the second group of amtracs on Enubuj Islet (Carlson). The landing on Kwajalein Island on D+1 would be made by two infantry regiments utilizing the remaining two amtrac groups. Twenty of the amtracs had been fitted with infantry flame-throwers which could be operated from inside the cab; these were distributed among the four amtrac task groups.

The artillery, all of which would be landed on Carlson Island on D-Day, would come ashore in DUKWs. Sixty of these amphibian trucks were available. These were organized into four groups of fifteen DUKWs each and assigned one for each of the artillery battalions, which provided five DUKWs for each 105mm howitzer battery. The artillery and accompanying DUKWs were loaded on LSTs on the basis of one LST per artillery battalion. An additional 40 DUKWs were preloaded with priority supplies and embarked on separate LSTs ready to come ashore to support the assault infantry. Several LSTs were also designated as DUKW maintenance ships in the same manner as those for LVT support. All in all, the Army's plans were straightforward, uncomplicated and thorough.

The 4th Marine Division plan for the landings in the north was based upon using two cargo/personnel-carrying amtrac battalions and one armored amtrac battalion. The 10th Amphibian Tractor Battalion with 110 cargo LVT(2)s, reinforced by 30 LVT(2)s of Company "A", 11th Amphibian Tractor Battalion and fourteen cargo amtracs from the 1st Armored Amtrac Battalion would land elements of the 25th Marines on four islets on D-Day. Subsequently, these amtracs would land the 75mm pack howitzer battalions of the 14th Marine Artillery Regiment on three of these islets. The amtracs would then be recovered aboard LSTs for servicing and refuelling in preparation for landing the 24th Marines on Namur Island on D+1.[3] The 4th Amphibian Tractor Battalion with 100 LVT(2)s was to land the 23rd Marines on Roi Island on D+1. The 1st Armored Amphibian Tractor Battalion would support the landings of the 25th and 24th Marines on D-Day and D+1 respectively with 36 LVT(A)1s from its "B" and "D" Companies. Support for the landing of the 23rd Marines on Roi Island on D+1 would be provided by 36 LVT(A)1s of "A" and "C" companies.[3]

To meet its multiple requirements, the 10th Amtrac Battalion had reduced its Company "A" to 10 LVT(2) and increased its "B" and "C" to fifty LVT(2)s each. In this manner, Captain Edgar E. Burks's "B" Company would land Lieutenant Colonel Clarence J. O'Donnell's 1st Battalion, 25th Marines on Mellu (Ivan) and Enneubing (Jacob) Islets on the early morning of D-Day. Company "C" commanded by Captain George A. Vradenburg, Jr. would land Lieutenant

Colonel Lewis C. Hudson's 2nd Battalion on Ennubir (Allen) Islet two hours later. At that same time, Company "B" LVTs would have returned to sea, embarked the troops of Lieutenant Colonel Justin M. Chambers' 3rd Battalion and landed them on Ennumenet (Albert) Islet. The reduced "A" Company of the Amtrac Battalion was to embark the 25th Marines' command group and some Division scouts and land them as and when directed.

Once these preliminary objectives were secured, Captain Harry T. Marshall, with thirty LVT(2)s of his Company "A", 11th Amtrac Battalion, plus the fourteen LVT(2)s provided by the 1st Armored Amtrac Battalion would land the three pack howitzer artillery battalions on Jacob, Allen and Albert Islets. The 4th Battalion of Artillery, equipped with 105mm howitzers destined for Ivan Islet, would come in by LCM since these weapons could not be carried by the amtracs. Once the artillery was ashore, the amtracs would build-up ammunition stocks there before proceeding to their LSTs for preparation of the next day's assault landing operations.

As is apparent, these plans were sufficiently complex to have taxed an experienced amtrac battalion, whereas, the 10th Amtrac Battalion, reinforced, had been created only one month before sailing. Equally serious, the 4th Marine Division itself was new and untried as were many of the LSTs upon which the amtracs were to depend as safe havens for the preparation of the next days' operations. As a final note, twelve LVT(2)s in each of the 4th and 10th Amtrac Battalions were equipped with 4.5-inch rocket-launchers which were damaged or whose firing circuits were drowned out during the landings . . . and the 10th Amtrac Battalion had the added aggravation of receiving the grapnel–mine-detonating device, previously mentioned, which, contrary to orders, was not installed lest it cause the modified amtracs to sink.

Below: *Tracked landing vehicles of the 10th Amtrac Battalion, armed with rocket-launchers and loaded with men from the 25th Marines, head for shore with the objective of occupying the small islands flanking Roi-Namur.*

Trouble in the north began on D-Day soon after the transports arrived off the objective area. The sea was rough and the wind strong. Troops in boats were soon soaked and the LVTs, heading for the rendezvous areas where the troop transfers were to be made, were having a hard time making headway. Most serious was the fact that their radios were systematically being drenched. Also disturbing was that the LVTs loaded on the upper decks of several LSTs had to be lowered on elevators that were shorter than the LVTs. Thus, wooden ramps had been built on the elevators to cant the LVTs so that the elevators could be lowered. The requirement to drive an LVT up a narrow wooden ramp at night on a rolling ship put a heavy strain on man and machine and the debarkation was understandably slow. Then, once in the water the LVTs had to find their guide boats to take them to the troop transfer areas and then to the line of departure. This was a difficult process because the initial launch was made just before first light some four miles out to sea. Then too, LVTs lie low in the water and the driver's range of vision is limited and his field is further reduced when peering through a periscope or slit in his frontal armor. It is not surprising to learn that the landings on Ivan and Jacob, originally scheduled for 0900 on 31 January 1944, were executed at 1015. Fortunately, opposition was light and both islets were secured in fifteen minutes. The artillery began to come ashore soon after.

Meanwhile, minesweepers had begun to clear passages into the lagoon. Just then, the destroyer *Phelps*, serving as the central control vessel, was diverted to another task. This caused a number of amtracs, whose drivers were using the ship as a reference point, to follow and thus move out of position. Brigadier General James L. Underhill, the assistant division commander, embarked in a subchaser (SC) to direct the D-Day landings, was able to intercede but, again, time was lost. That, and continuing bad weather adversely affecting amtrac navigation, caused the second series of landings from the lagoon side to be delayed from 1130 to 1500. Although off-schedule, the landings on Albert and Allen went off without trouble; the islets were quickly secured and the artillery followed with little delay.

It was at this point where yet another misadventure occurred. A modification of plans had directed Lieutenant Colonel Chambers to launch an attack from Albert Islet to Ennugaret (Abraham) Islet as soon as the first had been secured. This change of orders, however, had not reached the 10th Amtrac Battalion. Thus, when the infantry had been landed on Albert Islet, the amtracs, which by then were very low on fuel, went off looking for fuel boats supposedly in the transfer areas offshore. Before all had left, however, Chambers was able to commandeer four of them on which he loaded 120 of his Marines. His mortars then laid smoke on the near beach of Abraham Islet to cover the approach of the modest landing force. As it happened, resistance was light and the Marines were able to gain control over Abraham by 1900. With that, all objectives assigned on D-Day were in Marine hands . . . multiple difficulties notwithstanding. The travail of the 10th Amtrac Battalion, however, was not yet over.

The 110 LVT(2)s used to land the 25th Marines units on D-Day were supposed to return to their LSTs that night to be readied for the landing of the 24th Marines on Namur Island the next day. A number of problems were to arise to affect this plan. First of all, LVT(2)s had to depend on their engines to operate their bilge pumps. Thus, when several fuel boats failed to appear and the LVTs began to run out of gas, twenty-three were sunk. Further, in the course of the D-Day landings six of the LVTs had been swamped and overturned on the reef while seven others were reported missing. Of the surviving LVTs, many failed to find their way to their LSTs because these would not display the prescribed recognition lights. Moreover, several LSTs refused to embark LVTs that had originally been embarked on other ships. Thus, when the new day began, LVTs of the 10th Amtrac Battalion were scattered on five islets and several LSTs.

While the Marines had been struggling with their many difficulties in the north, the Army in the south was not finding all its plans working well either. The reconnaissance unit that was to land on Gea Islet at night by rubber boat found itself heading for Ninni Islet instead. Fortunately, they were able to change course and reach their proper objective, but the Ninni attack unit landed on nearby Gehh (Chauncey) Islet by mistake. There they encountered a tough Japanese detachment which caused considerable trouble. None the less, the soldiers were able to overcome the resistance and paddle over to their original target where they landed without difficulty. Later, the 17th Infantry, destined to land on Carlos and Carlson islets, had some difficulty assembling its LVTs into waves in the dark, but the landing was only delayed forty minutes and everything went well thereafter. By late afternoon of D-Day there were four battalions of artillery moving into firing positions on Carlson Islet. The next morning, 1 February 1944, assault units of two infantry regiments of the 7th Infantry Division loaded in fresh LVTs stormed ashore on the western end of Kwajalein Island. No serious opposition was encountered until the troops reached the end of the airfield. From then until the evening of 4 February when the island was secured, the Army mounted a series of deliberate co-ordinated attacks against skilled and stubborn enemy forces; the issue was never in doubt.

In the north, despite a night-long hunt, only half the amtracs needed by the 24th Marines were found. Orders were then sent to Captain Marshall whose amtracs had supported the artillery throughout D-Day, to report to designated LSTs to pick up infantry units. This, however, was a slow process because many LVTs still required fuel and the hunt for the specified LSTs among the many ships now in the lagoon was time consuming. Accordingly, the time of landing was delayed from 1000 to 1100. Meanwhile, the LSTs with the 4th Amtrac Battalion had moved into position and received the units of the 23rd Marines that were to load on the amtracs embarked. The LVTs with their troop loads had then been launched from the LSTs, formed into waves and led to the line of departure where they awaited the order to land. By this time the continued effort to round up 10th Amtrac Battalion machines had produced only enough of them to carry four of the six assault rifle companies. By 1100, after considerable reshuffling of units among the two assault infantry battalions, the organization of the 24th Marines had stabilized sufficiently for a landing to take place. By 1155, the first elements of the 24th Marines had set foot on Namur and two minutes later, the 23rd Marines landed on Roi. That regiment rapidly drove across the island and had all its objectives secured by nightfall. The 24th Marines, however, confronted a stronger defense and more difficult terrain with the result that it did not secure Namur until the next afternoon, 2 February. Two days later the Army finished at Kwajalein Island. In the final accounting it was discovered that the Japanese had suffered more than 8,000 dead. For the Americans, the unexpectedly swift victory cost them 486 dead and 1,295 wounded. This was well below half the price paid for the Gilberts and evidence that the lessons of Tarawa had been well learned.

As the intelligence staffs began to sort over the windfall of captured documents and navigation charts that would help advance the next operation, that against Eniwetok, the amphibian tractor battalions moved ashore to salvage amtracs on the reefs and continue their support of infantry units engaged in securing the remaining islands of the atoll. Then, as time permitted, the experiences of the amtrac personnel were collected to form the basis of reports intended to improve subsequent operations. Included among these observations was that the landings just completed had confirmed the need to avoid transferring troops from boats to amtracs at sea. Equally important was the need to strengthen the mechanisms for controlling the ship-to-shore movement. Landing diagrams of rendezvous, transfer or fuelling points and of boat lanes, lines of departure and other control features were meaningful only when marked at sea by identifiable boats, flags, buoys or other signal means visible and understandable to all the personnel concerned.

The performance of the amtrac units was also affected by maintenance limitations. No maintenance LSTs had been designated for the Marines as they had been for the Army. This needed to be corrected. Also needed were recovery amtracs able to operate on reefs and off-lying islets where they could approach unserviceable amtracs and tow them or repair them well enough so that they could be removed and returned to maintenance support areas. Further, amtracs urgently needed manual bilge pumps to help keep vehicles afloat when at sea without engines running. Also, a way had to be found to waterproof vehicle radios; virtually all radio sets had been drowned out shortly after the vehicles were in the water.

There were other technical and tactical comments and recommendations concerned with LVT performance and employment included in post-action reports. Most revealing of the human aspects arising from the new tactical role of the LVTs was the report written by Doctor Perry R. Ayres, the surgeon of the 10th Amphibian Tractor Battalion, under the heading of fatigue. Dr. Ayres wrote:

"It is estimated that about 75% of the personnel of this organization operated tractors 24 to 30 hours of the first 48 hours of the recent Kwajalein invasion. Continuous operation of tractors for 14 to 16 hours was not uncommon and several platoons participated in assaults on three separate islands in one day. Upon returning to their ships on the evening of D-Day, it was necessary for the tractor crews to refuel and service their vehicles in preparation for the assault on D+1. Thus, these men worked almost continuously at heavy labor during the period of the assault. No sooner were the assaults completed than these same men were called upon to operate their vehicles in transportation of supplies and troops. During the period of the assault, the men were, of course, under fire intermittently, and, following that period, they were subjected to the nervous strain incident to the organized confusion experienced in beaching supplies. Several officers have reported that men fell asleep at the tractor controls when they were not in operation and a few reported seeing men vomit from sheer exhaustion."[4]

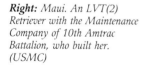
Right: The 10th Amtrac Battalion Camp at Maalea Bay on Maui in October 1944. A good view of the troops' living accommodation. (USMC)

Right: Maui. An LVT(2) Retriever with the Maintenance Company of 10th Amtrac Battalion, who built her. (USMC)

Right: Towing trials of amphibious trailers conducted in Hawaii, 1944. (USMC)

Tarawa had demonstrated that the cost to the men in amphibian tractor units of going from service troops to shock troops was high. The Kwajalein operation, where the shock effect of the amtracs was heightened by the introduction of the cannon-mounting LVT(A)1, revealed that demands placed on human endurance and courage were not lessened even though battle casualties had been far fewer.

In January 1944 the 2nd Marine Division had started planning the invasion of Eniwetok. Soon after, the 27th Infantry Division was alerted for operations against Kusaie in the Carolines. The target date for the Eniwetok landings was 1 May 1944, which would give time for Fifth Fleet units to support the 3rd Marine Division's invasion of Kavieng. But, the Kavieng operation was cancelled and the Kwajalein landings had gone off more rapidly and at lesser cost than expected. The force reserve had not been needed and hence was immediately available. Accordingly, Admiral Turner proposed using the 22nd Marines and the 106th Infantry, less the battalion used at Majuro, to move on Eniwetok as soon as the ships could be replenished. Admiral Nimitz agreed and a new target date of 17 February was set.

Rear Admiral Hill, who had commanded at Majuro, was assigned to lead the Eniwetok operation. His Expeditionary Troops, numbering 10,000 men under command of Marine Brigadier General Thomas E. Watson, was a modest force to use against an estimated 3,500 Japanese that included a newly arrived brigade. However, there was considerable comfort in having three battleships, two heavy cruisers and seven destroyers as a bombardment group and six carriers to provide air support. The operation plan, like that for Kwajalein, directed the seizure on D-Day of three islets upon which artillery could be deployed. The 22nd Marines would land the next morning, 18 February, on Engebi Island. Once it appeared that the landing was successful, the 106th Infantry would strike at Eniwetok Island and then move on to Parry Island. After the three main islands were secured, the lesser islets of the atoll would be cleared. These multiple landings were to be made in 102 LVT(2)s, which would be screened by seventeen gun-mounting LVT(A)1s. All of these amtracs were from the Army's 708th Provisional Amphibian Tractor Battalion which had just performed so well at Kwajalein Island. In addition, 30 DUKWs, also veterans of Kwajalein, would land artillery. All the LVTs and DUKWs were to be loaded on LSTs and all would be preloaded with emergency supplies or artillery as appropriate.

The first air strikes against Engebi on 30 January destroyed the fifteen Japanese bombers based there. Other raids followed on a daily basis until 16 February when the pre-D-Day bombardment began. By that time, most facilities above ground had been destroyed and the garrison weakened by shock and loss of sleep. While this pounding was building up to its climax, Task Force 58 had hit the major Japanese base at Truk. In two days of air attacks, 200 Japanese aircraft had been destroyed or damaged and 200,000 tons of shipping had been sunk. Meanwhile, Admiral Hill's ships entered Eniwetok lagoon on 17 February, passing within 200 yards of Parry Island without receiving any fire. There, he launched the V Marine Amphibious Corps Reconnaissance Company against the first two islets. The landings succeeded and the artillery quickly followed. That evening, the decision was made to send the 4th Marine Division's Scout Company in rubber boats to take the third islet. Unfortunately, the wind came up and turned what was to have been a simple task into an adventure that did not end until 0300 the next morning when the islet was finally secured.

Thus far the Japanese had done little to reveal their presence. Later, however, when the 1st and 2nd Battalions of the 22nd Marines hit the beaches at Engebi at 0845 on 18 February, they found the Japanese groggy but still willing to fight. It took the Marines until afternoon to sweep the island and declare it secure . . . although not free of survivors who would make the night difficult. At 0900 on the 19th, the 106th Infantry crossed the line of departure heading for Eniwetok Island. Upon landing they came up against a 9-foot embankment behind which the determined foe had dug a system of field defenses. The Army's advance, unavoidably slow, was temporarily held up by a Japanese counter-attack late in the morning. General Watson committed the 3rd Battalion, 22nd Marines to settle the issue and allow the advance to resume. That night, the Japanese commander found a gap between the Army and Marine units ashore and deployed an assault unit which nearly destroyed the Marine battalion command post. The attack was eventually shattered but it took until 21 February for Eniwetok Island to be cleared of its former tenants. That same morning, General Watson sent the two Marine battalions that had taken Engebi to seize the last objective, Parry Island. Once again the bombardment preceeding the landing so dazed the defenders that the Marines got ashore without difficulty. However, there was a full day of fighting before the island could be secured. The seizure of Parry Island ended the operation and gained for the Americans a sheltered anchorage large enough to accommodate the whole Pacific fleet. More important, the outpost line of defense covering the enemy's homeland had been breached. The Eniwetok operation cost the Americans 348 dead and 866 wounded which, like at Kwajalein, was an unexpectedly modest price to pay for the significance of the accomplishment.

The 22nd Marines left Eniwetok on 25 February for Kwajalein, where they were to replace the 25th Marines as garrison force. Their easy duty did not last long, however, for on 8 March the Regiment began a series of operations codenamed FLINTLOCK JUNIOR to clear the remaining atolls in the Marshalls that were undefended or lightly held. This task required 29 landings on twelve atolls and three islands. These were accomplished in the amtracs that had remained on Kwajalein with Company "A" of the 10th Amphibian Tractor Battalion and Company "A" of the 11th Amphibian Tractor Battalion. When FLINTLOCK JUNIOR was completed on 15 April, the 22nd Marines with its two amtrac companies went on to Guadalcanal where the 4th Amphibian Tractor Battalion and the 1st Armored Amphibian Tractor Battalion had been sent earlier. The 10th Amphibian Tractor Battalion, more fortunate, had been returned to Hawaii where it settled on the island of Maui with the 4th Marine Division.

Admiral King had long favored a move against the Marianas once the Marshalls had been taken. But this view was not shared by all concerned; even Admiral Nimitz, for a time at least, appeared to favor a thrust to the Palaus, followed by an attack against the southern Philippines. General MacArthur, understandably, had been delighted with Admiral Nimitz' views. The General's advocacy of a drive into the Philippines from New Guinea was well known and repeated whenever occasion permitted. More recently, a new voice had been added to the discussions. General Henry H. Arnold, commanding the Army Air Corps, had the new B-29 long-range bomber entering the inventory and wanted bases to complement those in China from which to mount an air offensive against the Japanese home islands. The Marianas appeared ideal for the purpose. These views were addressed during the SEXTANT conference in Cairo at the end of November 1943 where it was agreed to invade the Marianas on 15 November 1944. But, this schedule was not to hold.

While the invasion of the Marshalls was in progress, American reconnaissance aircraft reported an absence of activity on the Admiralty Islands northwest of Rabaul. General MacArthur reacted immediately and in five days organized and dispatched 1,000 men of the 1st Cavalry Division in APDs to take Los Negros Island. By amazing luck, the 4,000 Japanese defenders were concentrated elsewhere on the island when the Americans landed on 29 February. Thereafter, it became a race to decide who could mount an offensive first. The Americans won and, after shattering the Japanese defense, moved on to take Manus, the largest island in the group. By 3 March they had also secured Seeadler Harbor. Meanwhile, on 15 February, New Zealand troops occupied the Green Islands just north of Rabaul against light opposition. Rabaul, already isolated, was now completely encircled.

At the time the 1st Cavalry Division detachment was securing the Admiralty Islands, the 4th Marine Regiment with 66 amtracs from the 3rd Amtrac Battalion was sent to take Emirau Island in an unopposed landing. This marked the last amphibious assault operation of South Pacific forces. The JCS, meanwhile, had directed South West Pacific forces to take Hollandia in central New Guinea in April, and then undertake whatever other landings were needed to pave the way for later operations against the Palaus or southern Philippines. In the central Pacific, Nimitz was to strike the Marianas on 15 June to secure bases for use by the Army Air Corps and to protect MacArthur's flank.

While these events were unfolding, General Hyakutake, earlier encountered on Guadalcanal, had assembled 15,000 men with which he proposed to attack the American beachhead on Bougainville. Unknown to the Japanese, Major General Oscar Griswold had 62,000 men ready to receive them. The Japanese attack, launched on 8 March, did achieve an initial shallow penetration, but the Americans soon sealed it off. The Japanese regrouped and returned to the attack time and again, each time taking heavy losses and gaining no ground. Finally, by 23 March, the Japanese force had been spent and its few remaining survivors driven off. At approximately this same time, Lieutenant General Robert L. Eichelberger had embarked two divisions for the move on Hollandia and Aitape. The deep envelopment supported by four rocket-firing LCVPs, four rocket-firing DUKWs, two LCMs converted to anti-aircraft boats, and 43 amtracs had caught the enemy by surprise and enabled the Americans to gain their objectives by 26 April. At the same time, the 20,000 by-passed Japanese of General Adachi's Eighteenth Army, who had been expecting the Americans at Wewak, began a difficult march towards the American invasion forces. The trek took more than two months so that it wasn't until 10 July that the Japanese were able to launch an attack. Three weeks of intense fighting ensued and ended only when Adachi's force had been destroyed.

Coincident with these operations, other U.S. Army forces landed on Wadke Island just off the coast and attacked Sarmi, a town near Hollandia. Despite Japanese opposition, the airfield in the area was quickly taken and returned to operational status within 60 hours of the landing. Ten days later, the U.S. Army's 41st Infantry Division commanded by Major General Horace H. Fuller landed on Biak Island off the Vogelkop Peninsula forming the far western part of New Guinea. The 11,000 Japanese on the island resisted fiercely and gave the soldiers several difficult moments. Then, as the Americans were gaining the upper hand, a Japanese task force with reinforcements approached. But, as luck would have it, a Japanese scout aircraft reported strong U.S. naval forces in the area. The Japanese commander promptly withdrew without verifying the report; if he had he would have discovered that the Americans posed no threat. Still, the Japanese did not want Biak to fall into American hands so they tried again. This time the task force included the super-battleships *Musashi* and *Yamato*. But, no sooner had the force sortied, than the Americans landed on Saipan. That caused the Japanese to immediately recall the force to prepare the ships for the fleet action that would soon challenge the American incursion into the Marianas. Biak was left to its fate.

These brief notes summarizing General MacArthur's conquest of New Guinea fail to convey the full merit of the accomplishment. It had taken South West Pacific forces six months to clear the Japanese out of Papua, at the eastern end of New Guinea. It had taken a year to build the wall around Rabaul. Then, in three swift months, from March to May 1944, these same forces had advanced 1,400 miles to a point where they controlled the whole of New Guinea and were but a short distance from the southern Philippines. The trip had involved tough fighting and considerable risks but had achieved brilliant results. These in substantial measure were due to the presence of two Engineer Special Brigades and the ships of the Seventh Amphibious Force.

The 2nd Engineer Special Brigade, already encountered in the support of the Marines on New Britain, had arrived in the theater at the end of 1942. The 3rd ESB had followed in October 1943 and the 4th ESB would arrive in May 1944. These brigades, each with 550 landing craft distributed among three Boat and Shore Regiments, did much to supplement the meagre resources of "MacArthur's Navy" and make possible the succession of amphibious envelopments that characterized the campaign in the South West Pacific area. The landings at Biak, for example, well demonstrated the teamwork required. For that occasion, six LSTs with 63 LVT(2)s and 25 DUKWs of the 2nd ESB's 542nd Boat and Shore Regiment landed the first four waves of the 41st Infantry Division's assault rifle companies. The remainder of the assault force followed in fifteen LCIs. Immediately after, eight LCTs brought in the engineers who rushed to complete beaching sites for the LSTs carrying support units and supplies. Altogether, it was a well-executed landing. In like fashion, the assault on Saipan in mid-1944 would reveal the maturing technique of assault landing operations.[5]

In mid-March, Admiral Nimitz informed his principal subordinates of the JCS decision to seize the southern Marianas. Operations would begin on 15 June with landings on Saipan, the administrative center of the fifteen-island group and the site of a major airfield. Subsequent landings would be made on Guam and Tinian, the latter only three miles from Saipan and well within artillery range. Admiral Spruance, commanding the Fifth Fleet, was to exercise overall command of FORAGER. Vice Admiral Turner would again command the Expeditionary Force, which would be divided into the Northern Attack Force with the V Marine Amphibious Corps to seize Saipan and Tinian, and the Southern Attack Force with the III Marine Amphibious Force to take Guam. Lieutenant General H. M. Smith, embarked on Admiral Turner's flagship, was to command the Expeditionary Troops and share with the Admiral the added responsibility for the Northern Attack Force. Rear Admiral Conolly and Major General Geiger were to direct the operations of the Southern Attack Force. The troops available to land on Saipan included the 2nd and 4th Marine Divisions. The Southern Attack Force would include the 3rd Marine Division and the 1st Provisional Marine Brigade with the 22nd and 4th Marines; the latter made up of the raider battalions formed earlier in the war. The Army's 27th Infantry Division was to be embarked as the Expeditionary Force reserve, while the 77th Infantry Division would be held in Hawaii as the strategic reserve, prepared to move into the Marianas area after D+20 days.[6]

It is of singular interest that the attack on three strongly defended islands located 1,200 miles from the nearest friendly base would require more than 800 ships, and include troops coming from bases as far as 4,000 miles away. At the same time, another armada, also embarking five major units, would land on the beaches of Normandy, a brief nine days before the opening assault on Saipan. That two vast expeditionary forces would be launching amphibious attacks in mid-1944 against separate objectives half a world apart would have been inconceivable to the embattled soldiers, sailors and Marines who had first stopped the Japanese advance a scant two years before.

Mount Tapotchau, the 1,554-foot peak of Saipan's mountainous spine, rises first on the horizon as one approaches the island. Then the green of the heavy tropical vegetation emerges together with the regular pattern of sugar-cane fields. Finally, a line of breakers marks the edge of the reef which guards the approach to the white beaches. These are backed by ridgelines and hills and, in several places, by steep rock cliffs that front the shore. The 72-square mile island, some fourteen miles long and six miles wide, with sugar refineries and the orderly towns of Charan Kanoa and Garapan, plus scattered chamorro villages, had long enjoyed a quiet existence. This had continued even after the war had started since the Marianas were far from the scene of action and well within Japan's island outposts.

However, once the Americans had moved into the northern Solomons and taken the Gilberts and Marshalls, the vulnerability of the Marianas became painfully evident. Reinforcements comprising two divisions, two brigades and two regiments were dispatched from February to May 1944, but not all reached their destinations. American submarines took a heavy toll. One convoy lost half a regiment, another 1,000 men and, most recently, five of seven transports with

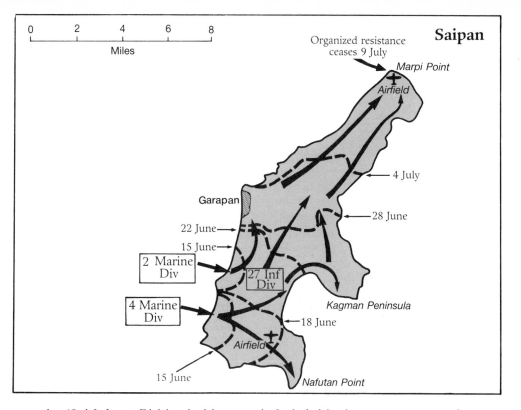

the 43rd Infantry Division had been sunk. Included in these severe personnel losses were large quantities of construction materials and cement essential for the development of suitable defenses. Still, by the time the Marines arrived, there were 30,000 Japanese troops on Saipan alone. There also were five operational airfields on the islands and five more under construction. Some of this was known to the Americans. But the tempo of operations had been such that there had been relatively few opportunities to obtain good photo coverage of the Marianas. As a result the highest estimate of Japanese strength on Saipan was only 17,600 men.[7] The terrain information was equally imprecise. The charts obtained in the Marshalls helped with details on the reef and its passages, but many questions affecting initial dispositions and early movements ashore remained unanswered.

The inadequacies in intelligence were compensated, in part, by the experience of the two assault divisions and the time that had been available for planning and rehearsals. These various activities had proceeded in orderly fashion but not without incident. On 14 May, rough seas caused three LSTs to lose their deck-loaded LCTs, resulting in two dead, seventeen missing and sixteen injured. Then, on 21 May, a 4.2in mortar round detonated while being unloaded from one of six LSTs nested at West Loch, Pearl Harbor. These ships, just arrived from the final rehearsal at Maalea Bay, Maui, were set afire and sunk. Much equipment was lost and the embarked units suffered 207 casualties. Fortunately, it was possible to find replacement ships and the 6th Base Depot was able to provide new equipment. Captain William E. Lunn, the Maintenance Officer of the 10th Amphibian Tractor Battalion, whose headquarters had been embarked on one of the LSTs, remained unhappy, however, because his spare parts trailer with its carefully selected contents ended up on the bottom and no comparable replacement parts could be found. Despite this spectacular disaster, the LSTs sailed only one day late and the time lost was made up en route to the objective.[8]

While the Expeditionary Force steamed west, preparatory air strikes and ship bombardments were directed at targets on the major islands of the Marianas. Carrier air had started hitting the islands in February, but on 11 June aircraft from sixteen carriers brought much increased intensity to the strikes. That tempo was maintained during the three and a half days that followed. Meanwhile, on the 13th, fast battleships added their salvoes to the bombs and rockets. Then, on the 14th, seven old battleships, eleven cruisers and 23 destroyers took over and positioned themselves to support the landing set for the next morning.

Plans called for the assault landings to be made over beaches on the southwest side of Saipan. The 2nd Marine Division was to land its 6th and 8th Infantry Regiments over Beaches Red and Green immediately north of Afetna Point. The 4th Marine Division was to land its 23rd and 25th Infantry Regiments over the Blue and Yellow Beaches to the south, opposite and just below Charan Kanoa. The landings of the 2nd Division's assault infantry and pack howitzer artillery units was to be made in LVTs of the 2nd and 5th Marine Amtrac Battalions, and the Army's 715th Amtrac Battalion. The Marines' 2nd Armored Amphibian Tractor Battalion would lead the assault infantry ashore. On the 4th Division front, the landings would be made in amtracs of the Army's 534th and 773rd Amphibian Tractor Battalions and the Marines' 10th Amphibian Tractor Battalion, less its Company "A" but with Company "C" of the 11th Amtrac Battalion attached. The Army's 708th Amphibian Tank Battalion would lead the assault ashore. There were a total of 773 amtracs of all types for the landing. In addition there were DUKWs to land the 105mm howitzer battalions.

A total of 47 LSTs were available to embark the LVT units. The assault troops that were to go ashore in amtracs were transferred to the LSTs carrying the amtracs during a stopover at Eniwetok. That meant that during the final six-day run to Saipan, living conditions on the LSTs would be very tight, but that inconvenience was nothing compared to the problems of transferring troops at sea. Artillery units would also be preloaded on their LVTs or DUKWs on the LSTs; the only exception was the additional 75mm pack howitzer battalion of the 14th Artillery Regiment which would come ashore in subsequent trips of LVTs or DUKWs as available.

Because Saipan is a large island, it could not be taken in a single assault. This meant that combat ashore would extend over several weeks and would require large stocks of supplies, replacement equipment and substantial maintenance support. Prolonged operations would also result in numerous casualties. Three LSTs modified to receive 100 wounded were designated to provide immediate aid during the assault landing phase; after D+3 regular hospital ships would become available in the objective area to take over this task.

In similar fashion, LVT casualties would be initially treated aboard designated maintenance LSTs. This would continue for some time since LVTs tended to attract enemy fire, and maintenance parks ashore required large land

Right: *LVT(A)1s drop off the ramp of an LST to form the first wave for the assault on Saipan; such LSTs were used to embark LVT units during the action.*

areas to permit proper vehicle dispersal. It was also anticipated that salvage operations would be facilitated because of the recovery vehicles that had been built by the amtrac battalions. The 10th Amtrac Battalion, for example, had taken the equipment off a winch-truck and installed it on an LVT(2), and had transferred the contents of its machine-shop trailer into an LVT(4).

Another lesson well learned by the 10th Amtrac Battalion in the Marshalls operation was the need for positive control of amtracs during the assault landing. To ensure that was done at Saipan, the battalion had task organized two companies of 49 LVT(2)s to land the two assault infantry battalions of the 23rd Marines on Beaches Blue 1 and 2. Each amtrac company had four platoons under an officer. Amtrac officers were also designated for liaison with the infantry regiment and assault battalion headquarters and with the Blue Beach Shore Party. The LVT company commanders were to land with the fourth wave and immediately return with their amtracs to the beach control boat stationed seaward of the reef to direct the transfer of support units from boats to returning LVTS. The amtrac battalion commander would set up an advance command post on the control vessel for the Blue Beaches; the battalion headquarters would remain aboard its LST to monitor LVT communications nets and maintain a status and location log of all the unit's amtracs. The battle experienced 2nd Amtrac Battalion under Major Henry G. Lawrence, Jr., was to organize a comparable command and control mechanism.[9]

The only other amtrac battalion with previous battle experience was the 708th which had performed so well at Kwajalein and Eniwetok where it had operated both cargo and gun-mounting amtracs. At Saipan, it had reverted to its original designation and was organized into four companies equipped with sixteen LVT(A)4s and 52 LVT(A)1s. Among the other five battalions without previous combat, the Marines' 2nd Armored Amtrac Battalion under Lieutenant Colonel Reed M. Fawell, Jr., had been formed at Camp Pendleton in California at the end of January 1944. Three months later it had sailed for Maui, where on 4 May it had received 70 LVT(A)4; the new armored amtrac with 75mm howitzer in an open turret. Shortly after, the battalion had sailed for Saipan. The 5th

Amtrac Battalion under Major George L. Shead also had been organized at Camp Pendleton, but not until March. It had been equipped with 72 of the new ramp-type LVT(4)s and had sailed minus its "C" Company for Saipan via Hawaii for liaison with the 2nd Marine Division.

The Army's 715th and 773rd cargo amtrac battalions had been organized as medium tank battalions and converted to amtracs in October 1943. The 715th carried 67 LVT(2)s and 33 LVT(4)s to Saipan; the 773rd had 99 of the older LVT(A)2s and LVT(2)s. The remaining cargo battalion, the 534th, had started as an armored infantry battalion and had been redesignated an amtrac unit in December 1943; it took 35 LVT(2)s and 64 LVT(4)s to Saipan. Notwithstanding their lack of combat experience, these Army units had been in existence for some time and had been able to profit from the lessons learned by the 708th Battalion. They were thus quite well prepared for the battle about to start.[9]

Among the myriad details addressed in the operations plan was the need for early seizure of the 0–1 line, a rise of ground extending some 1,000 to 1,500 yards inland which dominated the landing beaches. The original plan had called for the amtracs to proceed directly to the 0–1 line before discharging their troops. However, Major General Watson, commanding the 2nd Marine Division, doubted that the LVTs could move inland through the bombardment debris, climb the embankment backing the beaches and pass through the swampy terrain beyond the beach exits. Accordingly, he requested permission to have his assault units unload under cover of LVT(A) fire within 100 to 200 yards inland from the water's edge. After that they would make their way to the 0–1 line on foot. Major General Schmidt, commanding the 4th Marine Division, chose to keep to the original plan.

At 0542 on 15 June 1944, Vice Admiral Turner ordered "Land the Landing Force" and set H-Hour at 0830. By 0700 the 34 LSTs with the assault infantry had taken position 1,250 yards seaward of the line of departure and were opening bow doors in preparation for launching the troop-laden LVTs. Beyond them, twelve other LSTs with artillery units and four LSDs with tanks were readying the debarkation of their amtracs, DUKWs or LCMs. At this same time, control boats displaying flags corresponding to the beaches for which they were responsible, were siting themselves in their boat lanes. The naval bombardment, resumed at daybreak, continued its deliberate tempo until H-90 minutes, when

Left: An LVT(A)4 heading for the blazing shore of Saipan, 15 June 1944. (USMC)

carrier air took over for a 30-minute bomb and strafing attack. At H-60 minutes, the guns resumed their destructive fire, the full fury being turned on to the landing beaches at H-30 minutes; two battleships, the *Tennessee* and *California*, each pumped in 100 14-inch shells. Afetna Point, separating the two divisions' beaches, received 450 rounds from the 6in and 8in guns of the cruisers *Birmingham* and *Indianapolis*. All in all, eleven ships were standing within 2,500 yards of the shoreline delivering their salvoes. Just beyond the line of departure, 4,000 yards from the beach, 24 rocket gunboats, LCI(G)s, formed a wave behind which the gun-mounting LVT(A)1 and LVT(A)4s took position. Farther out, the troop-carrying LVTs were jockeying into their wave formations. At 0753, Admiral Turner delayed H-Hour ten minutes to allow the amtracs to complete the wave formations. At 0827, control vessels hauled signal flags down and the LCI(G)s crossed the line of departure at full speed; the LVT(A)s and troop-carrying amtracs followed close behind.

As the formation approached the reef, friendly fire lifted. Strafing attacks from 36 carrier aircraft took over the pummeling of the beaches until the troops were almost ashore, when all fire shifted inland. Despite the intensity of the fire and the previous four days of deliberate and systematic destruction, Japanese artillery fire began falling in the area of the control vessels as the first craft cleared the line of departure. Then, after the LCI(G)s launched their rockets and the first amtracs scrambled onto the reef, the enemy opened up with an intense fire from all weapons available, creating a dense cloud of spray and smoke into which the assault LVTs slowly disappeared. Seven hundred and nineteen LVTs had headed for the shore that morning . . . twenty never made it; four were overturned in the surf breaking on the reef, twelve were destroyed by direct hits while moving across the reef, and four broke down before making the shore. Still, in less than thirty minutes, 8,000 infantry had been deployed on to a beach in tactical formation, ready to fight.

The 2nd Marine Division had actually landed north of its assigned area. Heavy fire on its southern beaches had caused the amtracs to veer towards the north, and a north-setting current in the lagoon had added to the diversion. Then, all four of the assault infantry battalion commanders were wounded soon after landing. But, despite such early difficulties, the Division sorted itself out and moved forward as planned. The 4th Division, in the south, landed as planned

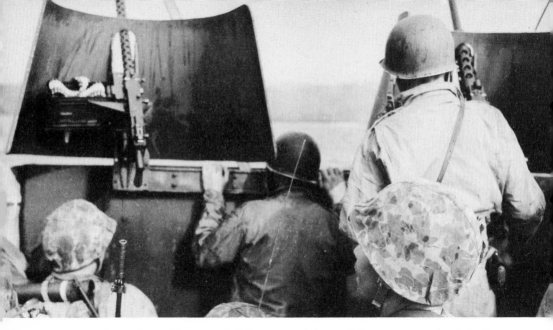

Above: Alert machine gunners look for targets as their troop-laden amtrac approaches the beach on Saipan. (USMC)

but the penetration inland never materialized. A number of amtracs did get as far as 700 yards inland but the advance was disorganized and the troops had to fall back later in the day. The problem, as General Watson had anticipated, was that there were too few clear exits for the LVTs to proceed inland. Moreover, heavy fire on the front and open flank of the 25th Marines prevented that unit's movement beyond the shore.[10]

Water and ammunition, which had been preloaded into troop-carrying LVTs, was dumped near where the troops had been unloaded. The cargo LVTs then spent the rest of D-Day ferrying in artillery, other support units and supplies. Indeed, the movement of supplies during the first two days was largely handled by amtracs, as was much of the casualty evacuation. LVTs routinely stopped at the Shore Party aid stations for a load of wounded on their way back to sea. This service began on the first return when an initial group of wounded were brought to a hospital LST at 1040; two hours later, two of the hospital LSTs had more than 200 wounded each and the third had little space left.

The armored amphibians supported the infantry throughout D-Day and that night took position on the reef to discourage Japanese infiltration. By that time, the 2nd Marine Division had landed most of its infantry and tanks, and two battalions of artillery. The 4th Division had done perhaps a bit better, but the beachheads of the two divisions were quite shallow. Still, a solid lodgement had been made. Later, Admiral Turner would note that "The Saipan landing . . . was much the most difficult of any I personally witnessed . . . The men who made it . . . did magnificently".[11]

While the Marines ashore awaited the Japanese counter-attack, Admiral Spruance received reports that the Japanese fleet was coming out to do battle and could arrive in the Marianas area by the 17th. This eventuality was not unexpected and led to a number of decisions. The first was that the landings on

Above: LVT(A)4s on the reef provide covering fire as Marine assault troops prepare to move inland on Saipan, 15 June 1944. (USMC)

Guam set for the 18th would be postponed. Second, the 27th Infantry Division in reserve afloat would be landed promptly and unloading would continue until the evening of the 17th when the ships concerned would withdraw to positions east of Saipan. Third, certain designated ships would join the main carrier force while the others, with escort carriers, would take station 25 miles west of Saipan to protect and support the troops ashore as needed. These measures had little immediate effect on the troops ashore, other than preventing the unloading of motor transport. This in turn placed the main burden of moving supplies on the amtracs, which they accomplished without difficulty but at high cost to road surfaces and ground-laid communications wire.

The Japanese did attempt several counter-attacks during the first night, but all were quickly thrown back. The next morning, the 16th, the remaining Marine combat units came ashore while the advance towards the 0–1 line was resumed. In doing so, they came upon the canefields which, earlier, had been set afire with phosphorous shells to expose enemy positions. Now, as infantry, amtracs, tanks and artillery advanced, the cane was crushed and its sugar released. The battle area was soon saturated in syrup particularly attractive to flies. These soon appeared in such numbers that it was impossible to open a can of rations without it being immediately covered by voracious competitors for its contents. It finally became necessary to spray DDT from aircraft to reduce the insect problem to tolerable proportions.

Progress on the 16th was modest. The gap between Divisions at Afetna Point was closed and Lake Susupe in the center of the Marine beachhead was flanked. The 4th Division had reached the 0–1 line in its zone, but the 2nd Division was still only halfway there after a hard day of fighting. That night the Japanese threw 44 tanks against the hard-pressed 2nd Division. The Marines stood their ground and systematically slaughtered the Japanese infantry accompanying the tanks under the eerie light of 5-inch star shells fired by destroyers. Other weapons hit at the armor; the 75mm howitzers of the 1st Battalion, 10th Marines fired 800 rounds in 75 minutes of violent action while, on the flank, one machine gun of Lieutenant Marion's platoon from "F" Company, 2nd Battalion, 2nd Marines ran through 40 belts of ammunition! Those tanks not destroyed in the night were finished off at dawn on the 17th. By 0700 it was all over, the ground in front of the Marine guns mounded with enemy dead.

The advance inland picked up speed on the 17th when both Divisions reached the 0–1 line and some units even got as far as 0–2. That afternoon Lieutenant General H. M. Smith moved his command post ashore in what remained of Charan Kanoa. In the enemy camp, a message from Premier Hideki Tojo in Tokyo reminded the beleaguered Japanese commander ". . . the fate of the Japanese Empire depends on the results of your operations . . ." Lieutenant-General Yoshitsugu Saito's headquarters on Saipan responded with a summary of the situation that could not have been reassuring. The next day, in a follow-on message, the chief of staff informed Tojo ". . . secret documents in the custody of 31st Army headquarters . . . were completely burned as of 1830 on 18 June . . ." That should have removed any doubt in Tojo's mind over the outcome of the battle for Saipan.[13]

That same day an American naval force of fifteen carriers, seven battleships, 21 cruisers and 69 destroyers was 90 miles northwest of Guam seeking contact with the enemy. At sunrise on the 19th, with no enemy in sight, Admiral Spruance decided to strike at Guam's airfields to deny the Japanese fleet any support from Guam-based aircraft or the use of its fields for its own aircraft. This action raised the curtain on the Battle of the Philippine Sea. While American and Japanese fighters were mixing it up over Guam, the action shifted 150 miles to the west where the first group of enemy carrier aircraft appeared on American

Below: Reserve Unit Marines transfer from LCVPs to amphibian tractors some 1,500 yards off-shore during the landings on Saipan. (USMC)

radar. By 1030, American fighters were on the way to intercept the Japanese force of 69 aircraft. Twenty-five were promptly shot down. The survivors pressed on and dropped one bomb on the *South Dakota*, which did little damage. In this brief action, sixteen more Japanese aircraft were shot down.

A second group of 130 enemy carrier aircraft was sent aloft at 0900. At that same time, the American submarine *Cavalla* sent the carrier *Shokaku* to the bottom while another submarine, the *Albacore*, fired a single torpedo into the fleet carrier *Taiho*; the ship disappeared within minutes taking three-quarters of her crew with her. The 130 enemy aircraft, meanwhile, ran into American fighters, which knocked 68 of them out of the sky. Yet another group of 47 Japanese aircraft missed their target but were found by Navy Hellcats, which destroyed seven of them. The final attack of the day was made by 82 aircraft launched from Japanese carriers at 1100. These too fell foul of the Hellcats and only nine returned. As these aerial actions were taking place, other American aircraft were hitting at the airfields in the Marianas to keep them from flying off aircraft to interfere in the "Marianas Turkey Shoot" at sea. The long-sought fleet engagement proved a disaster for the Japanese. The enemy losses were totalled at 346 aircraft and two carriers; the Americans lost 30 aircraft and had a battleship slightly damaged.

The next day, the Americans pursued the fleeing enemy and finally gained contact in the late afternoon. The Americans promptly launched 216 aircraft at 1620 knowing that they could only be recovered after dark. The enemy was located at 1840 and immediately attacked. Two fleet oilers, another carrier and 65 more aircraft were destroyed. The Americans lost twenty aircraft to the enemy, but 80 more ran out of fuel or crashed trying to land on their carriers after dark. Fortunately, the destroyers were able to rescue many of the downed aircrew so that despite the loss of 130 aircraft in two days of violent action, only 76 aircrew perished.

The victory at sea sealed the fate of the Marianas, but much bitter fighting remained until the 4th Division reached the 0–9 line at the northernmost tip of the island at 1615 on 9 July 1944. The twenty-five day battle cost the Marines and Army 3,144 dead, 10,952 wounded and 125 missing. Among these, 91 of the dead, 470 of the wounded and 33 of the missing were from amphibian tractor units. These also had lost 127 cargo and 57 gun-mounting amtracs of which 48 cargo and 26 gun vehicles had been salvaged and returned to depots. Of the Japanese garrison numbering 29,662 men, most were killed, others committed suicide and very few were taken prisoner. Particularly distressing to the Americans was the suicide of hundreds of civilians who hurled their children and themselves off the cliffs near Marpi Point because the Japanese authorities had told them the Americans would torture and kill them. General Saito himself had penned a last note to his men on 6 July which concluded with the statement:

> "As it says in the 'Senjishen' [Battle Ethics] I will never suffer the disgrace of being taken alive and I will offer up the courage of my soul and calmly rejoice in living by the eternal principle."[14]

Two hours later he was dead by his own hand.

The final episode in the battle for Saipan occurred at 1100 on 13 July when the 3rd Battalion, 6th Marines embarked in 25 LVTs of the 5th Amtrac Battalion preceded by five LVT(A)4s of the 2nd Armored Amtrac Battalion went ashore on Maniagass Island, 2,500 yards off Tanapag harbor. The assault, supported by 900 rounds of 105mm and 720 rounds of 75mm artillery ammunition, was unopposed. One hour later, fourteen defenders were dead and the remaining fifteen were taken prisoner. The Americans on Saipan could now rest and prepare for the move against Tinian which would begin ten days later. By that time, other Marines would have landed on Guam. These troops did not know that the government of Premier Tojo had fallen as a consequence of the loss of Saipan and some Japanese officials were considering peace overtures. It would be some time before the conquerors of Saipan would learn that they had just fought the decisive battle of the war.

The postponement of the Guam operation necessitated by the approach of the Japanese fleet was hard on the troops crowded on their ships. The delay, however, was not without compensation. Documents captured on Saipan and more time for aerial reconnaissance gave the Americans a far better picture of the situation on Guam than they had had of Saipan. Equally important, Admiral Conolly used the time to subject the island to an awesome bombardment. Surface and air attacks had been made against Guam from the first incursions of the U.S. Navy into the Marianas area but, beginning on 8 July, a systematic and sustained bombardment of Guam was initiated. This was intensified a week before the landings when Admiral Conolly arrived to take personal command; in this thirteen day period ammunition expenditures included 6,258 14in and 16in projectiles, 6,292 rounds of 6in and 8in and 16,214 5in shells. Then on W-Day, the day of the landing on Guam, the Admiral kept the guns firing while the final air attacks were delivered on the beaches just before the troops touched the shore; in that single preparation the ships fired 1,494 14in and 16in projectiles, 3,762 rounds of 6in and 8in, 13,130 5in shells and 9,000 4.5in rockets. In all other respects the invasion of Guam was to follow the same general pattern as that just ended on Saipan.

The assault units for the Guam operations had assembled at Kwajalein where the assault troops were transferred from their transports to the LSTs carrying the LVTs in which they would land. The force had sailed for the objective area ready to land on Guam on 18 June. Then, the landing had to be postponed because of the Japanese naval threat. Further pause was given by the stubborn defense of Saipan and the confirmation that Guam was defended by 16,500 troops with twenty battalions of artillery, a generous mix of anti-tank and anti-aircraft guns and a comprehensive inventory of mortars and machine guns. Because of this it was decided that no landing should be attempted until the 77th Infantry Division could be brought forward. The effect of these considerations was to move the date for the landing on Guam to 21 July 1944.

The plans of the III Marine Amphibious Corps called for separate landings above and below the Orote Peninsula on the west side of the reef-encircled island. The Japanese had prepared their defenses well for just such an eventuality; even after weeks of bombardment and the final blows of the pre-landing preparation, they remained well able to exact a heavy price of an invader. This would be paid, in part, by the 3rd Marine Division, which would land its three infantry regiments

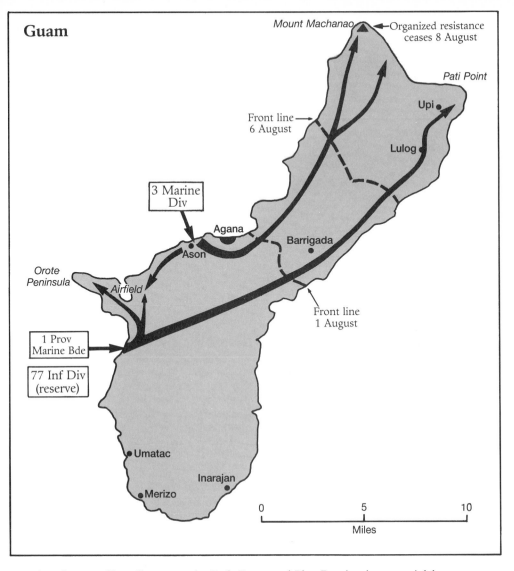

Guam

Mount Machanao

Organized resistance ceases 8 August

Pati Point

Front line 6 August

Upi

Lulog

3 Marine Div

Agana

Barrigada

Ason

Orote Peninsula

Airfield

Front line 1 August

1 Prov Marine Bde

77 Inf Div (reserve)

Umatac

Inarajan

Merizo

0   5   10

Miles

in columns of battalions over the Red, Green and Blue Beaches between Adelupe and Asan Points. The assault units would be carried in 193 LVT(2)s and LVT(4)s of Lieutenant Colonel Sylvester "Pete" Stephen's 3rd Amphibian Tractor Battalion with Company "A" of the 11th Amtrac Battalion, attached. Major Louis Metzger's 1st Armored Amphibian Tractor Battalion, less Companies "A" and "B", was to lead the troops over the reef with 36 LVT(A)1s. The artillery would follow in 60 DUKWs of the 3rd Motor Transport Battalion recently re-equipped with the amphibious truck.

The balance of the price of admission would be paid by the 1st Provisional Brigade under Brigadier General Lemuel C. Shepherd, Jr. Its two infantry regiments were to land abreast over Yellow and White Beaches near Agat village. The assault would be made in 180 LVTs of Lieutenant General Clovis Coffman's 4th Amphibian Tractor Battalion with Company "A" of the 10th Amtrac

Battalion attached. Captain Richard G. Warga with Companies "C" and "D" of Metzger's armored amtrac battalion would lead the landing with 37 LVT(A)1s. The Brigade's artillery was to follow in 40 DUKWs from the 3rd Motor Transport Battalion. Each landing force would also have nine LCI(G)s to saturate the landing beaches with rocket fire as the amtracs clambered up on the reef and headed for shore.

First light on W-Day, 21 July 1944, was at 0445. At 0535 four battleships opened fire against targets near the Orote Peninsula, while the other fire support ships took on their assigned targets elsewhere. At 0615, 26 carrier aircraft swept over the landing areas dropping bombs and firing rockets and machine guns. One hour later 200 carrier aircraft repeated the process in an hour-long shuttle of high explosives. At 0800 the LCI(G)s crossed the line of departure, 4,000 yards from shore, immediately followed by six waves of LVTs. When these reached 1,200 yards from shore, the Navy shifted the fire of their large guns inland while they increased to the maximum the rate of fire from the 5in guns on the landing beaches. At that moment, 32 aircraft came in for a final strafing of the landing areas. As at Saipan, the LVTs were to proceed to the 0–1 line before unloading their troops; as at Saipan the penetration inland failed because of debris and enemy fire. The troops were landed from 200 to 800 yards inland.

The intense preparatory fire did keep the Japanese from interfering with the organization of the wave formations and the movement to the reef. But, from the reef inland a curtain of enemy fire fell over the laboring formation. On the Brigade's front a 77mm gun on Gaan Point opened up and hit nine of Warga's LVT(A)1s; three more blew up on mines laid on White Beach. Coffman's 4th Amtrac Battalion had twelve of its LVTs hit or disabled by the coral as they made their way over the reef. On the 3rd Division's front, Stephen's 3rd Amtrac Battalion had 30 of its LVTs hit or damaged on the way to shore. Metzger, more fortunate, had only one LVT(A)1 hit on the way in, but four more of his armored amtracs were hit when they withdrew to the seaward side of the reef where they

Below: LVTs on the beach at Guam just a few hours after the assault landing on 21 July 1944. A destroyed amtrac lies in the background, one of twelve hit during the first run to the beach. (USMC)

were to meet the tanks being offloaded from LCMs and lead them across the reef to the beach.

Despite the heavy fire laid down by the Japanese gunners, all units got ashore within a few minutes of the scheduled 0830. By nightfall, two beachheads had been established and General Turnage and General Shepherd had their command posts ashore. The lodgement had cost the Marines 1,047 casualties among whom were 102 officers and crewmen from the amtrac units. The losses suffered in LVTs in the landing reduced the flow of supplies to the beach and delayed the landing of reserve and support units. The problem was aggravated by the need to transfer all personnel and supplies from boats to amtracs at the reef. Cranes were eventually set up on barges or directly on the reef to help in this tedious process and in some areas rafts and rubber boats were mustered into the transportation system. In this manner more than 5,000 tons of vehicles, equipment and supplies were brought ashore each day while the Marines were consolidating their beachhead.

The evening of W-Day was tense but quiet. Then, near midnight, Japanese infantry moved against the 4th Marines dug in on the Brigade right. The fighting soon became general and very personal; six Marines received bayonet wounds. Although the Marines brought in heavy supporting fire including that from ships offshore, the Japanese threw in attack after attack in an effort to penetrate the American position. The effort proved in vain. A few Japanese did reach the beach where they knocked out two weapons carriers and three amtracs, but by dawn the few remaining enemy were being systematically pursued and killed. At the same time, the Brigade quickly expanded its beachhead before the badly disorganized Japanese could pause, regroup and dig in. The sleepless night had cost the Marines 50 dead and nearly 100 wounded; the Japanese left 600 dead for the Marines to bury.

The situation in the 3rd Division area had been comparable. A succession of determined assaults were stopped by infantry weapons, artillery and naval gunfire

Below: *Amtracs and cargo trailers clutter the beach following the Marine invasion of Guam, a former American possession. The trailers will be taken inland towards the front whilst the amtracs will soon return to offshore ships for more men and supplies.*

directed by observers taking advantage of the flares that illuminated the whole battlefield throughout the night. By 0830, the Japanese counter-attack that had hit the Marines' left was spent and the weary survivors were withdrawing with the Marines in pursuit.

The efforts to expand the beachhead on 22 July were not all directed inland. At 1200 that day, 40 amtracs from the 3rd Battalion were ordered to the town of Tepunga to embark the 3rd Battalion, 9th Marines. This force, escorted by eighteen LVT(A)1s of Company "C" of the 1st Armored Amtrac Battalion, landed on Cabras Island, southwest of Asan Point. The landing was unopposed but the numerous mines scattered in the dense brush made the clearing of the island slow and dangerous. One LVT was lost in the process; luckily the vehicle had already unloaded its troops and only the three crewmen were injured.

Throughout these operations and those that followed, the cargo LVTs and DUKWs were in constant use. Hard-working maintenance crews kept up to 70 per cent of the vehicles in operation. The demands were particularly severe on the cargo amtrac crews who had to haul supplies all day and then spend the night on alert on the reef. The armored amtracs were no less taxed. During the day they supported the infantry working to expand the seaward flanks of the beachhead and at night they too served as outposts on the reef or on beach defense.

Once the beachhead was consolidated, the Marines moved against the Orote Peninsula. On 25 July the Brigade had closed its neck, bottling up 2,500 Japanese there. The next day the 4th and 22nd Marines began the costly reduction of the promontory, which was not completed until the evening of 29 July. Meanwhile, the 77th Infantry Division had come ashore and was advancing on Mount Tenjo, which dominated the landing beaches and the Orote Peninisula. The day before the Marine Brigade finished its fight for Orote, the 3rd Marine Division and the Army's 77th Division began their advance to clear the northern part of Guam. Intelligence had revealed that the southern part of the island was essentially free of organized enemy formations and could be sanitized at leisure later.

The final act of the drama occurred on the morning of 11 August, when the 1st Battalion, 306th Infantry attacked and sealed the caves occupied by the Japanese commander's headquarters. Sometime that same morning Lieutenant General Hideyoshi Obata atoned for his failure by taking his life in ritual suicide. Eleven thousand of his troops had already died on the beaches and fields of Guam; the other 6,000 men under his command had been entombed in caves or had fled into the jungle. The Marines had lost 1,570 men and the Army 177; together they had suffered 5,970 wounded. The price, always heavy in terms of personal value, was modest considering the strong defense and the rapidity with which the prize had been taken.

In World War II an infantry battalion normally landed over 500 yards of beach. Thus, a division going ashore in the conventional formation of two infantry regiments abreast, each with two battalions in assault, required a landing front of 2,000 yards. The 2nd and 4th Marine Divisions went ashore on Tinian over two beaches totalling 600 yards of which less than 200 yards could be used by LVTs and DUKWs. That alone made the Tinian operation unique. Another unusual fact was that the objective was only three and a half miles from the Marine's supporting base on Saipan. This meant that Tinian could be bombarded without regard for weather or visibility. It also meant that the island could be closely studied even to the extent of allowing battalion commanders to fly over the ground across which their units would advance. Finally, the logistic problem was simplified by retaining the supplies on Saipan and delivering only what was needed to maintain the desired tempo of operations on Tinian.

Colonel Keishi Ogata, commanding the 50th Infantry Regiment, had a total of 8,900 troops with which to defend the 50 square mile island. Tinian at that time also had a population of 18,000 civilians, mostly Japanese engaged in farming and the sugar industry. The terrain of Tinian was undulating with few hills; the highest, Mount Lasso, reaching 564 feet. The island also had few beaches. The best were near Tinian town on the southwest side of the island. Other less favorable beaches were at Asiga Bay on the east side. Lastly, two small beaches on the northwest side interrupted a series of coral ledges rising eight to ten feet above the sea.

Colonel Ogata had concluded that the Americans would land on the southwestern beaches or, less likely, at Asiga Bay. He had deployed two of his infantry battalions accordingly. Then, because he thought the northwest beaches might give entry to a raiding force, he sent one rifle company to cover the area. In addition to his infantry weapons, Ogata had ten 140mm coast defense guns, ten 120mm dual-purpose guns and three 6in British naval guns, most of which he sited in the south. Heavy anti-aircraft automatic weapons were concentrated around the Ushi airfield in the north.

The Marines sent swimmers to look over the Asiga Bay and northwest beaches, carefully balanced their resources and capabilities against the enemy's and concluded that landings over the northwest beaches were feasible and would prove less costly. The naval command agreed and set J-Day for the invasion of Tinian at 24 July 1944. Twelve days earlier General Schmidt had succeeded to command of the V Marine Amphibious Corps and Major General Clifton B. Cates had taken over the 4th Division.

The landings on Saipan had been launched with 588 cargo LVTs. After more than a month of hard usage, a surprising 453 of these vehicles remained serviceable. These and 130 DUKWs were carefully prepared for the attack on Tinian. The newly created Provisional Amphibian Tractor Group, V MAC, distributed the cargo amtrac assets among the four battalions that would make the landing. The 2nd Amtrac Battalion, now commanded by Major Fenlon A. Durand, would land the 24th Marines over Beach White 1 in 136 cargo LVTs. The Army's 773rd Battalion with a detachment from the 534th would land the 25th Marines over Beach White 2 in 136 cargo LVTs. The 23rd Marines, in reserve, would be landed when directed in 136 amtracs of the 10th Battalion reinforced by detachments from the 5th and 715th Amtrac Battalions.

Company "C" of the 2nd Armored Amtrac Battalion would lead the 24th Regiment ashore while Company "D" remained afloat under Division control. Two gun-mounting amtrac companies of the 708th Amphibian Tank Battalion would be attached to the 25th Marines and would remain afloat on call. On the logistic end of the preparations, the 534th Amtrac Battalion, with what remained

Left: Two LVT(2)s stand offshore on the reef as a column of DUKWs comes ashore on Tinian's White Beaches. (USMC)

Left: A column of troop-laden amtracs await guides who will direct their passage safely through the mined areas on Tinian Beach. (USMC)

Left: LVTs unload near the water while troops continue to clear numerous mines from the beach in order to prepare exits inland for the vehicles. (USMC)

Below: Early morning and the beach is lined with amtracs bringing in supplies. (USMC)

of its own assets and those of the 715th, would operate 45 cargo amtracs for the 4th Division's Support Group. Finally, ten LVTs were fitted with special ramps that were to be laid from the reef over the top of the coral ledges to enable small vehicles to clear the obstacle. Once these ramps were positioned, the amtracs were to become a salvage group whose mission was to keep the beaches clear of any disabled vehicles.

The 2nd Marine Division had a dual task. Its 2nd and 8th Regiments were to embark on seven transports and conduct a simulated landing off Tinian town to deceive the Japanese. The 6th Marines was to remain on Saipan prepared to move out on ten LSTs, which were to be returned from Tinian with 102 amtracs of the 773rd Battalion and 68 amtracs of the 2nd Battalion, after these had completed their assault landings. All other LVTs remaining at Tinian would work on clearing preloaded supplies from the ships offshore.

Tinian had been subjected to massive air and naval bombardments to which, beginning on 20 June, had been added artillery fire from guns based on Saipan. Just before the landing, Army P-47s joined in the destruction. Much of this was now centered on Tinian town to support the deception, which began at 0600 on 24 July 1944, when the Demonstration Group took position. The transports lowered boats; Marines scrambled down cargo nets . . . and quickly scrambled back up. The empty boats then formed up and headed for the beach. As they approached, coastal batteries opened fire causing them to withdraw, reform and begin another run towards the shore. When 400 yards from the beach, all landing craft turned and headed back for their transports where they were hoisted aboard. The feint went off without loss. However, at 0740, the *Colorado*, lying 3,200 yards off the town, came under fire from Ogata's 6in British guns. The battleship took 22 hits in fifteen minutes, which killed 43 and wounded 176. A destroyer seeking to protect her took six quick hits and had nine killed and 47 wounded. That deadly battery remained in action for four more days.

The situation off the White Beaches was far less dangerous. At 0600 the LSTs began to launch their LVTs, while two battleships, a heavy cruiser and four destroyers worked over the beaches to detonate mines. Fourteen Army planes joined in the effort at 0645. Meanwhile, thirteen artillery battalions on Saipan began pounding every conceivable target on Tinian. Smoke was also laid on Mount Lasso to deny the Japanese commander a view over the landing beaches. At 0720 eight LVTs of the 2nd Amtrac Battalion and sixteen LVTs of the 773rd Battalion crossed the line of departure 3,000 yards from shore and headed for White Beaches 1 and 2. The eight amtracs arriving off White 1 at 0745 found it wide enough for only four amtracs to land; the others had to butt up against the coral ledge and let the troops climb ashore. A detachment of Japanese that had survived the bombardment in nearby caves opened fire on the struggling Marines. Company "E" of the 24th Marines had a difficult moment but soon managed to clear the way for the other companies coming in to land in its rear. It was a bad few minutes, but by 0820, the whole of the 2nd Battalion, 24th Marines was ashore. Twenty-six minutes later the Regiment's 1st Battalion had landed, and by 0925 the 3rd Battalion was moving into an assembly area inland.

Ogata's concern over a possible raid had led him to organize light defenses and mine Beach White 2. Most of the mines had been undisturbed by the

Above: Hectic activity on Tinian's White Beach late on the day of the landing. (USMC)

bombardments and were plainly visible to the arriving troops. In order to avoid them, the amtracs were forced to carry their embarked troops to the coral ledges flanking the beach. Awkward as this was under the fire of surviving defenders, the 25th Marines pushed ahead and by 0930 the whole of the Regiment was ashore. The waiting Japanese had been destroyed in the landing, but the mines were not cleared until later in the day.

When the Marines stopped their advance to dig in for the night, they had all three infantry regiments ashore together with four battalions of artillery and all the tanks of the 4th Battalion; the beachhead was 3,000 yards wide and 1,500 yards deep. All of this had cost the Marines fifteen dead and 225 wounded among whom were seven dead and 31 wounded from among the amtrac crews. Twenty-one amtracs had been lost; three to mines and the others sunk because of coral damage or mechanical failure.

The day's events had not fully convinced Colonel Ogata that the Marines would not try another landing over the preferred beaches. Thus, the counter-attack force he assembled that first night did not include the units covering the other beaches. Still, he hit the Marines with 1,500 men and six tanks. In an action-filled night, five of the tanks were destroyed and the next morning the Marines found 1,241 Japanese dead in front of their positions. Despite these heavy losses and those already sustained in the preliminary bombardments, the Japanese retained plenty of fight which they demonstrated right up to and even beyond 1 August when the Americans declared the island officially secured.

With organized resistance ended, thousands of civilians emerged from caves as did several hundred die-hard soldiers of the Emperor. On 2 August, just before dawn, some 200 of these troops hit the command post of the 3rd Battalion, 6th Marines and killed the commanding officer, Lieutenant Colonel John W. Easley, among others. In a two-hour firefight that followed, 119 of the Japanese were killed. A similar attack hit the 2nd Battalion at the same time; the next morning, the 3rd Battalion was hit again. Such incidents continued until the end of the year by which time more than 500 Japanese dead had been added to the 5,000 killed in the battle for the island. American losses had been disproportionally low; 328 killed and 1,571 wounded. Three months later, on 24 November 1944, the first flight of one hundred B-29s took off for Tokyo.

As the thunder of naval guns yielded to the roar of aircraft engines over the Marianas, General MacArthur's forces in the South West Pacific continued to seize the bases they would need to support the thrust into the southern Philippines. Noemfoor Island fell on 2 July. Three weeks later, Cape Sansepor in western New Guinea was occupied. In mid-September, an attack would be directed against Morotai, from which the leap to Mindanao would be made. At the same time, other forces would strike at the Palaus to cover MacArthur's flank and provide bases to support landings in the Philippines.

The Palaus, an elongated group of islands lying within a great encircling reef, extend some 100 miles in a north-to-south direction. The adminstrative center was located at Koror, near Babelthuap, the largest island of the group in the north. Of more concern to the American planners were the two large islands in the south. Peleliu, the larger, some six miles long and two wide, resembles a lobster claw. It has a flat open area in the south, where the Japanese had built an excellent airfield, but the northern part was extremely rough. In the center of Peleliu, Mount Umurbrogol, an irregular hill mass pierced with numerous caves, rises to 550 feet. Landing beaches are plentiful but all are fronted by a coral reef. Anguar, the smaller island in the south, lies outside the reef. It is level, open, and readily accessible from several good beaches; the Americans would find it was well suited to become a bomber base.

The concept for STALEMATE as the invasion of the Palaus was code-named, was finalized on 7 July 1944. It called for operations in two phases, the first to be made against the southern Palaus on 15 September. The second phase, to begin about 5 October, would entail the seizure of Yap and Ulithi atoll, the latter to provide a major fleet base. Incident to the planning that followed, it was decided that a boat passage would have to be blown through the reef on Yap. This was to be accomplished by using three amtracs to tow a cable made up of high explosives which would be guided into position over the reef and detonated by underwater demolition team (UDT) personnel. The call for volunteer amtrac crews for this hazardous task went out to the 10th Amtrac Battalion which had just returned to its home base on Maui from the Marianas.

Contrary to the popular idea that troops never volunteer, virtually all the crewmen of the battalion did so. Indeed, several of the medical corpsmen also offered their services, arguing that someone might get hurt. The selection, as finally made, fell on Jack F. Tracy, acting gunnery sergeant of "C" Company. He and his nine-man detail departed Maui and disappeared into the western Pacific. Some time later, when it had been learned that the Yap operation had been cancelled, inquiries were made about the fate of the sergeant and his men. After some difficulty they were found in the Philippines where they had participated in the invasion of Leyte with the Army! They were returned to their parent battalion just in time to read four-months' accumulated mail and leave again for the Iwo Jima operation. None of the men got the week's leave in Honolulu that had been promised them, but Sergeant Tracy was later commissioned.[14]

Among the more important actions taken after the announcement of the STALEMATE operation was a succession of wide-ranging attacks by the Third Fleet under Vice Admiral Halsey. Beginning on 28 August and extending to 10 September, Halsey struck at the Bonins, Yap, the Palaus and Mindanao. Surprised by the weak enemy reaction, Halsey shifted his attacks to the central Philippines where his force downed 173 Japanese aircraft, destroyed another 305 on the ground and sank 58 ships. This success prompted Halsey to urge cancellation of STALEMATE and a direct move against the Leyte–Samar area. However, the JCS decided that because of the existing commitments to the invasion of the southern Palaus, the operation should go ahead.

Lieutenant Colonel Ellis, the prophet of the Pacific War, had met an untimely death on Koror in 1923 while searching for evidence that the Japanese were fortifying their mandated islands. The fact, however, was that although the Japanese had undertaken some improvements in the islands' infrastructure, the military did not use them as bases until after the war had started. Even then, it was not until the Americans had moved into the central Pacific that the Japanese took serious steps to prepare defenses. The most important such step was the deployment of their veteran 14th Division, under Lieutenant-General Sadae Inoue, to the Palaus in April 1944. The General had sent his 2nd Infantry Regiment with one battalion of the 15th Infantry to Peleliu where, with other attachments, they made up a combat force of 6,500 men augmented by 4,000 service troops. On nearby Angaur Island, south of Peleliu, Inoue stationed a reinforced infantry battalion of 1,400 men. The remaining Japanese forces, aggregating some 25,000 men, were stationed on other islands, principally Babelthuap.

The invasion of the southern Palaus was to be undertaken by two divisions, one Army and one Marine. The 1st Marine Division, under Major General William H. Rupertus, would strike Peleliu. Angaur would be taken later by the 81st Infantry Division under Major General Paul J. Mueller. The 1st Marine Division received its warning order at its camp on Pavuvu, in the Russells, where it had gone after its four-month campaign in New Britain. The Division had had a difficult time in the Russells where it had been required to build its own living accommodation and training facilities in an area suited to neither purpose. Pavuvu was as bad as Melbourne had been good . . . and the Division was ready to move on.

When its planners began to focus on Peleliu's southwestern beaches as the preferred landing sites, the question of overcoming the reef had to be resolved. This was a new problem for the Division since its landings at Guadalcanal and New Britain had been made by boat; now there would be five infantry battalions to land on beaches whose approach required crossing a coral reef. For such a task, at least 200 of the new LVT(4), able to carry 30–35 troops as opposed to the twenty men normally loaded in an LVT(2), would be required. However, the 1st Amphibian Tractor Battalion had come off New Britain with only 48 LVT(2)s and these were badly worn. This, however, was but one of the many problems that confronted the battalion commander, Major Albert F. Reutlinger.

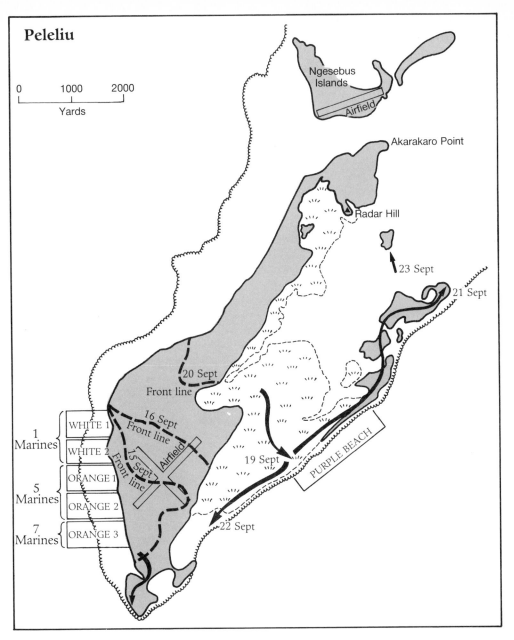

Peleliu

0   1000   2000
Yards

Ngesebus
Islands

Airfield

Akarakaro Point

Radar Hill

23 Sept

21 Sept

20 Sept
Front line

16 Sept
Front line

WHITE 1

1
Marines

WHITE 2

Airfield

15 Sept
Front line

5
Marines

ORANGE 1

ORANGE 2

19 Sept

PURPLE BEACH

7
Marines

ORANGE 3

22 Sept

The 8th Amphibian Tractor Battalion, recently formed at Camp Pendleton, was the only uncommitted amtrac unit available to the Marines. But, as reported by Lieutenant Colonel C. B. Nerren on 31 May, the battalion's combat readiness was only ten per cent.[16] Clearly the amtrac requirements of the Division for Peleliu would have to be met from its own resources. The solution adopted was to use two men from each of the experienced three-man crews of the 1st Amtrac Battalion as nuclei around which the 6th Amphibian Tractor Battalion (Provisional) and the 3rd Armored Amphibian Tractor Battalion (Provisional) would be formed. Additional personnel would be taken from the Division's motor transport and artillery units. Command of the 6th Battalion was given to Captain John I. Fitzgerald, Reutlinger's executive officer. Lieutenant Colonel Kimber H. Boyer was moved from the motor transport battalion to command the 3rd Armored. To compound the latter's task, the first of the armored amtracs to arrive in August were the old LVT(A)1 model with 37mm gun; the shipments that followed brought in LVT(A)4s with the 75mm howitzer. However, since the loading of the LSTs for the rehearsals and the move to Peleliu began in mid-August, there was little time to grieve over this from among so many other aggravations.[17]

When the Division mounted out the cargo amtrac units had been organized into an Amphibian Transport Group headed by Major Reutlinger consisting of his 1st Amtrac Battalion with 120 LVT(2)s and LVT(4)s and Fitzgerald's 6th Amtrac Battalion with 80 LVT(4)s. In addition, there was a detachment from the 8th Amtrac Battalion with 21 LVT(2)s. Fifteen of these were preloaded with artillery ammunition, the remaining six were assigned to the 1st Tank Battalion. These last were to guide the tanks, scheduled to land in the fourth wave, across the reef. This expedient was intended to keep tanks from being lost in holes in the coral. Finally, the 454th and the 456th Army Amphibian Truck Companies, each with 50 DUKWs to be used to land artillery, were also included in the Group. Of note is that three of Reutlinger's amtracs had been fitted with a heavy Navy-developed flame-thrower. The unit, under Ensign Melvin B. Thayer, promptly dubbed "Ensign Flame-thrower", quickly became a prize asset in the battle and was in great demand. Thayer, an energetic and engaging young officer accommodated all possible requests until he was killed in action. The armored amtracs were retained in a separate Armored Group.[18]

Carrier air struck the Palaus on a regular basis from 9 August until 14 September. Strikes by Army B-24 bombers began on 25 August. Then on 12 September, five battleships, eight cruisers and fourteen destroyers began the preliminary bombardment. Throughout these attacks the Japanese kept to their shelters and their concealed guns remained silent. On D-Day, 15 September 1944, the sky was clear and the sea calm. Naval guns opened the action at 0530 and continued through a strike by 50 carrier aircraft. At 0800 the troop-laden amtracs crossed the line of departure, preceeded by eighteen LCI(G) and Boyer's armored amtracs. At the same time, 48 fresh carrier aircraft came in for a final shot at the beaches.

Until this moment, the enemy had been quiet, confirming the Navy's optimistic reports of the effectiveness of its preliminary bombardments and the preparation. But, as the first LVTs approached the reef, the Japanese opened a devastating fire which demonstrated that their defenses had not been seriously impaired. Despite this heavy fire the first wave reached the shore at 0832. However, the reef was soon dotted with 38 burning amtracs followed not long after by a comparable number of DUKWs. Fortunately, the Division's plan to land tanks early succeeded even though fifteen of the thirty tanks sent in received from one to four hits in the ten minutes it took them to cross the reef. The arrival of heavy armor within the first thirty minutes of the landing was welcomed by the infantry which, until then, had relied on thin-skinned armored amtracs. That these were willing even though vulnerable was attested to by the 27 armored

Above: *Into the Jaws of Death. Landing craft carrying Marine assault troops head towards the fire-swept beaches on Peleliu following the combined naval and aerial bombardment, September 1944. (USMC)*

Right: *Marines seek cover from enemy fire behind a DUKW at Peleliu soon after coming ashore on 15 September. Amtracs burn in the background. (USMC)*

Right: *The approach to the airfield is a scene of destruction with an aircraft and a tank hit during a night counter-attack. (USMC)*

Left: Marines on Peleliu beach return Japanese fire from behind the shelter of an LVT(A) nicknamed "The bloody trail", which is what it became for those engaged here.

Left: The first assault wave heads for the beach of Ngesebus, 700 yards north of Peleliu, at daybreak on 28 September 1944. The attack was made with troops embarked in a company of amtracs supported by 18 gun-mounting armored amphibians. Heavy artillery, naval and aerial bombardment preceded the assault.

Left: Marines in the foreground clear a 200 pound mine from in front of a flame-throwing LVT(4) during the Peleliu advance in October 1944. This machine was capable of directing a stream of blazing napalm 150 yards. But, while highly effective, the thin-skinned LVT proved too vulnerable to enemy fire. The flame-thrower was subsequently mounted on the medium tank, seen in background, where it performed valiantly on Iwo Jima. (USMC)

amtracs lost to enemy action. Still, even with fresh tank support, the infantry's advance inland was being measured in feet rather than yards.

Brigadier General O. P. Smith, the assistant Division commander, set up an advance command post ashore shortly before noon. He had with him an experimental LVT fitted with mobile communications which proved most valuable in the confused afternoon and night that followed. The Japanese threw in three counter-attacks in the fading light, one supported by more than a dozen tanks. The Marine positions held each time, but by nightfall a shallow beachhead only 500 yards deep and 3,000 yards wide had cost more than 1,000 casualties. The 1st Marines on the left in the shadow of Mount Umurbrogol had been very badly hurt. The 7th Marines on the right had been unable to cross the narrow neck of the island as planned. Only in the center had the 5th Marines been able to push to the southern end of the airfield. Still, eleven batteries of artillery had been landed, which helped ensure that the multiple local attacks, repeated by the Japanese throughout the night, were systematically defeated. Even so, it was a bad night with considerable hand-to-hand combat between weary Marines and aggressive, well-trained Imperial soldiers adept at infiltration.

At first only the amtracs and DUKWs could bring supplies ashore. But, because of their heavy losses, these vehicles could not meet the demands for their services. Contributing to the problem was the long time needed by LVTs to carry wounded to ships offshore rather than, as had been done at Saipan, to hospital LSTs just off the beach. Another problem was that the LST designated for amtrac maintenance was filled with vehicles and could not embark the many others that were being damaged. Considering these and its many other problems, it is fortunate that the Division had planned to use nine barges as floating dumps where LVTs could be more readily loaded, and three other barges for LVT fueling services. There were also 60 amphibious trailers each preloaded with 4,500 pounds of ammunition, rations and medical supplies that had been towed by boat to the reef where amtracs had been able to hitch on to them and pull them ashore. Later, when passages were found in the reef, permitting boat access to the beach, the logistic situation ashore began to improve even more.

At 0800 the second morning, the Division launched a co-ordinated attack. Progress on the flanks again was slow, but in the center the 5th Marines made it to the airfield. From then on, the advance was at snail's pace. By the third day the 7th Marines had cleared the southern end of the island. Then, it took six more days to force the enemy off the ground dominating the airfield. These nine days of ceaseless combat had cost the Marines 3,946 men and had destroyed the effectiveness of the 1st Marine Infantry Regiment which had lost 56 per cent of its personnel . . . the nine rifle platoons of the 1st Battalion, 1st Marines totalled 74 men on the evening of 23 September!

While the Marines were locked in battle on Peleliu, the 81st Infantry Division received orders to land on Angaur on the 17th and Ulithi on the 21st. The landing on neighboring Angaur in amtracs of the Army's 726th Battalion went off as planned and three days later the island was declared secured. However, it would take another month for the 200 Japanese survivors to be hunted down. Meanwhile, the 81st Division had moved on to Ulithi which it took without trouble since the Japanese had already been withdrawn. The atoll soon became an important staging base for the Pacific Fleet.

On the same day that the Army took Ulithi, General Geiger, the III MAC commander, went ashore on Peleliu where he confirmed with General Rupertus his intention of relieving the 1st Marines with an Army regiment. The next day, the 321st Infantry came to Peleliu from Angaur and the 1st Marines moved to a quiet sector before leaving the island . . . it had suffered 1,672 casualties. In the battle's next phase, the 5th Marines drove up the west coast to the end of the island from where, on 28 September, its 3rd Battalion embarked in LVTs and, escorted by eighteen LVT(A)s, assaulted Ngesebus Island, 700 yards away. This brilliantly executed action gained an airstrip and closed the Japanese infiltration route; two days later only the Umurbrogol complex remained Japanese. By then the Marines had lost 5,044 men.

The reduction of the Umurbrogol hill mass was probably the most difficult task undertaken during the Pacific war; certainly the terrain was unlike that encountered elsewhere. The Japanese had taken full advantage of the caves and fragmented topography to organize formidable defenses. The 7th Marines set off to penetrate the redoubt, but after six days of costly effort they, like the 1st Marines, had reached the end of their effectiveness. The 5th Marines took over on 6 October and carried on. In ten more days of violent action, the 5th Marines had compressed the Japanese into an area 400 by 500 yards. By then, they too were finished as a fighting force. On the 15th of October, the 321st Infantry relieved the 5th Marines and five days later the 81st Division assumed responsibility for destroying the remaining enemy on Peleliu.

On the night of 24 November 1944, Colonel Kunio Nakagawa atoned for his failure by ritual suicide and, on 27 November, General Mueller announced that organized resistance on Peleliu had ceased. By that time the 1st Marine Division was back in Pavuvu where the 6th Amtrac Battalion had been disbanded; the 8th Amtrac Battalion had been sent on to Guadalcanal. More than 10,000 Japanese died in the prolonged defense of Peleliu. Their commander, Colonel Kunio Nakagawa, was advanced to the rank of Lieutenant-General posthumously in recognition of his leadership and their sacrifice. The U.S. Army, which came to the island on 23 September, suffered 1,393 casualties during its sojourn there; the Marines who arrived on 15 September and left a month later lost 6,526 officers and men, 1,252 of them listed as killed in action. It had been a costly operation indeed.

For Douglas MacArthur, return to the Philippines was the fulfillment of a promise made at the nadir of American fortunes in early 1942. For the Marines, the Philippines would provide Colonel Clayton B. Jerome and his pilots the opportunity of refining the doctrine and perfecting the techniques of close air support. The Joint Chiefs of Staff had never been fully supportive of the Philippines invasion. Because of this they had resisted MacArthur's calls for priority on the war resources allotted to the Pacific and had favored Admiral Nimitz' central Pacific offensive as leading more directly to the Japanese home islands. But then, in March 1944, the General was authorized to take Morotai, the southern entry to the Philippines, on 15 September and move against Mindanao on about 20 December. The directive also indicated that subsequent attacks would be made against Luzon or Formosa, or against Amoy on the China coast.

The Japanese, thrown on the defensive by the success of recent American landings, had devised several contingency plans to meet possible developments. One of these plans, SHO-1, envisaged a decisive battle for the Philippines, since their loss would deny Japan access to the oil of the Dutch East Indies. The Imperial Navy, however, was in reduced circumstances and little able to play the vital role envisaged in SHO-1. This had been clearly revealed in September when Admiral Halsey's forays had led the JCS to decide on by-passing Mindanao and striking directly at Leyte on 20 October 1944.

The invasion of Leyte was carried out by Lieutenant General Walter Kreuger's Sixth Army made up of the X Corps, with the 1st Cavalry and 24th Infantry Divisions, and the XXIV Corps, with the 7th and 96th Infantry Divisions. The 32nd and 77th Infantry Divisions were held in reserve ready to embark after D+3. Included in the assault force were 1,500 Marine artillerymen

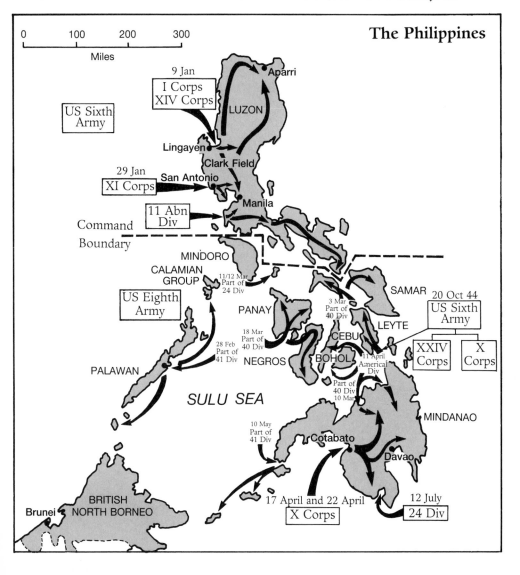

from the V Amphibious Corps under Brigadier General Thomas C. Bourke. The landings of the two Corps on an 18-mile front took place as planned on 20 October. Two days earlier, the Japanese fleet, alerted by American landings on the islands at the entry to Leyte Gulf, had sallied forth to do battle. Admiral Toyoda's plan called for a carrier force under Admiral Ozawa to decoy Admiral Halsey to the north while two powerful battleship and cruiser forces came through San Bernardino and Surigao Straits to destroy the shipping in Leyte Gulf, after which they would turn on Halsey.

The plan was complex but well conceived. It might have worked if the Japanese had still had the requisite air power, but Ozawa's four carriers could muster only 116 aircraft. First blood was drawn on 23 October when American submarines sank two cruisers and disabled a third. Then, a strike by Japanese land-based air sank the light carrier *Princeton*. The Americans responded by sending the battleship *Musashi* to the bottom. On 24 October, a classic surface action near Surigao Strait cost the Japanese two battleships, two cruisers and three destroyers. The Americans came away with only 39 dead and 114 wounded. Next, an equally incredible encounter occurred between a powerful Japanese surface force and six American escort carriers covered by four destroyers. The unequal contest cost the Americans two carriers and two destroyers. Still, the American force would have been annihilated had it not been that, at a critical moment, the Japanese commander, his force hard hit, his staff confused and news of the disaster in the south just received, decided to retire. The final encounter came when Halsey's aircraft struck at the lure early on 25 October and sank all four of Ozawa's carriers. That ended the Battle of Leyte Gulf and with it most of what remained of the Japanese Navy; its total losses in the various phases of the battle included four carriers, three battleships, ten cruisers, nine destroyers and one submarine. The threat of the once renowned Imperial fleet was finished!

These encounters had not discouraged Japanese attempts to reinforce Leyte. By 1 November the Americans had landed more than 100,000 troops on the island, but the Japanese had brought in 45,000 additional men and 10,000 tons of supplies. Since the Japanese had some 260,000 men already deployed in the Philippines, it was essential that the Americans stop any more from reaching Leyte. The U.S. Navy was forced to carry that burden longer than planned. The Army engineers ashore were pushing the construction of airfields as fast as possible, but the terrain was poorly suited to the purpose and the rains were incessant. As a result the Navy had to maintain its presence even though its men, ships and aircraft needed rest and replenishment. The difficulty was aggravated further when Kamikaze aircraft, which had first appeared during the Battle of Leyte Gulf, returned. Despite its weariness, the Navy was able to hit Luzon in November hard enough to destroy some 700 aircraft which the Japanese had sent down through Formosa, and to sink 134,000 tons of commercial shipping. A further welcome development that same month was the deployment of a Marine night-fighter squadron to Leyte. This was followed by the arrival of Marine Air Group (MAG)12 with four fighter squadrons. At the same time, the American Sixth Army was winding down its operations on Leyte. The day after Christmas, General Kreuger declared the capture of Leyte complete except for "minor" mopping-up. This, not unexpectedly, had to be continued until May 1945.[19]

Above: Coast Guard-manned LSTs bring in more men and supplies to Leyte, while the ship's personnel and soldiers fill sandbags to make gun emplacements for the beach defences. (USMC)

In the original plans, the Sixth Army was to finish on Leyte in time to move on to Luzon by 20 December. But, because of the delay in airfield construction, the start of the Luzon operation would wait until 9 January 1945. Meanwhile MAG 24 and MAG 32, with seven dive-bomber squadrons, were standing by for the Luzon invasion, where they would write the book on close air support.

The Army operations in the Philippines made full use of amphibian tractors. Some, as previously recorded, were manned by the Boat and Shore Battalions of the Engineer Special Brigades. The landings on Leyte were supported by the veteran 2nd Engineer Special Brigade which had already worked with the Marines on New Britain. Then, on 9 January 1945, the 4th ESB joined in the Sixth Army landings in Lingayen Gulf, Luzon. The Army also committed six cargo amtrac battalions and the 776th Amphibian Tank Battalion to the Leyte campaign. Several of these went on to Luzon. Notable among these was the 727th Amphibian Tractor Battalion which had fought at Hollandia before engaging in the Leyte operation, and had gone on to join in landings in Borneo after serving at Luzon.[20]

The third year of the Pacific War had returned the Americans to the Philippines, shattered Japanese air power, destroyed the Imperial Navy and brought the islands of Japan itself under continuing attack. The price had been high. But the shock of the losses at Tarawa had lessened as the campaigns in the Marianas and Palaus brought the realization that victory never comes cheap. The Marines, having broken through Japan's outpost line and penetrated deep into their defensive positions in the central Pacific, now stood poised with six divisions ready to move forward and finish the war.

Twelve equally ready amphibian tractor units were with these divisions. The 2nd Armored and the 2nd and 5th Amtrac Battalions were at Saipan with the 2nd Marine Division. The 1st Armored and the 3rd and 4th Amtrac Battalions were on Guam with the 3rd Marine Division. The 3rd Armored and 1st Amtrac Battalions were in the Russells with the 1st Marine Division. The 8th Amtrac

Battalion and the newly formed 9th Amtrac Battalion were on Guadalcanal where the 1st Provisional Marine Brigade had just become the 6th Marine Division by the addition of the 29th Marines. Lastly, the long-separated companies of the 11th Amtrac Battalion had been assembled and this newly constituted battalion together with the 10th Amtrac Battalion were on Maui, where the 4th Marine Division also was based. The only Division without amtrac units was the 5th Marine Division which had only just come to the big island of Hawaii where it occupied the camp formerly used by the 2nd Division. The 6th Amtrac Battalion, as noted earlier, had been disbanded after Peleliu and no 7th Battalion had ever been formed.

The experience gained by these units in the six major landings made in the central Pacific in 1944 were reflected in the refinements that had been brought to the technique of the amphibious assault. This information was finding its way into publications being prepared at the headquarters of the V Marine Amphibious Corps by Major Victor J. Harwick who had served at Guadalcanal and in the Marshalls and was then in G-3, Plans. Soon afterwards, he joined the 1st Provisional Tractor Group headquarters when it was formed by Colonel W. W. Davies, former head of the Dunedin detachment. Davies had taken his staff group to Saipan where they had planned the amtrac support for Tinian. A 2nd Provisional Tractor Group was later formed in the III MAC but too late to play any operational or planning role.[21]

By the end of 1944 the many details involved in the organization of a force landing from amtracs had been worked out. The command and control system for the ship-to-shore movement was now quite effective as were the procedures for the employment of amtracs after the initial assault landings. The maintenance and servicing of amtracs, however, remained a difficult problem, particularly in the first few days of an operation. Maintenance LSTs were of limited use since disabled LVTs could not be readily embarked and the confined space in the tank deck made it awkward to move vehicles about aboard ship. Then too, LST captains were reluctant to allow open-flame welding in their tank decks for safety reasons. Thus, as soon as there was space ashore, amtrac maintenance facilities were landed and the work carried on from there. The retrievers and amphibious shop facilities, built by the battalions, justified their existence many times over in their ability to go out to disabled vehicles wherever they were and bring them back.

The tactical role of the LVTs, first assumed at Tarawa, stimulated the imagination of innovators. Thus, 1944 witnessed a number of attempts to expand upon the LVT's combat capabilities. Rocket-launching devices and mine-detonating grapnels proved ineffective when not actually dangerous. Only the heavy flame-thrower, introduced at Peleliu, proved valuable. But, even then, its utility was limited by the vulnerability of the amtrac; the device only became fully effective when later installed in a tank. The most important development in the transition of the amtrac to a fighting vehicle was found in the use of the cannon-mounting model.

The initial introduction of these vehicles in the Marshalls had provided little opportunity truly to evaluate their potential. Then, in the Marianas, it became evident that the 37mm gun was too light for an assault gun, and the amtrac itself was too lightly armored to be useful in a light tank role. This was attested to at Saipan where the 2nd Armored and the 708th Amphibian Tank Battalions suffered 148 and 184 casualties respectively, while the 2nd and 4th Tank Battalions lost only eighteen and 59 men each. Major Metzger, whose battalion fought in the Marshalls and Guam, found the optimal solution when he received LVT(A)4s after the Marianas. While accepting the vehicle's primary role as a direct fire weapon platform in the amphibious assault, Metzger visualized its subsequent use ashore mainly as self-propelled artillery. Thus, he organized and trained his battalion to provide assault gun support to the infantry in the initial landing phase of the amphibious operation, and subsequently to furnish the support of twelve batteries of 75mm howitzers controlled by five Fire Direction Centers (FDC) tied in to the artillery fire control communications net. This innovation would prove highly useful at Okinawa.[22]

Cargo amtracs serving as tactical vehicles in the assault gave the embarked infantry a mechanized capability. Efforts to exploit this capability were made, but with little success. The operation order issued by the 23rd Marine Infantry Regiment for the landing on Saipan, for example, directed:

"1st wave [LVT(A)s] leads 2nd and 3rd waves [LVT(2)s] carrying troops to 0-1 . . . BLTs hold necessary LVTs in readiness prepared on RCT order to execute motorized infantry-mechanized attack with LVT(2)s, LVT(A)s and tanks to accomplish seizure of Aslito airfield . . ."[23]

As noted earlier, the plan had not worked, not because the concept was defective but because debris blocked the beach exits and enemy fire tended to focus on the large vulnerable target represented by the LVT. Still, cargo LVTs often got into fire-fights in efforts to support infantry. Army amtracs in the Philippines were involved in such actions quite frequently; the 727th Amtrac Battalion cites an incident on Leyte in October when one of its amtracs supported the attack of an infantry unit until disabled by a mine placed under it by Japanese soldiers the amtrac had overrun. Comparable incidents occurred elsewhere but, in general, after the initial assault, cargo LVTs reverted to logistic tasks . . . unless they got into a fight hauling supplies to front-line troops.

The cargo amtrac's logistic role was not without considerable danger since it involved the continuous supply of the fighting units in the first days of the operation. This, as demonstrated at Tarawa, the Marianas and Peleliu, required repeated trips across the coral while still within range of enemy guns. Movement inland was made equally hazardous by uncleared mines and the proximity of enemy defenders who found little difficulty in hitting the massive machines. The early logistic effort in a beachhead was supplemented by DUKWs which were more vulnerable to the reef than were LVTs, but much kinder to roadbeds and communications wire. DUKWs, however, were most often used for artillery ammunition supply and were not as readily available for the more general resupply operations as were the LVTs . . . and these had learned to cope with whatever each situation required.

In summary, 1945 would find experienced amphibious forces that had been tested in a succession of diverse and difficult operations and who were well prepared to overcome whatever last effort the enemy would make before his final capitulation.

Above: *The first flag over Mount Surabachi. A small flag carried by the 2nd Battalion, 8th Marines is planted atop Mount Surabachi at 10.20 on the morning of 23 February 1945. The famous Rosenthal photograph was taken later on after a Marine obtained another set of colors from LST 779 to replace the ones planted earlier. (USMC)*

5. Seasoned Assault Landing Troops

Iwo Jima and Okinawa, the last battle, 1945

A MOMENT ago in geologic time, the earth belched forth a mass of rock, ash and sulphureous gas into a lonely part of the western Pacific. This spasm brought forth the Volcano Islands which lie some 650 miles below Tokyo and midway from there to the Marianas. This phenomenon of creation was of interest to volcanologists and few others until late 1944 when American B-29 bombers based in the Marianas began their air campaign against Japan. Then, the Volcano Islands, notably Iwo Jima, suddenly became important. Japanese radar on Iwo Jima gave the home islands two hours of warning of the approach of the American bombers, and the airfields situated there enabled Japanese fighters to challenge the bombers' passage. In addition, the absence of a way station between the B-29 bases and their distant targets denied the big bombers fighter cover when most vulnerable, or sanctuary in the event of damage or distress. Clearly the Japanese presence on Iwo Jima was intolerable; the island would have to be taken. Thus, on 19 February 1945, 80,000 Marines landed on the black ash beaches of Iwo Jima to engage 20,000 Japanese entrenched there in the most elaborate defenses that human effort and ingenuity could devise.

The sulphur island of Iwo Jima is a waterless wasteland, a scant eight square miles in area. An extinct volcano, Suribachi, rises 550 feet at its southern end as a stark reminder of the island's origins. Towards the north, the island broadens into an open tableland where the Japanese had built two airfields and were building a third. The plateau is dotted with several hills, three of which reach above 350 feet. The surface throughout is very rough and interspersed with deep gorges and high ridges. The beaches in the north are fronted by rocky shoals and backed by cliffs or broken ground. In the south, they are clear and steep; there the high surf and sharp drop of the land into the sea create an everchanging pattern of terraces which further impede the movement of men and even of tracked vehicles over the volcanic ash. The island has little vegetation and even less animal life. A Japanese officer vividly described it as an " . . . island of sulphur, no water, no sparrow, no swallow."[1]

The Japanese garrison on Iwo Jima was small at first. But, as the Americans advanced westward in the central Pacific, the need for improved inner defenses became evident to the Japanese and Iwo Jima was greatly strengthened. By the end of 1944 there were more than 20,000 men on the island, supported by more than 360 pieces of artillery, 75 heavy and medium mortars, 33 naval guns, 94 anti-aircraft guns, almost 300 anti-boat guns and 70 rocket-launchers firing projectiles ranging from 200 to a monstrous 550 pounds.

The island's highly competent commander, Lieutenant-General Tadamichi Kuribayashi, had carefully noted the failures of his countrymen to repel American amphibious assaults elsewhere. Not for him the deployment of troops in vulnerable beach defenses, the precipitate counter-attack, or the glorious death of a banzai charge. Rather, the General planned an elastic defense from mutually supporting positions organized in depth and centered in the north. Ground was not to be yielded; if lost, it would be regained by counter-attacks launched at night. Such affairs were to be local in nature; no general counter-attack was contemplated. Further, when a landing appeared imminent, heavy weapons would hold fire until the enemy had deployed ashore. Then, a concentrated fire would be placed on the landing areas from concealed positions inland followed by a final withdrawal into the northern defense system. These measures, the General believed, would not ensure that the island could be held, but they would guarantee that the price for its conquest would be high.

The epic that would yield a dramatic photograph later immortalized in a bronze memorial in front of the Arlington National Cemetery, began on 9 October 1944 when Lieutenant General H. M. Smith was informed by Admiral Nimitz that Iwo Jima was the next target. The Expeditionary Troops that the General would lead would comprise the largest force of Marines assembled during the war; they would include Major General Harry Schmidt's V Marine Amphibious Corps with the 3rd, 4th and 5th Marine Divisions. This force seemed more than adequate since intelligence estimates based on captured documents and aerial photos were much too conservative. Terrain analysis, however, led to the realistic conclusion that there was little choice of landing areas and little room for maneuver ashore. Thus, it would be necessary to strike hard with maximum force and maintain the impetus of the attack. This would be difficult because of the steep terraces off the beaches, but the shock power of eight infantry battalions landing in 380 amphibian tractors, supported by 68 armored amtracs all preceeded by a saturation bombardment should provide the desired momentum. Kuribayashi would dispute this conclusion.

The invasion of Iwo Jima, code-named DETACHMENT, was originally planned to begin on 20 January 1945. But, operations near Leyte had involved the Navy longer than planned and the appearance of Kamikazes had resulted in losses that had reduced readiness. Thus, the start date for the Luzon landings had had to be moved to 9 January. This, in turn, had led to the postponement of the landing on Iwo Jima to 19 February and the selection of 1 April as the date for the invasion of Okinawa.

Such a rapid succession of amphibious operations placed heavy demands on the Navy. As a result, the carefully studied recommendations of Lieutenant Colonel Donald M. Weller of the naval gunfire needed to prepare Iwo Jima for invasion were not fully implemented. The Marines wanted ten days of deliberate bombardment to destroy weapons emplacements, known troop positions and military facilities . . . they got three! General Smith and General Schmidt urged the Navy to reconsider the decision several times, but without success. Iwo was only one of several competing operational requirements and neither its start date nor the associated bombardment schedule could be changed without altering the whole chain of events.

The limiting factors affecting the duration of the preliminary bombardment of Iwo Jima did not preclude the lavish expenditure of ordnance against the island. Carrier air and naval guns first struck at Iwo Jima in mid-1944. This was followed by massive bombardments on 11 and 12 November and somewhat lesser strikes on 8 December. A four-day operation over Christmas again brought the island under naval guns. Meanwhile, beginning on 8 December, bombers of the Seventh Air Force began 74 days of strikes against the Volcano Islands, principally targeting Iwo Jima. The Navy ships returned once more on 5 January and yet again on the 24th. But, while these attacks neutralized airfields, these were returned to operational status in short order. Moreover, the effectiveness of these strikes against Japanese ground forces dispositions was even more limited. Indeed, photo intelligence revealed that despite the violence of the preliminary attacks, Japanese defenses continued to improve. Thus, when Rear Admiral William H. P. Blandy's Amphibious Support Force arrived off Iwo Jima on 16 February 1945, there remained 724 known priority targets to be destroyed by the six battleships, five cruisers and sixteen destroyers under his command.

As Blandy's ships moved into position at daybreak on 16 February, other Navy forces were launching aircraft for a strike on Honshu. The raid against that Japanese home island had been intended to distract the Japanese from the imminent invasion of Iwo Jima, but unfortunately, this added claim on the Navy's resources detracted from its capabilities to heap more destruction on the invasion target. There, the bombardment began at 0800. Soon after, bad weather interrupted the schedule of naval gunfire and air attack. The next day, the 17th, dawned clear and the Navy set about supporting minesweeping and underwater demolition team operations. Japanese gunners, disturbed by these activities and contrary to orders, opened fire and thereby disclosed positions which were promptly brought under attack by the watchful Americans.

The first incident that day was light automatic weapons fire directed against the American minesweepers which had closed to within 750 yards of the shore. Then the battleship *Tennessee*, moving in to cover UDT operations, had four men wounded by a coastal battery which opened fire at 0900. Half an hour later, the nearby *Pensacola* took six quick hits which killed the cruiser's executive officer and sixteen crewmen, and wounded 120; the ship also took moderate topside damage. The most serious event occurred at 1100 when twelve gunboats moved to within 1,000 yards of the shore to cover 100 frogmen reconnoitering the beach approaches. The Japanese opened fire, hit all gunboats and sank six. A destroyer that dashed in to the rescue was damaged. Altogether, the over-eager Japanese cost the U.S. Navy an additional fourteen dead, 183 wounded and one frogman missing. The consolation was that the Japanese reaction had not only revealed previously unidentified weapons positions but had also convinced Admiral Blandy that heavier fire concentrations were required; ammunition allowances were increased accordingly. The ships, temporarily favoured by the weather, spent the rest of the day directing intense destructive fire against targets around Mount Surabachi and on the high ground dominating the beaches. That day too, carrier air was able to carry out its planned strikes. Still, at the evening conference, it was apparent that because of the poor results achieved on the 16th, much less had been accomplished than was needed. Weller urged that the final day be

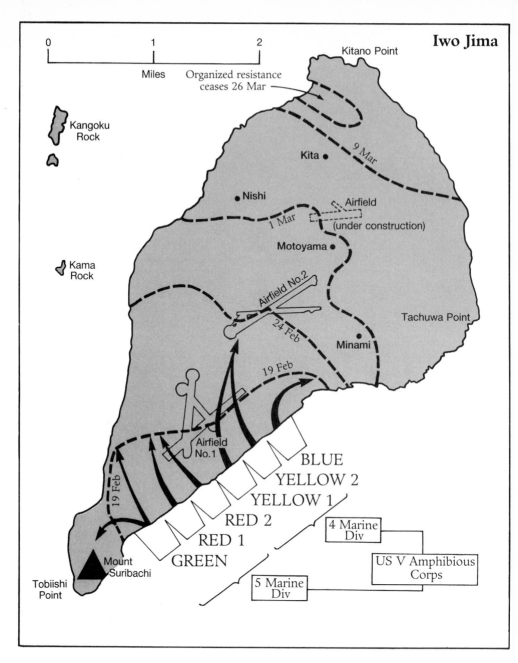

Iwo Jima

0   1   2
Miles   Organized resistance
ceases 26 Mar

Kitano Point

Kangoku
Rock

Kita ●

9 Mar

Nishi ●

Airfield
(under construction)

1 Mar

Kama
Rock

Motoyama ●

Airfield No.2

Tachuwa Point

24 Feb

Minami ●

19 Feb

19 Feb

Airfield
No.1

BLUE
YELLOW 2
YELLOW 1
RED 2
RED 1
GREEN

4 Marine
Div

US V Amphibious
Corps

Mount
Suribachi

Tobiishi
Point

5 Marine
Div

devoted to destroying targets within range of the landing beaches. Blandy concurred, but the weather again interfered. Visibility on the 18th was poor, with the result that by nightfall only 194 of the priority targets had been taken out. Fortunately, the majority of weapons included within the 201 priority targets in the landings areas had been hit. Marine infantrymen would have to do the rest.

Landing force plans called for the 4th and 5th Marine Divisions to land four regiments abreast over six of seven designated beaches totalling 3,500 yards on the southeast side of the island. The 5th Division under Major General Keller E.

Rockey was to come ashore in the shadow of Mount Surabachi. Its 28th Regiment was to land on Green Beach on the left with battalions in column, cover Surabachi and cross the island. The 27th Marines on the right was to land with two battalions abreast over Beaches Red 1 and 2, cross the island and swing north. The 4th Division, under Major General Clifton B. Cates, was to land against the island's main defenses. Its 25th Marines was to come ashore over Beach Blue 1 with two battalions abreast and pivot to the right to take Beach Blue 2. The 23rd Marines was to land two battalions abreast over Beaches Yellow 1 and 2, seize Motoyama Airfield No. 1 to the front and then swing north on the flank of the 5th Division's 27th Marines. The 3rd Division, under Major General Graves B. Erskine, was to remain aboard ship in reserve.

The lead wave on the 4th Division's front was to consist of 34 LVT(A)4s from Companies "A" and "B" of the 2nd Armored Amtrac Battalion. The assault infantry battalions of the 25th Marines were to be landed in 94 amtracs of the 5th Battalion. A similar number of amtracs would be provided by the 10th Amtrac Battalion for the assault infantry units of the 23rd Marines. The division artillery would be brought ashore by the Marines' 4th Amphibious Truck Company and the Army's 476th Amphibious Truck Company. On the 5th Division front, the other 34 armored LVT(A)4s from Companies "C" and "D" of the 2nd Armored Amtrac Battalion would precede the landing. The 28th Marines were to come ashore in 93 amtracs of the 11th Battalion under Lieutenant Colonel Albert J. Roose, and the 27th Marines would be landed in 90 amtracs of the 3rd Battalion. Artillery was to be carried ashore in two DUKW companies, the 5th Marine and the 471st Army. All amtracs and DUKWs were to be embarked on LSTs, nineteen of which were assigned to each assault division. The infantry was to be transferred to the LSTs with amtracs after the final rehearsal in the Marianas on 14 February. In addition, all of the 4th Division's tanks were to be loaded on sixteen LSMs. The 5th Division had only twelve of these small ships for its tanks, but received an LSD to make up the difference.

Many of the LSTs were assigned supplementary functions. Four were positioned 2,000 yards off the beaches as casualty evacuation stations. Another 28 LSTs were loaded with 200 tons each of priority supplies to be brought ashore by amtracs returning from the initial run to the beach. To ensure further flow of supplies to the units ashore, 42 DUKWs and 28 amphibious trailers, each preloaded with ammunition, rations, water and medical supplies, were also embarked on LSTs. An additional 50 of the 3½-ton amphibious trailers of the type first used at Peleliu, were embarked in a Landing Ship, Vehicle (LSV), a converted 6,000-ton minelayer with stern ramp. Finally, a light-weight tracked vehicle, the M29C "Weasel", made its first combat appearance. Although mechanically fragile, the Weasel could carry a ½-ton of cargo over soft terrain; it was widely used on Iwo Jima for the emergency supply of front line units beyond the reach of the more cumbersome LVTs.

The Navy control organization provided clearly identifiable control vessels and guide boats; the amtrac battalions paralleled the control organization with liaison officers as in previous landings. In the 4th Division area the commander of the 10th Amtrac Battalion served as Division Amphibian Tractor officer to co-ordinate LVT operations. In addition, that Battalion's supply officer, Lieutenant

Above: A dramatic aerial view of the landing assault at Iwo Jima during the early hours of 19 February 1945. Some 68 gun-mounting amtracs followed by 380 cargo amtracs loaded with the Marine assault elements storm towards the beaches.

Donald E. Kramer, was assigned duties as Shore Party Liaison Officer. The lieutenant had been left in the rear echelon during the Battalion's previous operations and had specifically requested to be allowed to participate in at least one landing operation so that, as he put it, he would have something to tell his children. Kramer went ashore early in the morning on D-Day and lived through the storm of fire that was to engulf the landing areas for several days; whatever he later told his children would not be an exaggeration. Another officer who volunteered to land early was Dr. Perry R. Ayres, the 10th Battalion's medical officer. The doctor had been through the operations in the Marshalls, Saipan and Tinian, but had remained aboard ship until the Battalion headquarters went ashore, which usually was a day or more after D-Day when there was sufficient area available to provide the large vehicle park required. Ayres believed the capabilities of his medical section should be exploited for the benefit of the assault troops in the early hours of a landing and requested that he supplement the casualty evacuation facilities to be established by Company "C" of the 4th Medical Battalion. This, as will be related later, exposed the doctor and his corpsmen to a trying ordeal compensated for by the numbers of wounded saved by their presence ashore.

The 2nd Armored Amphibian Tractor Battalion, under Lieutenant Colonel Reed M. Falwell, Jr., mountd out with each of its four companies equipped with seventeen LVT(A)4s and two cargo LVTs modified for maintenance and supply support. The four cargo amtrac battalions shared 181 LVT(2)s and 222 LVT(4)s. Of these 403 LVTs, 380 were used in the assault and the remaining 23 were retained as battalion support vehicles. All cargo amtracs were conventionally configured; i.e., there were no specially armed or adapted vehicles. The only innovation were two hand-made scaling ladders carried in each amtrac for use by the troops in the event that the terraces encountered off the beaches were too steep to be climbed easily. These, fortunately, were not required.

In short, the landing plan for the assault of Iwo Jima was uncomplicated and depended for its execution on veteran amtrac units. The same situation, unfortunately, did not apply to a number of the Navy ship's crews who were new to the demands that such operations placed on amphibious ships, particularly LSTs. Because of this, some of the difficulties experienced in the invasion of Kwajalein were to appear again off the beach at Iwo Jima. How all this would work out was about to be decided with the first light of dawn at Iwo Jima on 19 February 1945. It was 0539 and the sea was calm.

The night quickly dissolved into a clear bright day and at 0640 27 bombardment ships opened a last effort to destroy the guns covering the beaches. On the tank decks of the LSTs, LVT crews removed vehicle lashings and started engines. Heavily burdened infantrymen made their way to their assigned vehicles along the narrow passageways between them. All weapons, equipment and the vehicles themselves had been checked and serviced in the four days since the rehearsals at Saipan. While the tank decks were shuddering with the roar of

Below: A rolling barrage is delivered from the 5in guns of a battleship as amtracs head for the beach at Iwo Jima on 19 Feb 1945. (USMC)

Bottom: The first wave of LVT(4)s drives past a rocket-firing LSM on their run to the beach at Iwo Jima. (USMC)

seventeen amtrac engines and the ship's exhaust fans, the LSTs reached their amtrac launch positions, 1,500 yards seaward of the line of departure. The LSTs opened bow doors, lowered ramps and all was ready.

The order to launch vehicles came at 0725. Within twenty minutes 448 amphibian tractors were afloat, formed into waves and moving towards the line of departure behind their guide boats. At 0805, 72 carrier aircraft struck against positions on Surabachi and others dominating the landing beaches. As these aircraft left, 48 more came in to repeat the performance. During these strikes, the fire support ships moved in closer to the shore to deliver the final neutralization fire. At 0830 the armored amtracs crossed the line of departure, 4,000 yards from the beach; the gunboats were already on the way in, the troop-carrying amtracs following in orderly waves at the prescribed intervals. As the formation moved shoreward, the ships opened an intense fire, soon supplemented by a deluge of 4.2in rockets from the gunboats. Finally, just before the LVT(A)s touched land, a last strafing run was made over the beaches by carrier aircraft. At 0902 the armored amtracs passed through the surf line and down-shifted gears as their tracks ground into the soft ash. Two minutes later, the troop-carrying amtracs, arrived and the infantry swiftly disembarked below the protection of the first terrace. The cargo amtracs then returned to their LSTs where they loaded priority supplies. The LVT(A)s meanwhile, had moved off to the flanks of the landing beaches from where they were delivering fire to support the continuing arrival of

Left: *The M29C Weasel, light tracked cargo carrier, saw action for the first time on Iwo Jima. It is shown here loading 5-gallon water cans for delivery to front line troops. (USMC)*

Left: *An M29C on Iwo following the securing of the island. (USMC)*

Right: *A wave of amtracs loaded with assault troops makes its way to the beach. (USMC)*

the troop carriers; some LVT(A)s, masked by the terraces, had moved back outside the surf line in order to bring their weapons to bear on enemy targets.

Within thirty minutes' of the first wave's landing, the assault elements of eight infantry battalions were fighting their way inland over shifting sands and steep terraces. The enemy had done nothing to interfere with the organization of the landing or the movement towards the beach. But, five minutes after the first wave reached the Yellow beaches, fire began to fall on them and within minutes all landing areas were being subjected to a growing volume of mortar and artillery fire. This slowed the advance of the infantry whose progress was already hampered by the soft sand. Meanwhile, the tempo of the ship-to-shore movement was maintained and the beaches were becoming increasingly congested. The intense Japanese fire was hitting boats, amphibious vehicles and shore parties trying to organize the beaches to facilitate forward movement.

On the left flank, men from Company "B", 1st Battalion, 28th Marines drove across the narrow neck of the island and reached the opposite shore by 1030. The remainder of the Regiment was then deployed so as to isolate the menace of Surabachi. The effort of the 28th Marines facilitated the advance of the 27th Regiment; by 1130 advance elements of the Regiment were on the southern edge of the airfield and by 1500 they had reached the opposite beaches. Soon after, the 26th Marines serving as the Division reserve, landed and went into assembly areas south of the airfield. Tanks had been a help in much of the fighting, but

their presence had been a mixed blessing because they tended to draw fire. The division artillery had a particularly difficult time in getting ashore. With the beaches remaining under fire, the artillerymen suffered heavy losses aggravated by the need to get LVTs to tow the loaded DUKWs through the sand which they could not negotiate unaided. By evening the 5th Division had only one battalion of artillery ready to fire. However, the other three battalions managed to land during the night and set up so that they too were ready to contribute their support in the second day's fighting.

On the 4th Division front, the 23rd Marines under Colonel Walter W. Wensinger had brought its tanks in by 1000 and its reserve battalion in by noon. Then, with its full strength committed, the Regiment reached the airfield by late afternoon. One battalion of the 24th Marines, the Division reserve, landed in time to dig in with the 23rd Marines for the night. On the Division's exposed right, the 25th Marines used its 1st Battalion to drive directly inland towards the airfield on the right of the 23rd Marines. The 3rd Battalion landed on the flank, pivoted to the right towards Beach Blue 2 and ran into a wall of fire. As the 1st Battalion advanced west, the 3rd Battalion inched north towards the heights dominating the quarry and the beach. This opened a gap between the two battalions which Colonel John L. Lanigan plugged with his reserve, the 2nd Battalion. With this additional support a co-ordinated move was launched which brought the persistent Marines to the heights overlooking the quarry and Blue Beach 2 by 1830. By that time the 3rd Battalion, commanded by Lieutenant Colonel Justice M. "Jumpin' Joe" Chambers, was down to 150 men; it was relieved at nightfall by the 1st Battalion, 24th Marines. By 1900 the last battalion of Colonel Walter I. Jordan's 24th Marines had come ashore and occupied positions on Beach Blue 2. This put all the Division's infantry on the beach.

The 14th Marine Artillery Regiment of the 4th Division was accorded the same reception as its 5th Division counterpart. First, the artillery reconnaissance parties, landed early to select battery positions, had suffered disruptive casualties. Then, at 1400 when the 1st and 2nd Artillery Battalions were ordered ashore, "regardless of beach conditions", they found the DUKWs incapable of moving over the volcanic ash.[2] The 1st Battalion solved its problem by manhandling its 75mm howitzers into firing positions on Beach Blue 1. The 2nd Battalion, which had come ashore over Beach Yellow 1, was equipped with the 105mm howitzer which could not be manhandled and had to rely on the ubiquitous amtracs to get into firing position. In this manner, the 4th Division had its combat strength largely deployed ashore by the end of the first day. The Marines had a beachhead, and even though they had paid for it with 2,420 casualties and their landing areas remained under fire, they were ashore to stay.

Contrary to the Marines' expectations, the Japanese failed to launch their usual counter-attack, but they did keep up mortar and artillery fire throughout the first night. The next morning Colonel Liversedge, of Raider fame, turned his 28th Marines to the task of taking Mount Surabachi. The Regiment had suffered 385 casualties on its first day ashore; the climb to the top of Surabachi would take four days and would cost another 510 men. But, the flag planted on the summit on the morning of 23 February electrified all Americans present, none more then Navy Secretary James V. Forrestal who had just set foot on the beach.

Above: Engineers clear mines and mark the passage with tape during the assault landing as enemy shells rain down and burst in the water off the beach at Iwo Jima. (USMC)

Below: Amtracs coming ashore on 4th Division beaches at Iwo Jima. (USMC)

Left: An LVT(2) delivers wounded Marines to a floating aid station off Iwo Jima beaches. (USMC)

Below: Marines carry wounded to an amtrac for evacuation to the floating aid station situated on a hospital LST offshore. (USMC)

Less spectacular and even more bloody was the steady penetration of the island's main defenses in the north which began at 0830 with an attack by seven infantry battalions on a 4,000-yard front. The advance was agonizingly slow through minefields and against incessant mortar and artillery fire. Still, by the end of the day the airfield was firmly held and the front lines had been moved forward another 500 yards. It was in the afternoon of this difficult day that 50 Japanese aircraft stormed against the ships offshore. One light American carrier was sunk and another damaged. In addition, the *Saratoga* was hit hard enough to have to return to Pearl Harbor for repairs. Two other ships were also damaged. Fortunately, one of these, an LST with the 3rd Division's tanks, was able to beach and discharge its cargo undamaged.

That same day the Corps commander wanted to get the 21st Regiment of the 3rd Marine Division ashore, but conditions on the beaches were so bad that the Regiment, already boated, was ordered to return to its ships pending further word. Less lucky was the 4th Battalion of the 14th Artillery Regiment, which tried to get ashore late in the day. Seven of its overloaded DUKWs, each carrying a 105mm howitzer and ammunition, rolled off the ramps of their LSTs on which they had been loaded and continued straight down to the bottom. Two more loaded DUKWs broached in the surf and were lost. Fortunately, the 3rd Battalion managed to come ashore without loss. In that manner, the 4th Division had all its artillery, except for that at the bottom of the sea, ashore by the end of D+1.

The day before the flag went up on Surabachi, the 21st Marines came ashore and relieved the 23rd Marines. Two days later, on 24 February, General Erskine set up the command post of the 3rd Marine Division ashore; the next day his division took position between the 4th and 5th Divisions and joined in the killing advance to the north. The move from pillbox-to-cave-to-dugout-to-pillbox-to-cave-to-dugout in endless succession continued until the island was officially secured at 1600 on the 16th of March 1945. By that time the 4th Division was loading ships in preparation for its return to Maui. The 5th Division left on the 27th bound for Hawaii. The 3rd Division began loading that same day, but its units sailed for Guam separately, the last leaving Iwo Jima on 12 April.

The B-29s were not long in taking advantage of the changed ownership of Iwo Jima. The first actually came early. It landed, on its belly, on 4 March and stopped just before reaching a Japanese position which had been troubling the Marines for some time. Two days later, 28 P-51 Mustangs and twelve P-61 Black Widow night-fighters arrived to take up residence. By the end of the war, 2,250 more B-29s had made emergency landings on the island. The 25,000 airmen making up their crews had good reason to appreciate the 22,000 Marines and 3,000 Navy casualties suffered to make those landings possible. Only 1 per cent of the Japanese garrison of 20,000 survived as prisoners. This was the first time that the Marines had paid more to take an island than the Japanese had lost in defending it.

Among the 448 amtracs in the assault landing, D-Day losses had been surprisingly light, thanks largely to the density of the neutralization fire from carrier aircraft and naval guns immediately preceding the initial run to the beach. Many amtracs had been hit by small-arms fire on their way in, but only one LVT(A) was destroyed by a Japanese gun. That situation did not last, however.

Within the first two hours ashore, seven more LVT(A)s were knocked out by gunfire. That night, two more were destroyed by enemy guns while on beach defense. For the next 22 days the armored amtrac battalion continued to provide direct fire support to infantry in the daytime and join in beach defense duties at night. These latter services were particularly effective in preventing such incidents as an attempted barge landing over the western beaches on D-Night and an infiltration by swimmers over the 5th Division beaches on D+3 night. Beyond these routine tasks, the armored battalion engaged in a number of patrols along the coast. In the performance of these many duties the 2nd Armored Amphibian Tractor Battalion suffered 67 casualties and lost twenty LVT(A)4s. Of these, thirteen were destroyed by enemy fire, and sixteen sank because of mechanical failure or lack of fuel. Most annoying, and reminiscent of the unfortunate experiences during the landings in the northern Kwajalein islands, was that the loss of five of the LVT(A)s could be attributed to the refusal of LSTs to provide fuel or take the vehicles aboard.

The cargo amtracs at Iwo Jima once again revealed the unique qualities that had earned them front row places in the amphibious assaults of 1944. Once they had deployed the infantry ashore and dropped off the 700 pounds of ammunition and water each assault LVT carried, the vehicles had returned to designated LSTs where they had taken on balanced loads of emergency supplies for delivery to combat units ashore. The shuttle continued for four days without cease. It was during this period that amtracs were also used to position artillery, drag DUKWs and other vehicles over the volcanic ash terraces and generally help to clear the badly cluttered beaches. By the fifth day, when the intensity of the fire on the beaches lessened, the amtracs returned to more routine tasks where they could be rotated for servicing and whatever crew rest the congested beachhead could provide. One such routine task required the delivery after dark of urgently needed mortar ammunition to a forward position by an amtrac of the 10th Battalion. The route crossed an area where heavy mines already had blasted several of the battalion's amtracs. To avoid a similar disaster, Lieutenant Lyman D. Keown took it upon himself to lead the loaded amtrac on foot, while prodding the sand for mines. The ammo was delivered safely; Keown received a well-deserved Silver Star.

The cargo amtrac battalions continued their logistic services into the third week in March when they were ordered to return to their rear bases. The 11th Battalion went to Hawaii while the 3rd, 5th, 10th and 2nd Armored went to Maalea Bay on Maui. At that time, a recapitulation of amtrac losses revealed that one-third of the number landed had been lost. Of these, 14 per cent had been lost to enemy fire, another 23 per cent had been lost coming through the heavy surf and 4 per cent had been destroyed by mines. The heaviest losses, 59 per cent, were vehicles that were sunk . . . among which were several which had been unable to find a safe haven aboard inexperienced LSTs. Personnel losses among the four cargo battalions numbered 122, 20 per cent of which were incurred when men of the 3rd and 11th Amtrac Battalions were used for mopping-up operations in areas by-passed by the infantry.

Reference has been made earlier to the practice of amtracs to stop routinely at beach evacuation stations to pick up wounded for removal to ships offshore.

Right: Amtracs destroyed by mines. The Japanese laid "yardstick" mines over buried aerial bombs. When detonated these were powerful enough to lift 30 tons of LVT and cargo, and blow a hole in the vehicle's bottom. (USMC)

Right: Having reached the airfield on Iwo, Marines of the 4th Division seek cover among the shattered aircraft. (USMC)

Right: Swamped boats lie in the water as LSM 202 unloads tanks onto the beach at Iwo Jima while an LVT hauls vehicles away.

It was just such an evacuation station that Dr. Perry Ayres had set up between the Blue and Yellow Beaches shortly after noon of D-Day. The doctor and his medical section had remained aboard LST 761 awaiting the call to land. By noon, having failed to receive the long-awaited call, the doctor embarked his detachment in an LVT and made his way ashore. There he found that the aid station he was to have joined had been knocked out by shellfire which continued to sweep the beach. Without hesitation, the doctor began to treat casualties in the immediate vicinity and directed his corpsmen to recover additional wounded on the beach. Soon word spread that a doctor was ashore and, despite the continuing enemy fire, wounded began to gather where Ayres was diligently working. By that time, Ayres had found a bomb crater which provided a minimum shelter. There he organized an aid station that was to function without letup for the next five days. The Medical Annex to the After-Action Report of the 10th Amphibian Tractor Battalion records that 240 casualties were treated at this rudimentary aid station. A footnote explains that the figure excludes casualties treated during the first 24 hours because these were "not properly logged due to intense fire and continual aid work required for all personnel".[3] On an island where, as Admiral Nimitz later stated, "Uncommon Valor was a common virtue", that displayed by Perry Ayres ranks with the highest; certainly none of the Marines who survived their wounds because of his presence ashore would deny him that place.[4]

Below: *A view from the Suribachi volcano shows U.S. supplies being moved onto Iwo Jima beaches.*

The battle for Okinawa is recorded in superlatives as befits what was to be the last amphibious operation of World War II. The battle was fought by the American Tenth Army, commanded by Lieutenant General Simon Bolivar Buckner, Jr., whose four Army and two Marine Divisions worked in close and harmonious collaboration throughout the four-month campaign. Army, Navy and Marine close air support was available to all, as was the fire of 42 warships and 33 battalions of artillery. Beyond the magnitude of the men and resources engaged in this final climactic battle is the fact that Okinawa first brought American troops into contact with Japanese culture.

The Chinese had strongly influenced the early development of the Okinawan people. The Japanese, who followed in the 17th century, shared in the process until 1871 when the King of Okinawa was made a Marquis of Japan. Thereafter, Chinese influence declined as Japan's dominion over the kingdom became firmly established. In 1879, Okinawa became a Prefecture of Japan; in 1943 that Prefecture was joined to seven others to form the District of Kyushu. Despite the close ties to the home islands, the Okinawans were considered inferior to the Japanese. The resulting resentment, while evident, did not serve the American effort. On the contrary, more than 20,000 Okinawans fought with the Japanese against the Americans. Most memorable is the valiant resistance offered by 1,500 civilians when the island of Ie Shima was attacked by the Army's 77th Infantry Division. The Okinawans might resent the Japanese, but that did not mean they were prepared to support the Americans.

Okinawa, like other Japanese possessions close to the home islands, was little affected by the early war years. Then, as Japanese defenses in the Pacific crumbled, Japan began to strengthen its inner bastion. Thus, on 1 April 1944, the 32nd Army was established on Okinawa and systematically built up to a force of 75,000 combat troops including two divisions, an independent brigade and Navy units. In addition, 18,000 Okinawans in the Home Guard were absorbed into the 32nd Army together with 6,000 other natives organized into special engineer and miscellaneous units. These forces were concentrated in the southern third of the island in three successive defense lines: the Kakazu Ridge, the Shuri Castle, and the Yuza Dake and Yaeju Dake line. The defense plan reflected the understanding of the Japanese commander, Lieutenant-General Mitsuru Ushijima, that the American amphibious assault was too powerful to be resisted. Thus, the northern two-thirds of the 60-mile long island would be covered by two provisional regiments, while the remainder of the force would be deployed in strong positions in the south where it was thought the American landings would be made.

North of the 2-mile wide Ishikawa Isthmus, Okinawa is heavily wooded, sparsely populated and has broken terrain rising to 1,500 feet. The beaches there are poor and lead to a wild interior with few communications. The south, in contrast, is relatively well developed, and the terrain, although precipitous in several areas, is more open and undulating and does not rise above 500 feet. There are several stretches of good but reef-fronted beaches on both the east and west coasts. Following a careful terrain analysis and study of Japanese dispositions, the Americans concluded that an assault landing by four divisions over the Hagushi beaches on the west coast just below the Ishikawa Isthmus was preferred because, among other advantages, it led directly to two airfields. Vice Admiral Turner, designated to command the Joint Expeditionary Force, favored the eastern beaches because of the shelter they offered. However, he finally agreed to a landing on the west provided that, in addition to the landing on nearby Kiese Shima to emplace artillery, a landing also be made in the Kerama Retto to provide a sheltered anchorage for the Navy force; these landings were both to be accomplished before the main landings on Okinawa itself.

The assault on Okinawa was to begin on 1 April 1945 with the III Marine Amphibious Corps, under Major General Roy S. Geiger coming in over beaches north of Hagushi village. Major General John R. Hodge would land his XXIV Corps over beaches south of that same village. The scheme of maneuver ashore envisaged the early capture of Yontan airfield by General Shepherd's 6th Marine Division, which would then continue its advance towards the northwest. The 1st Marine Divisions under Major General Pedro del Valle, was to take Yontan and then drive directly east towards the Katchin Peninsula thrusting out into Nakagusuku Bay. The Army's 7th Infantry Division, under Major General Archibald V. Arnold, was to land immediately below Hagushi village, move directly towards Kadena airfield and continue to the east coast of the island where it would turn south. The 96th Infantry Division, under Major General James L. Bradley, was to land on the Tenth Army right, turn south and advance in concert with the 7th Division against the main enemy defenses.

At the same time that the four divisions were landing in the west, the 2nd Marine Division would feint a landing against the Minatoga beaches in the southeast. Also afloat on L-Day, the day of the main landings, would be the 27th Infantry Division as Tenth Army reserve. Finally, land-based tactical air support would be provided by Major General Francis P. Mulcahy's 2nd Marine Air Wing which would move to Okinawa as rapidly as airfields could be made available. The two airfields featured in the initial assault plans were to become operational by L+4 and two more were to be in service by L+15 days.

Each of the four assault divisions planned to land with two infantry regiments abreast. This would require the equivalent of two cargo amtrac battalions per division to enable four assault battalions to land simultaneously over the reef. In addition, one armored amtrac battalion was required to form the first wave in accordance with what had by then become standard practice. In the III Marine Amphibious Corps the requirement was to be met by the assignment of Lieutenant Colonel Coffman's 4th Amtrac Battalion to land the 22nd Marines, and the 9th Amtrac Battalion, under Major Theodore E. Watson, to land the 4th Marines. The 1st Armored Amtrac Battalion, under Lieutenant Colonel Louis Metzger, would comprise the lead wave on the 6th Marine Division landing front.

The 5th Marines would be landed by the 1st Amtrac Battalion, commanded by Lieutenant Colonel Maynard M. Nohrden; the 7th Marines would come ashore in LVTs from Lieutenant Colonel Charles B. Nerren's 8th Amtrac Battalion. The 3rd Armored Amtrac Battalion, under Lieutenant Colonel John I. Williamson, would form the first wave on the 1st Marine Division landing front. Amphibian tractor support for the U.S. Army's divisions would be provided by the 708th and 776th Amphibian Tank Battalions and by the 536th, 728th, 773rd

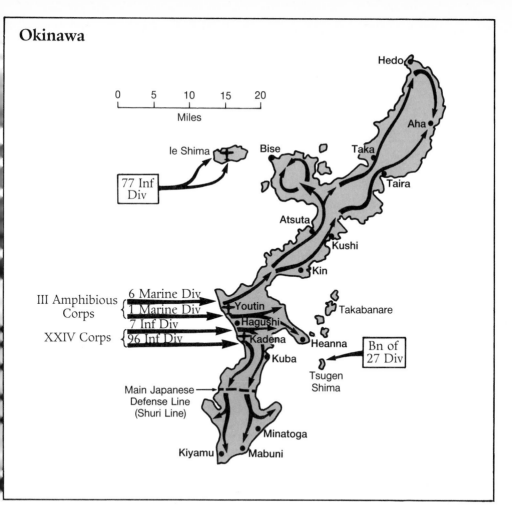

Okinawa

0 5 10 15 20
Miles

Hedo
Aha
Ie Shima
Bise
Taka
Taira

77 Inf Div

Atsuta
Kushi
Kin

III Amphibious Corps
6 Marine Div
1 Marine Div
Youtin
Takabanare

XXIV Corps
7 Inf Div
96 Inf Div
Hagushi
Kadena
Heanna
Bn of 27 Div
Kuba
Tsugen Shima

Main Japanese Defense Line (Shuri Line)
Minatoga
Kiyamu
Mabuni

and 788th Amphibian Tractor Battalions. Lastly, the feint to be made by the 2nd Marine Division would utilize tractors from Major Fenlon A. Durand's 2nd Amtrac Battalion.

The 9th Amtrac Battalion had been organized at Camp Pendleton in May 1944 and deployed overseas in October. Okinawa would be its introduction to combat. Equipped with 103 LVT(4)s, the battalion would log up to 400 operating hours per vehicle in that demanding campaign. The 8th Amtrac Battalion had been represented at Peleliu, but Okinawa would be its first combat operation as a complete unit. This battalion, equipped with 106 LVT(4)s, would also find ample scope for its capabilities in the long battle to come. The veteran 1st and 4th Amtrac Battalions had each been re-equipped with 108 and 102, respectively, of the new Borg-Warner LVT(3)s. This latest model amtrac with two Cadillac engines and hydramatic drive, provided a larger cargo compartment which could accommodate as many as 35 troops. The vehicle would prove its worth at Okinawa and would be retained as the standard landing vehicle of the Marine Corps throughout the Korean War.

The two Marine armored amtrac battalions were veteran units. Both were equipped with the LVT(A)4 mounting a 75mm howitzer in an open turret.

Lieutenant Colonel Metzger, with early training in artillery, had seen the potential of these vehicles as other than direct fire weapons and, with the concurrence and support of the 6th Marine Division, had trained his battalion as self-propelled artillery capable of both direct and indirect fire missions. The 3rd Armored also had acquired this expanded capability. As a result the two Marine armored amtrac battalions, already well prepared to carry out their assault gun roles in landings and subsequent support operations on the reef and on the flanks of the beachhead, were also trained to support their respective Divisions with the added fire-power of an artillery regiment. This represented a substantial increase in the overall artillery support available and a well-conceived means of fully exploiting the capabilities of the LVT(A)4.

The seven days of preliminary naval gunfire bombardment planned for Okinawa was based on the assumption that the enemy would have strong beach defenses which would have to be destroyed. Had the Americans known that would not be the case, they might have applied some of the resources expended on Okinawa against such priority targets as had had to remain untouched on Iwo Jima. But, lacking prophetic vision, the Americans first hit Okinawa with a carrier air strike on 10 October 1944. This was repeated twice in January 1945, then once again in February and March. By that time B-29s were also working over the island and submarines were helping keep the garrison isolated. The next blow was struck by Task Force 58 which threw its full weight against targets on Honshu, Shikoku and Kyushu in a wide-ranging attempt to disrupt Japanese air operation capabilities from home bases. The Japanese retaliated with Kamikaze attacks which damaged five American carriers.

By 24 March, the Navy's bombardment ships had appeared off the coast of Okinawa. Rear Admiral Morton L. Deyo, with his gunfire and covering force, opened the action with his fast battleships. By the day of the landing, the bombardment force had fired 27,226 projectiles at ground targets on Okinawa and carrier aircraft completed 3,095 sorties. On 31 March, Admiral Blandy, commanding the Navy's Amphibious Support Force, reported with confidence; "The preparation is sufficient for a successful landing." Unlike, the situation at Iwo Jima, this time the confidence was well founded.[5]

The preliminary landings of the 77th Infantry Division which began on the Kerama Retto on 26 March went off as planned . . . after a slight modification. The Division had planned to use boats for its landing, but underwater demolition team personnel had reported all beaches fronted by reefs. The Division had then arranged to use amtracs instead. This had created no difficulties and, by the first night, Division units had taken three islands and landed on two others. The last island of the group was taken on the next day, the 27th. During the next two days, the Army mopped-up on the Kerama Retto while the Navy blasted channels through the reef bordering Kiese Shima. Then, early on the morning of 31 March, the 2nd Battalion, 306th Infantry landed on that island. The infantry was quickly followed by the 420th Artillery Group whose 155mm guns were in position to begin registration that same night. In six action-packed days the 77th Division had gained an anchorage that would save many ships hit by Kamikazes in the days to come, and had secured an artillery base that would cause the

Above: Landing ships laden with Marines and tanks move towards Iheya Shima off Okinawa as it is pounded by an air assault. (USMC)

Right: A wave of LVTs moves across the line of departure bound for the beach, while an Idaho *class battleship fires in the background.*

Right: The seizure of offshore islands near Okinawa was a hazardous and costly process. Note LVT(3) and LVT(4) in the foreground and LSM unloading at the reef; an LCVP lies stranded off the beach. (USMC)

Japanese 32nd Army considerable grief . . . all at a cost of 31 dead and 81 wounded. Most significant, the seizure of the Kerama Retto had uncovered 350 suicide boats fully prepared to intercept the American landing . . . their effect against Tenth Army shipping might well have proved disastrous.

On 1 April 1945, Easter Sunday in the Christian world, more than half a million American fighting men embarked in 1,300 ships appeared off the coast of Okinawa to open the last major offensive of World War II. The enemy reacted with scattered air attacks. These were turned back by ships' guns, but not before the transport *Winsdale* and *LST 884* carrying troops of the 2nd Marine Division had fallen victim to two suicide planes. Sixteen Marines were killed and 37 wounded in this attack; the casualties were shared by the 2nd Battalion, 2nd Marines and Company "C" of the 2nd Amtrac Battalion which also lost twelve of its amtracs. These were heavy losses for a force that was only to engage in a feint. Despite that and other Kamikaze attacks, the planned events unfolded off the eastern and western beaches on schedule.

With daylight, ten battleships, nine cruisers and 23 destroyers began to pound the landing areas. The Japanese responded with scattered artillery and mortar fire. Only a vicious counter-battery fire directed against the 155mm guns on Kiese Shima proved disturbing. The Navy's preparation moved to its climax at 0800 when the amtracs crossed the line of departure. The 4,000-yard run to the beach was accomplished without loss against sporadic small-arms fire. Just before the lead amtracs came ashore, 138 carrier aircraft swept the 8,600 yards of landing beaches with rocket and machine gun fire. At the same time, the 2nd Marine Division units feinting against Minatoga beaches reversed course and returned to their ships.

The main landings went off as planned. The Marines had trouble with an unexpectedly rough reef, but otherwise no LVTs were lost or damaged in the assault that deployed their eight battalions of infantry ashore in good order within thirty minutes. Once ashore, the troops moved inland at a rapid pace. Before noon the 6th Marine and 7th Army Divisions had reached Yontan and Kadena airfields respectively. Tank units, many guided over the reef by LVTs, went ashore soon after the infantry to join in the drive to expand the beachhead. Divisional artillery came ashore in DUKWs and was in position by late afternoon; the DUKWs and some LVTs were busy building up ammunition stocks by the guns while the remaining amtracs shuttled between the beach and the ships offshore with additional troop units and supplies. By 1530 the reserve units of both Corps were ashore and by 1600 on 1 April, 50,000 troops were digging in ashore in anticipation of an enemy counter-attack . . . which did not materialize. A beachhead 15,000 yards wide and 5,000 yards deep, had been gained at a cost of only 159 casualties.

The next morning the 2nd Marine Division made another feint before sailing off to Saipan to await possible recall. Meanwhile, the Tenth Army went on to expand its beachhead and begin the build-up of supplies ashore. High tide provided water deep enough for boats to reach the shore. Even so, many of the supplies brought in from ships and barges offshore and delivered to the rapidly advancing units were carried in amtracs and a few DUKWs. The only serious problem was that the supplies were coming ashore faster than trucks could move

Above: An LSM(R) fires a salvo of 4.5in rockets at the Hagushi beach to prepare the way for the landing on Okinawa, 1 April 1945. (USN)

them inland. As a result the amtracs were required to continue in the round-the-clock effort which emptied 32 transports in the first four days. Two days later the tally showed thirteen more transports unloaded and an overall total of sixty LSTs completely discharged.

The Kamikaze menace, which had already hit the American Navy hard in mid-March, continued. From 1 to 5 April eight transports and one LST had been hit in scattered raids as had one battleship, one escort carrier and two destroyers. Then on 6 April, 200 suicide aircraft struck in a massive 2-hour long attack which sank two destroyers, two ammunition ships, one minesweeper and an LST. An additional eighteen ships were damaged. In contrast, the situation ashore remained relatively favorable. All units of the Tenth Army were a week or more ahead of schedule. The 6th Marine Division had crossed the Motobu Peninsula in the north, the 1st Marine Division was overlooking Nakagusuku Bay and the XXIV Corps had positioned its two divisions facing south at the threshold of the main Japanese defenses. It was time to open the eastern beaches, but before this could be done, it would be necessary to take the offshore islands guarding their approaches.

The Fleet Marine Force Reconnaissance Battalion was tasked with making the initial probes of the islands on 6 and 7 April. These revealed that only the 2,500-yard long Tsugen Shima was defended. Its garrison included 250 men, three 6in naval guns, two 75mm and two 57mm guns. The armament was powerful, but the troops modest in number. Accordingly, it was decided that the 3rd Battalion of the 105th Regiment of the 27th Infantry Division could handle the job. The attack was set for 10 April, two days after the 27th Infantry Division had been ordered ashore to reinforce the XXIV Corps. The Tsugen Shima assault force loaded up on four LSTs on 9 April along with armored amtracs from the 708th Battalion and cargo amtracs from the 534th Battalion. The landing went off well, but by the afternoon a heavy rain began which quickly slowed down what became a vicious firefight that lasted all night and continued into the morning. Finally, at the end of the second day the island was secured and with it access was gained to another sheltered anchorage and a clear stretch of open landing beaches.

In the week that followed, the 6th Marine Division moved into the Motobu Peninsula where 1,500 Japanese were determined to make a stand. The advance of the Division to that point had been unexpectedly rapid. Because of this, the Division's 15th Artillery Regiment would have been hard pressed to provide the continuity of support needed by the rapidly advancing infantry had it not been for the 1st Armored Amphibian Tractor Battalion. Five of its platoons with their LVT(A)4s helped overrun Yontan airfield, while its other units were directing their fire against all targets holding up the infantry's advance. Then, when the artillery regiment's headquarters landed, the armored amtrac battalion was attached to the artillery. As such, it joined in the action that secured the Motobu Peninsula on 19 April, after having moved two of its companies to the base of the Peninsula by LST. Beginning on the 21st, the 1st Armored's amtracs made a succession of landings on the islands off the Motobu Peninsula with each of the vehicles carrying four to six Marines riding behind the turret. The same day that this tedious operation began, the 22nd Marines reached the northern end of Okinawa. Unfortunately, there followed a period of guerrilla actions involving surviving Japanese troops and Okinawan Home Guard units that did not end until civilian control was tightened and patrolling greatly intensified.

The gains made by the 6th Marine Division in the north made it possible for Admiral Turner to set an early date for the planned attack against Ie Shima, a rectangular, 5 x 2½-mile island lying a short three and a half miles west of Motobu Peninsula. The 77th Division was given the mission of landing on the island on 16 April, seizing the airfield there and destroying the Japanese garrison

Below: Sugar Loaf Hill in Okinawa looking directly south.

estimated at two infantry battalions. The Division, at that time, was aboard ships some 300 miles off Okinawa where it had been circling since it had finished with the Kerama Retto assignment. The monotony of the two-week cruise to Nowhere had been interrupted only once . . . but that was enough! On 2 April a Kamikaze attack hit three transports. The *Henrico* lost its captain and 48 crew; the embarked troops lost the commander of the 305th Infantry Regiment and most of that unit's staff. Despite this tragic loss, the command group had been replaced and the Division was ready for its second amphibious assault in less than a month.

Major Masashi Igawa had done a magnificent job of camouflaging the dispositions of his 2,000-man force. He had also so inspired the civilian population on Ie Shima that the 1,500 men and women who fought at the side of the Japanese troops did so with equal skill and valor. The test of his preparations began on 13 April with an American reconnaissance of Minna Shima followed by the landing of three battalions of the 77th Division's artillery. Then, on 16 April, a landing force made up of the 305th and 306th Infantry Regiments left its anchorage off the Hagushi beaches, during an unsuccessful Kamikaze attack, and took position off Ie Shima. By 0725 the target island was shuddering from the impact of shells being fired by two battleships, seven destroyers and seventeen mortar boats. Then, as ten rocket-firing gunboats led the first wave of armored amphibians toward the beach, sixteen fighters came in to give the landing area a final pounding. A few minutes later, the amtracs came ashore and the assault troops of both Regiments unloaded and began to move inland. By nightfall the 306th, on the left, had advanced 3,500 yards; the 305th, however, had encountered much stronger resistance and had gone in only 500 yards. On 17 April, the reserve regiment, the 307th, was brought in by LST and made an assault landing in the center of the island. Intense fighting continued for five days until on 21 April the island was finally overrun. The Americans counted 4,706 enemy dead; their own losses included 239 dead, 879 wounded and nineteen missing. Among the dead was Ernie Pyle, the famed war correspondent, who fell to a Japanese machine gun covering the zone of action of the 3rd Battalion, 305th Infantry. His war had begun long ago in North Africa, half a world away from where it would so tragically end.

While these events were unfolding in the north, the XXIV Corps in the south had come up against the 32nd Army's main defenses. At this point, the Japanese commander began to synchronize his counter-attacks with the major Kamikaze strikes: while valiant airmen were sacrificing themselves against American ships, equally valiant Imperial soldiers would endeavor to blunt the advance of the American ground force ashore. In this fashion, reasoned General Ushijima, the American troops on the island would be cut off from their bases, ground down by incessant losses and eventually reduced in strength to the point where they could be disposed of. It was a good plan, but the Americans were unwilling to co-operate.

As an immediate measure, General Buckner assigned his 27th Infantry Division to the XXIV Corps. This enabled the U.S. Army troops to gain control over the first defense line, the Kakazu Ridge on 24 April. A week later, the 1st Marine Division was ordered to the southern front where it relieved the 27th Infantry Division on the west of the XXIV Corps zone of action. Five days later,

the 6th Marine Division took position to the left of the 1st Marine Division. With these moves, the Tenth Army was deployed on a two Corps front, each with two divisions on the line. These dispositions had been made in response to the strongest counter-attack the Japanese launched during the whole campaign.

That drama opened in the early evening of 3 May when Yontan and Kadena airfields were subjected to an inaccurate high-level bomber attack. This was followed by an equally ineffective strike of 60 bombers seeking to disrupt the Tenth Army rear area. Then, shortly after midnight, the 3rd Armored Amphibian Tractor Battalion found itself in the way of a 700-man Japanese landing force. In the words of the battalion's after-action report:

> "Shortly after 0130 [on 4 May] the 1st Marines informed us that approximately one battalion of the enemy had landed on our left flank and were in control of the low ground between the seawall and the ridge 400 yards inland . . . Lieutenant Hale took a platoon of Able Company vehicles through the seawall at 0145. Lieutenant Boudereaux was sent with three vehicles to cover the rear of his platoon . . . Lieutenant Hale immediately took the Japs on the reef under fire with devastating results. He fired ninety-five rounds of direct fire, mostly ricochet bursts. In the meantime, Baker Company vehicles stationed along the seawall fired on enemy boats to their front. One Type A landing barge later found to have been carrying 100 men was sunk by 75mm and .50 caliber fire . . . Patrols were dispatched at daylight . . . eighty-three bodies were counted on the reef . . . it is estimated that 150 Japanese were killed by this battalion . . . our casualties . . . just two wounded . . . "[6]

While this action was taking place in the west, a similar landing attempt by 500 Japanese on the east was being foiled by troops of the 7th Infantry Division. Then, as these amphibious envelopments were being thwarted, Japanese artillery fire intensified into a half-hour preparation to pave the way for the attack of their 24th Division. This began at first light, with Japanese infantry advancing through their own fire. When, at last, the Japanese fire lifted, the Americans replied with 28 battalions of artillery, accompanied by naval guns and an early flight of supporting aircraft. These last returned several times during the day to dump 70 tons of bombs and expend 450 rockets and 22,900 rounds of .50 caliber machine gun ammunition against the doomed Japanese. By noon the threat of the

counter-attack was over. But, while the 32nd Army had suffered heavily in this attempt, it still retained very strong defense capabilities, as events would soon demonstrate.

On 11 May, the Tenth Army, with the 96th, 77th, 1st and 6th Divisions deployed east to west across Okinawa, began to drive against the Shuri line, the heart of the Japanese defense system. The advance was agonizingly slow, with much of the fighting reminiscent of that against the cave complexes at Peleliu and Iwo Jima. Still, by 18 May, the 6th Marine Division had taken the Sugar Loaf, the western anchor of the Shuri line overlooking the city of Naha. It would take another eleven days for the 1st Marine Division and the 77th Infantry Division to gain possession of the Shuri bastion itself. The Japanese defenders, as always, had been skilled and tenacious, but the heavy rains which saturated the battlefield also helped slow the pace of advance of the American infantry.

The 9th Amphibian Tractor Battalion referred to the latter problem:

"The missions of this battalion were varied, but in the main consisted of transporting ammunition, water, rations and other high priority cargo to front line troops, and the evacuation of the casualties from the front. However, the heavy rains made the roads impassable and immobilized motor transport to a great extent. Consequently, this organization was assigned the additional mission of transporting men and supplies from the rear areas by water. As the rains continued in intensity, motor transport was almost completely stopped, and amphibian tractors became the only means of moving men and materials overland. . . ."[7]

At the beginning of June, the 6th Marine Division had been relieved by the 1st Marine Division and directed to carry out a shore-to-shore operation against the Oroku Peninsula, just below the city of Naha. It soon became evident that there were not enough amtracs remaining in serviceable condition to land assault units of one regiment. The 9th Amtrac Battalion reported only 16 per cent of its vehicles operable and the 4th Amtrac Battalion was in similar straits. Assistance was requested of the Army and with it, a provisional amphibian tractor group was formed under Lieutenant Colonel Coffman, the commander of the 4th Amtrac Battalion. The group included a Marine amtrac company under

Captain R. H. Lage with thirty cargo amtracs contributed by the 4th and 9th Battalions, an Army amtrac company with 29 LVTs from Lieutenant Colonel G. H. Hufford's 788th Amtrac Battalion, and a reserve platoon of fourteen cargo amtracs from the 4th and 8th Battalions, under Lieutenant J. C. Morecroft. Company "B" of the 3rd Armored Amtrac Battalion would provide the direct fire support for the landing.

The 1st and 2nd Battalions of the 4th Marines designated to make the initial landings on the Oroku Peninsula embarked in their LVTs at 0300 on 4 June. At 0500 a detachment of the 708th Amphibian Tank Battalion with troops of the 6th Reconnaissance Company landed on the tiny island of Ono Yama in the estuary between Naha and the Oroku Peninsula. At the same time, gunfire ships opened on the landing area and troop-carrying LVTs formed up behind the line of departure. By the time that simple manuever had ended, nine amtracs assigned to the 1st Battalion had broken down, but the landing went ahead. The movement went off without difficulty and by 0630, the whole of the 2nd Battalion was ashore. Thirty minutes later, two tank companies were ready to support the infantry. Meanwhile, the 1st Battalion was shuttling its troops over as fast as its remaining LVTs allowed. By 1000 the beachhead was large enough for the Division to order the 29th Marines to cross over . . . and then the skies opened and the rains fell. But, by then the Marines had well established themselves on the Peninsula and would make the best of it despite the weather. Even so, it would take ten days of hard fighting and 1,608 casualties to clear the area. The Marines would also lose thirty of their tanks to the most elaborate minefields yet encountered.

While the 6th Marine Division had been preparing for its move against Oroku, the 8th Marines on Saipan had been detached from the 2nd Division. The reinforced Regiment under a command group headed by Brigadier General Leroy P. Hunt, had been ordered to return to Okinawa, prepared to land on Iheya Shima and Aguni Shima. These islands, some twenty miles north and thirty miles west of Okinawa, were to be used for long-range radar and fighter director stations to help reduce the heavy losses being suffered by the picket ships then providing such services. The landings were to be made in 29 LVT(2)s and 73 LVT(4)s of the 2nd Amtrac Battalion supported by eighteen LVT(A)4s from Company "D'" of the 3rd Armored Amtrac Battalion. On 3 June 1945 the landing on Iheya Shima was executed without difficulty or opposition. Six days later, after a delay occasioned by the bad weather, the operation was repeated against Aguni Shima with the same pleasing results. The 8th Marines, both objectives secured, was ordered to the Oroku Peninsula on 15 June to join the 1st Marine Division in the final actions of the campaign.

On 4 June 1945, 30,000 Japanese were crowded into the Kiyamu Peninsula. Perhaps 6,000 of these were remnants of Imperial units, the remainder were rear area personnel or home guards with little training. Ammunition was low, four out of five machine guns had been lost and only a few artillery pieces and mortars remained. The 32nd Army had been reduced to an empty shell held together by tradition and discipline. But, while the enemy would find it virtually impossible to continue organized resistance, he still had courage and determination. General Buckner assessed the situation and shifted the boundary between his Corps to the west. Then, while the 6th Marine Division had been freed to make its landing on the Oroku Peninsula, the 1st Marine Division was ordered to isolate that peninsula and continue its advance to the south, clearing the Kunishi and Mezado ridges on the way. The XXIV Corps was also to continue south and seize the commanding Yuza Dake and Yaeju Dake escarpment on the way. By 18 June, these last organized defenses had collapsed and the end was near. On that same day, General Buckner visited the 8th Marines' observation post to witness a battalion advance in the valley below. Alert Japanese, presumably attracted by the arrival of the visitors, fired five artillery rounds and mortally wounded the Tenth Army commander; it was three days short of the end of the campaign. General Geiger assumed command and directed operations until organized resistance ceased at 1305 on 21 June 1945. On that tragic note the last great battle of the Second World War ended.

Tenth Army casualties suffered during the Okinawa campaign amounted to 39,420 men of whom 7,374 were killed in action. This grievous loss was fairly shared among the major units engaged. The Navy, in addition, paid the unprecedented price of 4,907 dead and 4,824 wounded when 36 of its ships were sunk and 368 damaged. Then too 763 aircraft must be added to the final tally of American losses. Strangely, while the overall price exacted by the Japanese for Okinawa was high, that paid by the amphibian tractor units amounted to well below 1 per cent of the amtrac personnel engaged. Moreover, the high vehicle losses that had become the accepted norm during operations in the central Pacfic were not evident at Okinawa. Amtrac losses to enemy action were insignificant while losses in the surf, on the reef or at sea from other than enemy action were in the order of 10 per cent. There was, however, severe wear on amtracs of all types due to the heavy usage and that factor, coupled to the limited availability of spare parts, reduced the effectiveness of the cargo battalions more and more as the campaign progressed.

On the Japanese side, 107,539 dead were counted and 10,755 prisoners were taken. An additional 25,000 men were entombed in caves and subterranean defenses. Among the many dead, as many as 42,000 may have been civilians who had fallen victim to area fire or had been on conscripted service in the local defense forces. The three-month period from April to June also cost the Japanese 7,830 aircraft, of which 2,000 were the Kamikaze suicide aircraft that had hurt the U.S. Navy so seriously. Also included in the foregoing total were 602 aircraft shot out of the sky; the remaining losses representing aircraft destroyed on the ground in the far-ranging strikes by U.S. Army and Navy aircraft. Finally, the Imperial Navy, already decimated, lost the mighty battleship *Yamato* and fifteen other fighting ships, bringing to its end what once had been among the world's greatest fleets.

Japan's loss of the Prefecture of Okinawa in the District of Kyushu opened the door to the home islands only 350 miles away. Thenceforth, whatever battles remained would have to be fought on soil that had never suffered a foreign invader. For the Americans, the tenacity of General Ushijima and his 32nd Army confirmed that the invasion of the home islands would be difficult, long and extremely costly. Under the circumstances, neither side could find comfort in what the future promised after the battle for Okinawa had ended.

Above: *The British "Mulberry" Operation in June 1944; an artificial harbour created by sinking concrete caissons to form a breakwater. (US Maritime Commission)*

Below: *Amtracs of the 79th British Armoured Division in operation near the Scheldt Estuary in October 1944. (FMC)*

6. The European Area of Operations

Casablanca to Normandy; Amtracs in the Lowlands

T HE amphibious doctrine which became the focus of Marine Corps interest after World War I was not confined to any particular world area. However, with the passage of time, Marines became increasingly concerned with the geography of the Pacific. Because of this they were alert to the potential of the amphibian tractor as a means of overcoming the reef obstacle guarding many of the military objectives in that vast ocean area. The reef obstacle also exists in the Atlantic and Mediterranean areas where numerous landings were made in World War II. But the reefs there are not as limiting as they were in the Pacific. This is borne out by the record which shows that of the 34 major landings made during World War II in which amphibian tractors were used, 30 of them took place in the Pacific. Of the remaining four, LVTs were used in a seaborne landing only in North Africa. There, four LVT(1)s were assigned to each shore party engineer company. They proved useful in getting stranded boats afloat, but were too unreliable mechanically for any continuous service. The other three operations that featured amtracs all were concerned with river crossings.

This does not suggest that innovativeness in the amphibious operation was confined to the Pacific. On the contrary, the European Theater of Operations sired its fair share of devices and techniques to facilitate or augment amphibious warfare capabilities. Notable among these are the artificial ports laid down off the Normandy beaches and the family of special tracked vehicles devised to assault beaches larded with mines or barred by multiple man-made obstacles. The venerable DUKW appeared in Sicily as the artillery's prime landing vehicle and enjoyed that status in many other landings in Europe as in the Pacific. Finally, while the amtrac was not needed to land assault troops from the sea, it proved most useful where lakes, rivers and swamps impeded the progress of Allied forces.

Because of these considerations, a short commentary on the landings that took place in the Mediterranean and Atlantic areas during World War II and a brief narrative of operations where amtracs were used, will complement the record of similar operations carried out in the Pacific.

The entry of the United States into the Second World War was welcomed by the British. Yet, while the event heightened prospects for ultimate victory, it raised several concerns. One of immediate importance was the extent to which American mobilization would lessen the flow of lend-lease supplies needed by the British to help sustain their war effort. Another, with strategic implications, was how far anti-Japanese sentiment born of the sneak attack against Pearl

Harbor would influence the American Government to shift the weight of its attention to the Pacific. Clearly, the progress of the war would be affected by the answers to these and related issues. An early concert of views on the actions to be taken was needed and this could best be attained at a meeting of the political leaders and their principal advisors.

The British Prime Minister, as was his nature, did not labor the matter overlong. The day following the Pearl Harbor attack, Winston Churchill addressed his King with a proposal for an immediate trip to Washington. The next day, with Royal assent in hand, the Prime Minister telegraphed President Roosevelt his intentions. Three days later, with a warm welcome assured, Churchill and his entourage embarked in the *Duke of York* and proceeded to Hampton Roads. From there, a short flight took him to Washington where he landed on 22 December for the three-week visit that set the pattern for the Anglo-American collaboration that was to endure throughout the war.

Churchill had used his time at sea to write down his personal views on the prosecution of the war. In these, he held that 1942 should be devoted to seizing control of North Africa to open the Mediterranean for subsequent Allied operations. On the Pacific "front", the Prime Minister conceded the initiative to the Japanese "for the time being" but called for stubborn resistance where attacked and a strong effort to "fight them at every point we have a fair chance, so as to keep them burning and extended."[1] At the same time, he urged that a superior battle fleet centered around aircraft carriers be built to carry the war to the enemy in the Pacific in mid-1943. Finally, he proposed that Europe be invaded in 1943 to bring an end to German military power.

These views and a comprehensive agenda of related subjects became the substance of the "Arcadia" conference. British concerns over war production were allayed when President Roosevelt increased 1942 goals to eight million tons of merchant shipping, 45,000 operating aircraft and a like number of tanks, and set the 1943 production levels at ten million tons of shipping, 100,000 aircraft and 75,000 tanks. Also settled was the question of priority of effort. Germany would remain the principal opponent.

There was also agreement that the defeat of Germany would require an invasion of the continent. The staffs examined the general requirements for such an invasion and concluded that 48 divisions were needed, six of them in an assault force supported by 7,000 landing ships and craft and 5,800 aircraft. In short, the effort would have to be massive and not attainable until the spring of 1943. The Americans could not argue over these requirements but urged that, as a minimum, plans be made to enter the continent somewhere between Brest and Cherbourg in 1942 in the event that Germany should collapse or that the Russians should suffer a reversal. Later, in April 1942, General George C. Marshall, the U.S. Army Chief of Staff, went to London to develop the idea of a cross-Channel invasion in 1942 to establish a lodgement that would be exploited by a major effort in 1943.

A month after the Marshall visit, the Russian envoy Vyacheslav Molotov arrived also to press for a landing on the continent in 1942. The British Prime Minister received him, as he had General Marshall, listened to the arguments and agreed in principle. The problem was that such an early thrust would, initially, have to be made mainly with British forces, and these were already heavily engaged in the Middle and Far East. Moreover, the British had been fighting the Germans since 1939 and had learned to respect the fighting qualities of the German forces. An amphibious assault of northern France would not be easy; and then too, there was the problem of landing craft availability. In sum, the arguments against a cross-Channel invasion in 1942 were substantial. But, the Americans were not convinced that North Africa offered an acceptable alternative since that would entail a diversion of resources and thus, they thought, a delay in the cross-Channel operation. The discussion and staff exchanges continued until July 1942 when President Roosevelt decided that the main American effort that year would be made against North Africa . . . Operation TORCH was on!

The Americans had made it clear from the outset that they intended to engage their forces in active operations as rapidly as they could be organized and trained. The U.S. Army, moreover, had made a strong plea for direct action against western Europe. At the same time, it had agreed to provide 41,000 men to garrison several Pacific islands. It had agreed also to provide other forces for operations against the Japanese, but these were not of priority concern. What was pressing was that regardless of where its forces were to be engaged, the Army needed landing craft. Officially, these were to be provided by the Navy; practically, the question remained open.

According to U.S. Army and Navy agreements, the Navy was to "provide and operate all vessels when naval opposition is to be expected."[2] The Navy was also to operate all boats used for assault landings. The truth was that at the start of the war the Navy's amphibious warfare resources were not equal to the 36 transports it had estimated necessary under its war plans. The numbers of landing craft, while growing rapidly, were notably modest. Under the circumstances, the Navy was unable to satisfy Army needs. On this advice, the Army turned to its Corps of Engineers.

The engineers, already aware of the situation, were quite prepared for the task. They quickly set up an Engineer Amphibious Command (EAC) at Camp Edwards in Massachusetts to direct the effort of organizing and training Army units to man boats in shore-to-shore operations. The command became operational on 5 June 1942. Ten days later, the 1st Engineer Amphibious Brigade (1st EAB) was activated. The 2nd EAB followed on 20 June and the 3rd EAB was authorized on 8 August. These units were equipped with the 36-foot landing boat and the 50-foot tank lighter. The Army had also wanted to operate the 105-foot LCT but the Navy had not agreed. It had, however, agreed to train the amphibious brigades for shore party tasks as well as in boat handling.

The amphibious brigades were intended to support shore-to-shore operations of an infantry division at a distance of up to 100 miles. For this purpose, each brigade comprised 7,000 men organized into a Boat regiment of three Boat Battalions each with 120 LCVP and twelve LCMs, and a Shore Regiment made up of three Shore Battalions, each with 600 men to work the beaches. This basic organization revealed itself unwieldy and was modified in November 1942 to provide three Amphibious Regiments each with one Boat Battalion and one Shore Battalion.

In August 1942, at the same time that the 3rd EAB was organized, the EAC established a Development Section to test amphibious equipment including the DUKW and LVT. The Army, its interest centered in Europe with well-developed land communications, found the DUKW better suited to its needs than the LVT. Moreover, the DUKW had many parts in common with those of the standard 2½-ton Army truck. Following these tests 36 DUKWs were added to the EAB's inventories; amtracs were also used but mostly in the Pacific and on an as-needed basis. That same August, the 1st EAB was sent to Scotland, ready to support cross-Channel operations. When these were set aside in favor of a landing in North Africa, the EAB lost its basic purpose. The situation was not helped when General Eisenhower decided that the Navy would be responsible for all amphibious training in the European theater. Soon after, the 1st EAB disbanded its Boat Battalions but retained its shore units. It then went on to provide shore party services during the landings in North Africa, Sicily, Italy and France. After the landings in Normandy, the Brigade headquarters was sent to the Pacific where it controlled shore party operations for the XXIV Corps on Okinawa.

The fate of the 1st EAB was seen, for a time, as the portent of the future of the other amphibious brigades. But, when the Navy informed General MacArthur that it could not meet his requirements for landing craft and crews, the engineers saw an opportunity. With the active support of Andrew Higgins, the amphibious command was able to set up a boat assembly facility in Australia to meet the South West Pacific Area Command's needs. The EAC also urged that command to use its three uncommitted brigades. This was agreed, and the 2nd EAB began its deployment in late 1942 to New Guinea where it soon justified its existence. The 3rd EAB followed within a year and the last organized, 4th EAB, arrived in May 1944. These units saw extensive service in New Guinea, the Philippines and on other islands where, as noted earlier, they operated DUKWs and LVTs as well as landing boats.

As these events were unfolding in the Pacific, the Navy increased to the point where it could assume responsibility for satisfying the Army's landing craft requirements. Accordingly, at an Army-Navy conference held on 8 March 1943, the Army agreed to turn over amphibious training responsibilities and related facilities to the Navy. The Army, however, retained the four amphibious brigades already activated although their designation would be changed to Engineer Special Brigades (ESB) to reserve the term "amphibious" for Navy usage. Subsequently, the Army did form the 5th and 6th ESBs but these were without boat units and were specifically intended for shore party purposes in Europe. These two brigades with six DUKW companies served on Omaha Beach during the assault landings in Normandy; the 1st ESB served in a similar capacity on Utah Beach.

The assault landings in Normandy, which marked the beginning of the end for Germany, occurred at the same time as the invasion of Saipan, which toppled the government of General Tojo in Japan. But, where in Europe only one more major amphibious operation would follow Normandy, the assault on Saipan marked the beginning of the major landings that were still to be made there. Related to this comparison is the fact that of the 170 amphibious operations conducted during World War II, 90 per cent took place in the Pacific, but only one-third of those involved more than a regimental landing team. Thus, while there were fewer assault landings made in the Mediterranean and Atlantic areas, most of those made were on an imposing scale.

The Army's 18th Infantry Regiment and two battalions of the 7th Field Artillery had participated with the Marines in Fleet Exercise Four (FLEX-4) in the Caribbean in 1938. Army interest in amphibious operations was again manifested in the summer of 1941 in a joint exercise involving the 1st Marine and 1st Infantry Divisions. This was shortly followed by other joint training enabling three more Army divisions to gain some amphibious experience. Thus, when the United States Army entered the war, it had four divisions familiar with the intricacies of the amphibious assault. It also had a procedural doctrine for such operations in Field Manual 31-5, a publication based upon the Navy's FTP-167, itself derived from the Marine's Manual For Landing Operations. These were precious assets, for the introduction of U.S. forces to France in 1944 would be far different from what it had been in 1917. In World War I, the American Expeditionary Force (AEF) came ashore in a friendly port to find a warm welcome. In World War II, the Army would land in France on a fire-swept beach defended by battle-seasoned troops . . . and would do so only after having endured a succession of other opposed landings that had begun in 1942.

The first of these, Operation TORCH, was a considerable enterprise for green troops, particularly since the French were expected to resist. France's armistice with Germany limited the German occupation to northern France, on the assurance that France would defend her unoccupied territories from any invader. Thus, France would be obliged to defend North Africa, since any hesitation to do so would invite immediate German occupation. These facts, known to the Allies, meant that TORCH would require more than a token landing force. Because of that, the United States assigned 84,000 soldiers to the landings in North Africa. These would include 35,000 men coming directly from the United States, and the remaining 49,000 coming from bases in Britain. In addition, 23,000 British troops would also participate. These forces were organized into three groups that converged on their objectives from British and American ports. Considering the distances and numbers involved, and the seriousness of the submarine threat, it is amazing to discover that only one transport was damaged by enemy action in the movement.

The Western Task Force, commanded by Rear Admiral H. Kent Hewitt, mounted out of Norfolk with the troops under command of Major General George F. Patton. The landings were made at Safi, 150 miles south of Casablanca, at Fedhala, near Casablanca, and at Port Lyautey, near Rabat, by boat and without naval gunfire preparation on the night of 7/8 November 1942. At Safi, two old destroyers with 350 troops were able to dash into the harbor and disembark their troops directly ashore before the French reacted. The Americans quickly gained control of the port and were able to bring in the ships carrying the bulk of Patton's armor. That was unloaded and directed toward Casablanca on the morning of 10 November, just as the French proclaimed a ceasefire.

The group that landed at Fedhala was attacked by French surface forces after daylight. The French lost four destroyers and a light cruiser in an uneven action which cost the Americans damage to one cruiser. As this action was in progress, the landing of 8,000 men from the 9th Infantry Division continued against light opposition. By 1700 all the Americans were ashore and heading for Casablanca in good order. The landings near Port Lyautey ran into strong opposition centered in a fortified citadel at the mouth of the Sebou River. The destroyer *Dallas* solved the problem by embarking 75 troops, forcing a passage past the citadel and landing the soldiers without loss to outflank the French and link-up with a battalion of the 2nd Armored Division, which had come overland. The two units then went on to seize the airfield, which was quickly opened to Army aircraft flown in from escort carriers offshore. The success of these three landings in the west was marred only by the fact that 150 of the 350 landing boats used were lost to surf, tide and inexperience.

The Eastern Task Force, under Rear-Admiral Sir Harold M. Burrough, RN, carried 23,000 British and 10,000 American troops coming from Great Britain to seize Algiers. Here again the boat crews had little training with the result that 98 of the 104 boats used were lost. Fortunately, the landings were unopposed. The Center Task Force, under Commodore Thomas Troubridge, RN, brought in the 1st Infantry and part of the 1st Armored Divisions which also had been based in Great Britain. The landing of this force near Oran was not easy. A 400-man landing unit embarked in two Royal Navy cutters attempted to dash into the port of Oran as had been done at Safi. But, unlike the situation at Safi, the French at Oran were alerted and the American group was virtually annihilated. Luckily, the main landings fared much better so that when the ceasefire came, the Americans had already entered the city.

The German reaction to TORCH was swift. No sooner were reports received of the landings than German forces were ferried to Tunisia while other units moved into unoccupied France. This latter move led to the scuttling of 73 ships of the French Navy in the port of Toulon to keep them from falling into German hands. It was a final tragedy in the chain of events that destroyed France's naval power. For the Americans and British in North Africa, the winter would bring bad weather and a campaign that would last until 13 May 1943 when the British Eighth Army coming from Egypt, joined by the First Anglo-American Army in Tunisia, would close the net on 250,000 Axis troops at Cape Bon. Four days later the first Allied convoy left Gilbraltar for Egypt; it was the first such convoy since 1941.

The prolonged campaign in North Africa led to the decision to abandon the idea of a cross-Channel invasion in 1943. At the same time, it was decided to mount an all-out offensive against the German submarine menace and intensify the aerial bombardment of Germany. Beyond that, the Americans and British were of differing views. The British argued for a landing in Sicily, followed by an attack on Italy to drive that country out of the war. The Americans looked upon this as further dissipation of resources needed for the invasion of France. As far as they were concerned, it might be better to bring greater strength against the Japanese before they had more time to consolidate their gains in the Pacific, rather than attack another peripheral area in Europe. But, having said that, the Americans came to agree that the Allies could not go on the defensive in Europe and expect the Russians to carry the war by themselves. On that basis, agreement was given to the invasion of Sicily although the decision on follow-on actions was left open.

Operation HUSKY was launched on the night of 9/10 July 1943. The forces involved were impressive. The Americans fielded four divisions embarked in 580 ships while one Canadian and four British divisions were embarked in 795 ships. Admiral Hewitt with the Western Attack Force would land General Patton's Seventh Army on beaches in the southwest of Sicily. The Eastern Attack Force, under Vice-Admiral Sir Bertram Ramsey, RN, would land General Bernard Montgomery's Eighth Army on the beaches around the southeastern tip of that 10,000-square mile island. On the night of the landings, the wind was strong and the surf high. Despite the difficulties, the landings went well except at Scoglitti, where the wave organization was broken up by a reef causing, among other mishaps, the loss of five of the seven boats in the third wave. Elsewhere, the new LSTs, LCIs and LCTs were of great help, as were the DUKWs, that had made their first appearance there.

The toughest opposition in the Sicily landings was reserved for Major General Terry Allen's 1st Infantry Division at Gela, where the enemy had control of the air over the landing area. As a consequence, a German Messerschmitt destroyed an LST carrying the Division's anti-tank guns. Then, the LSTs carrying the Division's tanks was unable to beach because of sand bars. These events set up the American division for the German tank-infantry attack that soon materialized. In the ensuing ten-hour action, two American cruisers and

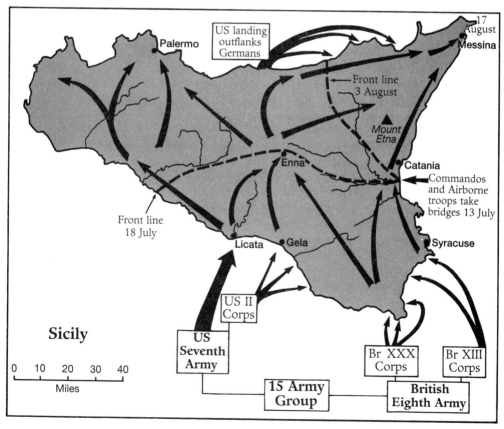

eight destroyers took on the German force, shattered its tanks and dispersed its infantry. The Army's gratitude extended up to General Eisenhower who joined in the loud praise of the Navy gunners. But, another disaster was not to be averted.

In the final hours of 11 July 1943, a flight of 381 enemy aircraft attacked Allied shipping off the Sicily beaches. It was the twenty-fourth air attack that day. Unfortunately, as the German aircraft appeared so did 144 American transport aircraft towing gliders. In the ensuing confusion 23 American planes were shot down and 37 more were badly damaged. It was a shocking and costly mishap.

Shortly after their landing, the Allied formations moved inland. Within one week twelve airfields had been taken and German air units on the island had been reduced to 25 serviceable aircraft. By 22 July, progress was sufficient to allow General Eisenhower to agree to move against Italy, but without commitment as to time or place. Then, on 25 July, Mussolini fell and the need for a quick move into Italy became imperative. The next day, Eisenhower received the order to land at Salerno as rapidly as possible with resources available. But, for these to be adequate, it was necessary for the campaign in Sicily to end. This came with the fall of Messina on 16 August. In 38 days, an Axis force of thirteen divisions aggregating 405,000 men had been well and truly beaten in the field by an Anglo-American force of lesser numbers.

The move against Italy proper began on 3 September when units of the 5th British and 1st Canadian Divisions crossed the Strait of Messina and started up the Italian boot. However, the main landings of Operation AVALANCHE at Salerno did not begin until 0330 on 9 September. The Allied force retained the same commanders as at Sicily and, again, was formed into two attack forces. The Northern Attack Force with the X British Corps, was to land just below Salerno, while the Southern Attack Force with the VI U.S. Army Corps was to land at Paestum. The two Corps made up General Mark W. Clark's Fifth Army. The landing plan, as in earlier operations, continued the Army's preference for coming ashore at night without preliminary bombardment "to gain surprise."[3] But the German commander in Italy, Field Marshal Kesselring, had anticipated the Allies and dispatched his 16th Panzer Division to Salerno on 6 September; it had nearly three days to prepare a suitable reception.

Unlike the Marines in the Pacific, who had a healthy respect for naval gunfire and believed it better to land by the dawn's early light, the Army in Africa and Europe thought it best to arrive at night without explosive introduction. The problem is that boat engines can be heard from afar. Those off Salerno were readily picked up by German listening-posts which alerted the gunners. Thus, when the assault infantry of the U.S. 36th Infantry Division hit the beach, they came under heavy fire which destroyed ten of the eleven boats lost. None the less, the troops pushed inland and the DUKWs soon followed with the artillery; 123 trips were made by these amphibians to bring in the howitzers, their crews and ammunition. The Division's tanks, unfortunately, could not be landed because of offshore sand bars which kept the LSTs from beaching. Thus, when the German armor appeared, as it had at Gela, it was the naval guns, complemented by the Division's artillery that kept it at bay. Support was provided by two cruisers and four destroyers whose fire was directed by shore fire control parties, the cruisers' seaplanes and, on two occasions, by Army P-51s operating from airfields in Sicily.

On the British landing front, the 46th and 56th British Divisions had come ashore and established a beachhead. But, by nightfall the seven-mile gap between the two Corps remained. In the seven days that followed the Germans threw three divisions against the gap in an effort to destroy the Allied beachhead, but each attempt was blunted by naval gunfire, artillery and the enduring infantry. By 16 September, the Germans concluded that the Allies were there to stay. That afternoon, patrols from the Eighth Army, advancing overland from the south, finally made contact with the U.S. VI Corps in the beachhead.

On 1 October the Fifth Army entered Naples. From there to Rome was a short 100 miles, but it would take the Allies eight months to make the trip. Hitler had ordered his forces to hold Italy and the terrain north of Naples was admirably suited to such purpose. The stalemate that resulted was to be broken by an end run of two divisions landing at Anzio, thirty miles below Rome. On 12 January 1944, the Fifth Army began the advance intended to draw the Germans' attention away from the amphibious force steaming toward its objective. The scheme worked well. Operation SHINGLE began at 0200 on the morning of 22 January when the 1st British and 3rd U.S. Infantry Divisions began landing over the Anzio beaches. Twenty hours later there were 36,000 men and 3,000 vehicles ashore. No opposition had been encountered; the enemy had been caught by surprise. Then, things began to unravel.

What Major General John P. Lucas, commanding the VI Corps at Anzio, did not know was that only two battalions stood between his force and Rome. Field Marshal Kesselring, however, was well aware of the fact and lost no time in dispatching two divisions to block the way. This had little effect on General Lucas whose main concern was to consolidate his beachhead and bring in his supporting troops and armor before making any moves. Finally, on 30 January when he was ready to move, the Germans had eight divisions in the area. After eleven days of inconclusive fighting the VI Corps had taken 6,923 casualties and had accomplished little. On 16 February the initiative passed to the Germans who launched a four-division attack backed by 350 guns against the beachhead. The Germans were driven off after three days of heavy fighting. They tried again at the end of the month and again they were driven off. The situation then stabilized. The Allies brought in additional troops, making for a total of six divisions jammed in the area. Finally, on 11 May, after an overture played by 2,000 guns, the curtain was raised on a major offensive by the Fifth and Eighth Armies. General Truscott, who by then had assumed command of the VI Corps at Anzio, broke out of the beachhead on 24 May in an attempt to block the retreat of German forces pressed back by the Allied offensive. The Germans, however, avoided the trap and made good their escape. Rome was finally reached on 4 June 1944, only two days before the invasion of France.

The assembly of the armada needed for the cross-Channel invasion had taken much time, effort and diplomacy. The Americans had reluctantly agreed to enter the European war through North Africa and had agonized over the worrisome demands of the prolonged Italian campaign, But now at last they had massed

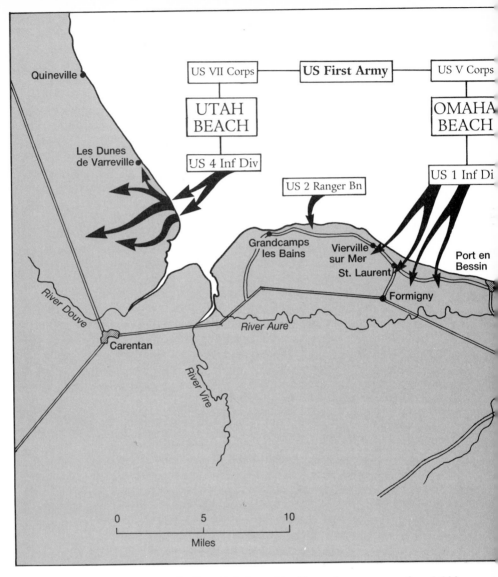

more than 1,500,000 men in Great Britain and had brought over more than 1,000 ships and landing craft manned by 50,000 sailors into British ports. The decisive operation of the war in Europe was about to begin.

The original plan for NEPTUNE, the amphibious phase of OVERLORD, was to land three divisions in assault. All agreed that this was a dangerously weak force, but no more landing craft were available for the landing, then scheduled for May. Eisenhower solved part of the problem by pre-empting the shipping that had been set aside to land one division in southern France, where Operation ANVIL was to be carried out at the same time as NEPTUNE. Then, by delaying NEPTUNE until June, production schedules indicated shipping for another division would become available. In this manner, the beach assault force was set at five divisions. Three of these in the British Second Army would sail in the Eastern Attack Force

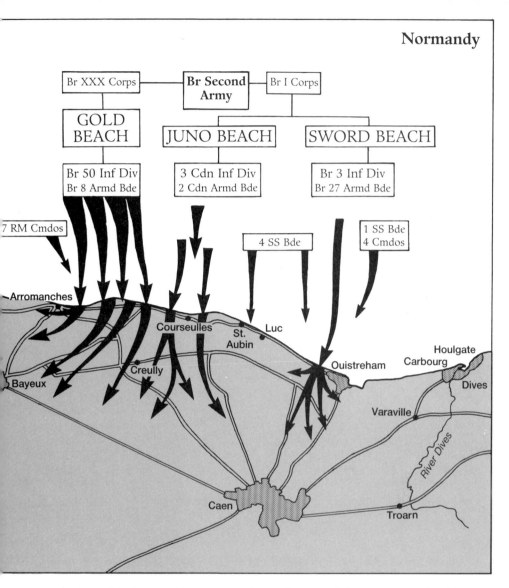

Br XXX Corps — **Br Second Army** — Br I Corps

GOLD BEACH — JUNO BEACH — SWORD BEACH

Br 50 Inf Div
Br 8 Armd Bde

3 Cdn Inf Div
2 Cdn Armd Bde

Br 3 Inf Div
Br 27 Armd Bde

7 RM Cmdos

4 SS Bde

1 SS Bde
4 Cmdos

Arromanches

Courseulles

St. Aubin

Luc

Houlgate

Carbourg

Creully

Ouistreham

Dives

Bayeux

Varaville

River Dives

Caen

Troarn

under Rear-Admiral Sir Philip Vian, RN. The other two divisions, actually the 4th U.S. Infantry and major elements of the 1st and 29th Infantry Divisions, would comprise the assault echelon of the American First Army embarked in the Western Attack Force under Rear Admiral Alan G. Kirk. Complementing these forces were three airborne divisions that were to drop the night before the landing.

The Germans had been awaiting the blow without knowing where it would fall. They had six armored and nineteen other divisional formations deployed between the Pas-de-Calais in the north and the mouth of the Seine River. Of these, one armored, two infantry and three "static" divisions were in the area where the landings were to be made. The weather on 5 June had been bad and the forecast was that it would continue so. Thus, even when the first blips appeared on the German radar at 0300 on 6 June 1944, there was no immediate alarm. There had been no bombardment to suggest anything unusual was about to happen and even when the ships appeared offshore, there was no assurance that this was the prelude of a landing in force. The deception plan which had created a fictional army under General Patton, poised in eastern Britain for a thrust across the narrow waist of the Channel, kept the German high command undecided. Meanwhile Allied formations were fighting their way ashore in Normandy on a broad front.

In the west, 805 aircraft with the 101st and 82nd Airborne Divisions encountered heavy cloud cover and anti-aircraft fire. Twenty aircraft were lost and several formations became disorganized. As a result the 101st was scattered over a 400-square mile area; the 82nd, more fortunate, landed 75 per cent of its men within three miles of their designated zones. Meanwhile, off the coast, minesweepers had started the dangerous job of clearing areas for transports, gunfire support ships and boat approach channels. Soon after, bombardment ships opened fire and the boats moved toward the beaches. The first wave at UTAH Beach landed at 0630, a mile south of its intended landing point. But there was little opposition and by the end of the day 21,000 troops and 1,700 vehicles had come ashore at a cost of only 197 casualties. On OMAHA Beach, however, the story was different.

There, the troops came up against strong defenses and no airdrop had been made in the vicinity to disorient the enemy. More serious, the 424 heavy bombers that were to blanket the beach defenses had missed their targets. Then, 27 of the 34 tanks that were supposed to swim in with their flotation devices sank; the remaining tanks loaded on LCTs came under German artillery fire and were decimated. While this was happening, the infantry, required to wade as much as 100 yards in the surf before reaching the shore and then cross 300 yards of flat sand beach before coming to the first cover, was taking heavy casualties. By 0800 the beach was congested and the situation confused. Offshore the underwater demolition teams were still working to clear boat channels through the obstacles, while three LCIs loaded with troops were lying off the beach in flames. The final blow came when most of the DUKWs bringing in artillery were lost in the surf; only one battery got ashore and went into action that day. Throughout this agonizing period, naval guns kept up supporting fire whose effect became discernible by midday when the drumbeat of German guns lessened. By nightfall a semblance of order had been attained . . . at the exceptional cost of 3,000 casualties.

On the British front, the 6th Airborne Division seized the bridges over the Orne and Caen Canals, while the landing force waited for the flood tide to rise high enough for the boats to make the shore. This delay gave the bombardment ships the time to take German positions under deliberate fire, a fortunate circumstance which greatly eased the task of the infantry when it came ashore. Also helpful were the specialized tracked vehicles of the 79th British Armoured Division which were used to clear paths through minefields, overcome obstacles and assist in the assault of fortified positions. Then, too, the British had reduced the running time to the beach by bringing their troop-carrying ships close to shore. The Americans' ships had been kept farther out and the extra time needed to reach the beach had added to the fatigue of the troops and had contributed to the navigation errors which put some units in the wrong landing areas.

The Allied build-up began in earnest on 7 June. By D+12 (18 June), 314,514 troops, 41,000 guns, tanks and other vehicles, plus 116,000 tons of supplies had been landed over the American beaches. The British beaches had handled 314,247 men, 54,000 tanks, guns and other vehicles, plus 102,000 tons of supplies during the same period. This massive effort had been greatly facilitated by the use of two artificial harbors, Mulberry A and B, made up of concrete caissons sunk in place. These had been complemented by five "Gooseberries" or breakwaters composed of blockships, 23 "whales" or floating piers, and a cross-Channel pipeline for fuel named PLUTO. On the 13th, the weather, never really good, blew a gale which destroyed Mulberry A. The other artificial harbor off the British beaches survived as did all the Gooseberries. In this fashion, the offshore support system continued to function until after 25 June when the American VII Corps took the port of Cherbourg. That same day the British Second Army struck at Caen, which fell on 9 July. Ten days later, the American First Army took St-Lô. Three weeks after that, General Patton broke through the last German defenses in France and was on his way to the Rhine. That long-awaited event was coincident with the last major landing to take place in Europe during World War II.

Operation ANVIL, intended to seize the southern French port of Marseilles, had been planned to occur at the same time as the landings in Normandy. The requirements of ANVIL, however, had been subordinated to those of the Italian front and of OVERLORD, with the result that ANVIL had to be delayed until 15 August. Before dawn on that easy summer day, 400 transport aircraft dropped a provisional airborne division behind the beaches soon to be crossed by the three American divisions and a French commando force. The landing was carried out by four assault groups that came ashore beginning at 0800 on a 30-mile front between Fréjus and Saint Tropez. Despite the presence of 30,000 Germans in the area, all landings went well and only one of the assault groups encountered serious resistance. In short order, the Allied force was assembled ashore and started towards Toulon and Marseilles, which were entered on 28 August. Five days later, the southern invasion force, which had been built up into the American Seventh and French First Armies, reached Lyons in the Rhône valley. There, the two armies became part of Lieutenant General J. L. Dever's Sixth Army Group and took their place on the right flank of the Allied forces engaged in crossing the Rhine for the final push into Germany.

The Navy had supported the Army well from its early days in North Africa to its final assaults over the French beaches. Now, even though the amphibious operations had ended, the services of the Navy remained in demand. The call came in September 1944 when General Omar Bradley, commanding the Twelfth Army Group, asked for Navy help in moving his forces across the Rhine. The Navy responded by immediately organizing four boat units each with 24 LCVPs. An additional 45 LCMs were formed into a pool unit for assignment as required. The 1st Boat Unit was used in March 1945 in the First Army's zone of action, where the 9th Armored Division had captured intact the bridge at Remagen.

Initially, the 1st Boat Unit was limited to providing supplementary ferry services. But, when the bridge collapsed on 17 March, the 1st Boat Unit really became busy; on that day six of its LCVPs moved 2,000 men across the Rhine. In the ten days that followed, 14,000 more troops and 400 vehicles were ferried across that last barrier to Germany.

Meanwhile, General Patton's Third Army was also approaching the Rhine. The 2nd Boat Unit, ordered forward to assist in the crossing, arrived at Oppenheim at 2200 on 22 March just as the Army's lead units began to cross the river in assault boats. The Navy had three of its LCVPs in the water by 0300; three hours later all 24 of its boats were busy moving troops across the river in a shuttle service which continued for 72 hours. By then the engineers had thrown three pontoon bridges over the river and the boats were released for service at three other crossing sites in the Third Army's zone. The most difficult of these was at Mainz, where twelve LCVPs and six of the pool LCMs were used. The enemy had the river covered by fire so that when the initial group started across in twenty assault boats at 0100 on 26 March, most of the boats were destroyed. At 0330 the Army held up further attempts at getting across, but the Navy did not get the word and sent one boat over. By lucky error the boat landed without mishap some 500 yards below the site covered by fire. The Army quickly exploited the unexpected success and, by 0630, there were enough Americans on the German side of the river to clear the remaining defenders away.

Unlike the dashing manner in which the First and Third U.S. Armies forced the Rhine barrier, the crossing of Allied forces in Field Marshal Montgomery's 21st Army Group was meticulously planned. Thus, on 23 March 1945, some 23 hours after General Patton's troops had swept over the Rhine, the 1st Royal Marine Brigade embarked in amtracs of the 77th Squadron, Royal Engineers, began shore-to-shore operations. Meanwhile, U.S. Navy Boat Unit 3 with 24 LCVPs and a like number of LCMs reached its assigned crossing site at Rheinburg at 0100 on 23 March. After two hours of artillery preparation, the Army assault boats with the first waves moved out followed by the Navy's LCVPs . . . all in conformance to a precise schedule. Despite some German fire, a lodgement was secured and, in the hectic days that followed, the Navy ferried over some 3,000 troops, 454 tanks and guns, 500 wheeled vehicles, 180 "Weasels" and fifteen bulldozers. Somewhere in this procession, an LCM crossed the Rhine with the British Prime Minister, two Field Marshals, and Lieutenant General Simpson, commanding the Ninth Army, then in the 21st Army Group.

The 4th Boat Unit remained at Le Havre and did not participate in the crossings of the Rhine since the Seventh American and First French Armies had sufficient assault boats to carry them across the upper part of the river. The British, on the lower Rhine, utilized yet another unique organization for their crossing of the Rhine and operations over the extensive inland waterways that characterized the terrain in their zone of the western approaches to Germany.

The Americans had been disappointed at the British opposition to an invasion of France in 1942. But, the 70 per cent casualties suffered by the 6,000-man Anglo-Canadian force which made the amphibious raid on Dieppe in August of that year, gave them a better understanding of the British position. Beyond that, the raid convinced the Germans that the Allied amphibious threat was real and justified the commitment of 45 divisions to the defense of western Europe. That was useful to the Russians. Of use to the Allies was a greater appreciation of the importance of naval gunfire support, the need for armor ashore to support assault infantry shortly after its landing, and the absolute requirement for effective over-the-beach supply support capabilities.

Recognition of the latter fact led to the development of the devices used at Normandy, particularly the Mulberry harbors, an idea first advanced by Winston Churchill in 1917. The value of naval gunfire was soon confirmed in Sicily and during the Italian landings with the result that the force eventually assembled to support the Normandy landings included seven battleships, 27 cruisers and 164 destroyers, most of which were British or Canadian. Lastly, the recognition of the need for armor ashore early in an amphibious operation led to the restructuring of the British 79th Armoured Division to meet that and related specialized requirements.[4]

It was fortunate that the Division was commanded by Major-General Sir Percy Hobart, a pioneer in the development of armor tactics. He had commanded the first tank brigade organized in Great Britain in 1934 and, four years later, had formed the 7th Armoured Division in Egypt. Ironically, Hobart had been seen as too unconventional to fit well into the conservative pre-war British Army and, despite his accomplishments, had been forced into early retirement in 1940. He was rescued from duty as a Corporal in the Home Guard by Winston Churchill, who put him in command of the 79th Armoured Division when that unit was first formed in 1942.[5]

The concept underlying the reorganization of that Division was to group within a single command all special assault tank and engineer units that would be required by British forces in the invasion of Europe. Accordingly, its subordinate units were equipped with a number of strange vehicles that had been developed largely as a result of combat lessons learned at Dieppe and in North Africa. These included tanks fitted with large searchlights (CDLs), flame-throwers (Crocodiles), or mine-clearing flails (Crabs). Also included was a tracked armored vehicle of the Royal Engineers (A.V.R.E.) equipped with various attachments or launchers to permit it to lay fascines over soft ground or into ditches, bridge narrow waterways, or fire various types of explosive charges and projectiles to detonate mines. A further valued innovation was a tank flotation device (DD) which had been invented by a Hungarian, Nicholas Straussler, and accepted by the British Army against Royal Navy opposition. The Army had wanted 900 tanks equipped with the device, but because the Navy questioned its seaworthiness, the program had been kept in low gear. General Eisenhower interceded, however, and had 300 tanks converted in the United States for the invasion of France. Finally, several 79th Armoured Division units were equipped with armored personnel carriers (Kangaroos), amphibian tractors (which the British nicknamed "Buffalos") and amphibian trucks (which the Americans called DUKWs and the British "Terrapins"). These diverse units were used by elements of the First Canadian Army and the Second British Army making up the 21st Army Group in operations extending from the beaches of Normandy to the final surrender of German forces on 5 May 1945.

The 21st Army Group operated in two European countries with exceptionally dense inland waterway systems. Belgium, whose land area of just under 12,000 square miles ranks it among the smallest countries on the continent, enjoys a diversity of terrain. The forested hills of the Ardennes in the southwest present a vastly different aspect from the Vlaanderen Plain which borders the North Sea from France to the Scheldt River. Several major rivers dissect the country and most of these are linked by canals able to accommodate barges with capacities ranging from 1,350 to 2,000 tons. The somewhat larger Netherlands, in contrast, has a uniform topography . . . all of it flat. The country encompasses just under 16,000 square miles, 6,000 of which lie below sea level and are kept from being inundated by a system of dikes. The country is laced with some 3,500 miles of inland waterways, most interconnected. Western Belgium and all of Holland offer an advancing army a succession of obstacles that are resource-demanding and time-consuming to overcome, even when not defended. It was in anticipation of these difficulties that the 79th Armoured Division had organized its amtrac and DUKW units. The employment of these vehicles in the lowlands of northwestern Europe is an interesting complement to their service in the Pacific.

On 5 September 1944, just twelve days before the British I Airborne Corps was to make its historic drop at Arnhem, the 11th Armoured Division captured the major port of Antwerp. The Germans, however, retained control of the approaches to the port through the Scheldt estuary. The Canadian 3rd Division was given the mission of clearing away the German defenders remaining on the south bank of the Scheldt. A direct assault against the enemy defenses appeared difficult, but an amphibious envelopment of the German flank offered excellent prospects of success at little cost. The problem was the Savoyaard Plaat, a broad channel leading into the Scheldt. The 79th Armoured Division, called upon for assistance, provided the 5th Assault Engineer Regiment with 88 LVT(4)s and twelve LVT(2)s, and the 82nd Assault Squadron of the 6th Regiment, with forty "Terrapins" (DUKWs). These were to land the Canadian 9th Infantry Brigade.

The plan was for the amtracs to load the troops below the town of Ter Neuzen, proceed up a small canal to the main waterway, bypassing damaged locks by using locally built wooden ramps to allow the LVTs to get around them. The ramps broke down after a few LVTs had used them, and the remaining amtracs had to be winched over the lock. This delayed the operation for 24 hours. Finally, at 0200 on 8 October 1944, two groups of loaded amtracs set off behind a boat guide which led them to two previously selected beaches. The troops got ashore without incident and established a beachhead before the Germans realized what had happened. By daylight, when the Brigade's reserve battalion was brought over, the Canadians began receiving artillery and long-range machine gun fire, which proved ineffective. Throughout the day the amtracs continued bringing in support units while the DUKWs ferried supplies. Then, on 10 October, the 7th Brigade was brought over to relieve the 9th and continue the advance. Two days later, when the amtrac unit was relieved, it was credited with having carried 200 loads of personnel and 680 loads of weapons and vehicles while suffering only four dead and 25 wounded. LVT losses were equally light, one LVT destroyed in a collision and two lost to enemy action. Most of the

Above: Amtracs of the same Division climb up dikes during the landings in the Scheldt estuary.

Below: American troops load a gun into an LVT(4) along a Belgian road. (US Army)

remaining vehicles, however, had been rendered unserviceable by their continuous use . . . a situation not unfamiliar to the amtrac units in the Pacific.

The clearing of the south bank of the Scheldt by the Canadians was but half the solution to control of the waterway. The other half lay on the north bank, formed by two German-occupied islands, Walcheren on the west and Beveland on the east. The Canadian 2nd Division, advancing from the east, had encountered strong resistance on the causeway linking Beveland to the mainland. Rather than continue a costly frontal assault, the decision was made to land two brigades of the British 52nd Division on South Beveland, directly in the German rear. The landing would be made in 78 amtracs of the 5th Assault Engineer Regiment augmented by 96 amtracs of the 11th Royal Tank Regiment. Added support would be provided by eighteen tanks fitted with the DD flotation devices from the Staffordshire Yeomanry.

The first echelon of troop-carrying amtracs moved out at 0245 on 25 October behind a guide LCVP. The 9-mile journey was made in total darkness without incident, and the landings began on Amber Beach within five minutes of scheduled time. A few surprised Germans were driven off, while the amtracs proceeded directly inland for about a mile before unloading their passengers. By that time the Germans were alerted and had opened a brisk mortar fire on the landing area. The second echelon with units of the 156th Infantry Brigade came in over Green Beach under fire but without excessive losses. By late morning the remainder of the Brigade had been brought in over the Amber Beach followed by the eighteen tanks equipped with the flotation gear. These last had great difficulty climbing over the dike fronting the landing area, and moving through

Below: U.S. Army tank carriers loaded with LVTs move to assembly areas in preparation for a river crossing operation. (US Army)

the soft ground beyond. It was not long before fourteen of the tanks were bogged down or otherwise out of action.

The next day, amtracs and DUKWs brought up support units and supplies, while the infantry expanded the beachhead and pushed out patrols. On 27 and 28 October, the 157th Infantry Brigade was brought in by LVT to join in the final clearing of Beveland. That was completed on the 30th with the help of a detachment of amtracs from the 11th Royal Tank Regiment. Meanwhile, on 28 October, the remaining amtrac units had been relieved to allow them time to service their vehicles for the next operation, the landing on Walcheren Island.

The reduction of Walcheren was to prove a difficult enterprise. The Germans held the island with a composite force from the Army, Navy and Air Force numbering 10,000 men. Despite their diverse service origins, the men were united in their determination to keep the Allies from using Antwerp. They were well equipped for the purpose with 150mm coastal batteries, reinforced concrete weapons emplacements, extensive minefields and belts of obstacles covering the more accessible landing areas. The Royal Air Force had earlier breached the dikes, flooding the inner part of the saucer-like island; only the coastal villages and the central town of Middleburg, linked to Flushing by a causeway, remained above water. This limited terrain options for the defender, but made movement more difficult for the attacker.

The British plan called for simultaneous assault landings from the south, near Flushing, and from the west, at Westkapelle. Troops of the 4th Commando Brigade and the 155th Infantry Brigade were to land from LVTs brought off the landing beaches from Ostend in LCTs. The 5th Assault Engineer Regiment and the 11th Royal Tank Regiment were to furnish 104 amtracs while other units of the 79th Armoured Division were to bring in two medium tanks, ten flail tanks (Crabs), six A.V.R.E. fitted for bridging and the laying of fascines, and four bulldozers.

On 1 November 1944, in weather bad enough to keep aircraft grounded, reconnaissance patrols landed from LCVPs at night near Flushing. They found the area clear and called in No. 4 Commando which had also traveled by boat. By that time the Germans had discovered the incursion and were fully alert. Thus, when the 155th Brigade arrived in its amtracs, it was met by such a heavy fire that 15 per cent of the men and machines were put out of action. Despite this violent reception, the troops pushed inland and undertook the murderous task of driving the enemy from his defenses. Meanwhile, in the west, a heavy naval bombardment had started at 0830 aimed at silencing the coastal batteries and destroying the fortified positions covering the beaches. Support craft then closed the beach to within 1,000 yards to pour direct fire on the defenses. This gallant act resulted in three out of four LCAs being sunk by German gunfire.

Under cover of this fire, the amtracs made for the gap in the dike opened by the earlier RAF air strike. Two Commandos were landed astride the gap. Three LCTs with special vehicles then headed for the beach, but two of these were hit on the way. Of the special vehicles embarked, only four of the flail tanks landed; two of the four bulldozers fell victim to mines ashore as did six of the engineer vehicles. After great difficulty the two tanks accompanied by two A.V.R.E., two flail tanks and two bulldozers reached Westkapelle where the Commandos had

Above: U.S troops, embarked in an LVT(4), keep their heads down as they head for an unfriendly river bank in Germany.

arrived a short time before. The losses in armor and of fifteen amtracs had been high, but the surviving vehicles proved decisive in driving the enemy from his positions in the west.

In the south, Flushing was taken after two days of severe fighting. It then took three more days to inch up the causeway to Middleburg. The town was finally occupied on 6 November by a force embarked in eight amtracs, two of which were destroyed on the way. Organized resistance soon ended and by 12 November all of Walcheren was in friendly hands . . . as were 8,000 demoralized German prisoners. It was later acknowledged that the seizure of Walcheren Island, which opened the port of Antwerp to Allied use, could not have been accomplished without the amphibian tractors whose crews "were highly praised by all concerned for their gallantry and endurance."[6] The clumsy amtrac was obviously appreciated as much in Europe when the going got tough as it was in the Pacific, and for the same reasons.

The port of Antwerp was reopened on 28 November as the British and Canadian forces prepared to continue their advance. Then, on 16 December, the Germans opened their offensive through the Ardennes aimed at Antwerp. They never came close to achieving their objective, but they did disrupt the Allied schedule. Thus, it was the end of January before the British XXX Corps was able to cross the Maas River in amtracs. From there to the Rhine, the Corps had to breach the Siegfried Line and fight its way over extremely difficult terrain made more so by an early thaw. Thus, it did not reach the Rhine until March where it completed preparations for the crossing on the 24th of that month. At that time the 79th Armoured Division, already the largest in the British Army, had grown to 21,430 men and 1,566 specialized vehicles, among which were 425 amtracs organized into four regiments (U.S. battalions). These played an important role in the assault crossing of the lower Rhine and of the other waterways remaining in the way of the 21st Army Group; the last of these, the

Elbe River, was crossed on 29 April 1945, a week before the war ended in Europe.

In that same spring of 1945, the American 755th Tank Battalion was re-equipped with 119 LVTs to enable it to join units of the Royal Army Service Corps in supporting operations of the British 9th Armoured Brigade in the Lake Comicchio area near Venice. Then, a short time before the war ended in Europe, four amtrac companies were used in the assault crossings of the Po and Adige Rivers. In this fashion the enemy was made to surrender in Italy as in Germany. Thenceforth, the vanquished in Europe could sift through their ashes and begin the painful process of reconstruction. But, the victors still had Japan to crush. In anticipation of this task, on which the Allies could now center their attention, the British organized yet another innovative unit as well conceived as the 79th Armoured Division, but on a lesser scale . . . that was the 35th Amphibian Support Regiment of the Royal Marines.

The British had not used gun-mounting amtracs in Europe. However, they had experimented with cargo amtracs fitted with 4.5in rocket-launchers and flame-throwers. These appeared to offer promise, as did the LVT(A)4, for the fire support of landing forces that were soon to be engaged in Burma, Malaya and, with the Americans, in the Pacific. The Royal Marine amphibious support unit, organized for that purpose in 1945, was made up of a headquarters and four batteries. Two "Support Batteries" each had 24 LVT(A)4s organized into three "troops" (U.S. platoons) of eight vehicles. The "Rocket Battery" included three "troops" of four LVT(4)Rs making a total of twelve vehicles each able to launch 72 rockets per load. Finally, a "Flame-Battery" had two "troops" of five LVT(4)Fs fitted with a WASP flame-thrower. The Regiment, to be first used in the invasion of Malaya, never saw action.

The combat effectiveness of such a unit can only be a matter of conjecture. More certain is the fact that in the Pacific as in Italy and Germany, the amphibian tractor in many guises brought the war to the enemy, often where least expected. These operations, of great diversity, had encouraged tactical and technical innovation and had provided a reservoir of experience that would serve in other wars that were to follow and in which the process would be continued.

Above: U.S. Marines of V Marine Amphibious Corps land on Kyushu, Japan on 30 August 1945. (USMC)

Below: The 1st Marine Division heads for Blue Beach at Inchon in LVT(3)s on 15 September 1950. (USMC)

7. Short Peace and New Wars

Korea, Indochina and Vietnam

THE abrupt end of the war with Japan left the Marine Corps with six divisions and four air wings deployed in the Pacific. The Corps, only 28,000 strong in mid-1940, had multiplied seventeen-fold in five years. It had also amassed $400 million in property in depots from Hawaii to Okinawa and was continuing the build-up in anticipation of invading the Japanese home islands. With the end of the war, the process not only had to stop; it had to be put into reverse.

The urgency of the United States to dismantle its immense military organization as soon as the war had ended was in keeping with the nation's historic tradition of maintaining only minimal peacetime forces. But, the emotional release of accelerated demobilization had to be tempered by the need to guard against any continuation of Japanese militarism. The Emperor, on 14 August, had called upon his troops to lay down their arms. The Allied experience, however, had been that Japanese troops did not surrender easily. There was, therefore, an understandable concern over how well the 4,000,000 Japanese remaining in the Imperial forces would accept the Imperial edict. In the American view, the question could best be settled by the prompt deployment of combat-capable occupation forces to the home islands and other Japanese-held areas.

Two task forces from the Marianas and Marshalls Area Command were speedily organized and dispatched to receive the surrender of 100,000 Japanese troops and 50,000 enemy civilian nationals in those areas. The first surrender took place on Mille Atoll on 22 August 1945. The following month, the 4th Marines landed at the Yokosuka Naval Base, while the V Amphibious Corps, with the 2nd and 5th Marine Divisions, landed on Kyushu to share with the U.S. Army in the occupation of Japan. Also in September, the III Amphibious Corps, with the 1st and 6th Marine Divisions, the latter less its 4th Marines, moved into north China. During this same period the 4th Marine Division on Maui and the 3rd Marine Division on Guam were kept in readiness to intervene should that become necessary. But the Japanese proved to be as docile and co-operative in peace as they had been cruel and fanatical in war. Thus, when these unexpected qualities were affirmed, the 4th Marine Division was returned to the United States and deactivated on 3 November 1945; the 3rd Marine Division was deactivated on Guam the following month.

The New Year brought further steep reductions in the Corps. In February 1946, the 5th Marine Division was disbanded and the 2nd Marine Division lost the third battalion in each of its infantry regiments. In March, the 6th Marine Division was deactivated. Then on 24 June the 2nd Marine Division sailed for the United States and its new home at Camp LeJeune, North Carolina. Four days earlier, the 1st Marine Division had left north China for San Diego and permanent basing at Camp Pendleton, California. These last moves represented the intention of the Marine Corps to retain a minimum effective combat capability while accommodating itself to the government's demobilization process.

During this same period, $207 million in excess property was disposed of by the Marine Corps, and an additional $68 million identified as surplus. The latter made for a particularly trying problem. The reductions in personnel had left the Marines' Service Command woefully undermanned and incapable of maintaining the equipment and spare parts which its depots and service battalions were holding. It was possible to reduce the stock levels at the 6th Base Depot on Oahu and the service battalions on Maui and Hawaii in somewhat orderly fashion because the weather was reasonable and the required shipping and minimum manpower were available to transfer selected equipment to the continental United States. Then too, a tidal wave which struck the Hawaiian area on 1 April 1946 had dramatically helped dispose of some of the surplus property held at Kahului and Hilo. This, however, was not a reliable way of disposing of government property, even if surplus. On Guam, the situation at the 5th Field Depot was more difficult. The weather, even without tidal waves, was hard on equipment. Then, too, the place was remote, its facilities primitive and access to shipping limited. Not the least of the problems confronting the harassed Depot commander were 372 LVTs deteriorating in the open.

The solution to that last problem was found in the reactivation of the 1st Amphibian Tractor Battalion at Camp Pendleton in May of 1946. Major Henry G. Lawrence, Jr., who had taken over the 2nd Amtrac Battalion at Tarawa when Major Drewes had been killed and had gone on to win the Navy Cross there, was given command. His executive officer was Major Eugene Siegel who had been Drews' supply officer on Tarawa where his services had earned him the Silver Star. In September, after three months of preparation, the Battalion sailed for Guam. There, for the next nine months, the Battalion identified, segregated, inventoried and warehoused a mountain of LVT parts. In addition, Companies "A" and "B" under Captains Tom Barker and Bill Stoll processed the cargo amtracs for long-term storage; Captain Bernard Thobe and his Company "C" did the same for the armored amtracs. On 1 June 1947, with its work well done, the Battalion was deactivated on Guam, and the last amtrac unit in the Pacific War passed into history. That same month the Marine Corps reached a personnel strength of 92,222 offficers and men.

This abrupt decline in manpower was but one of the challenges confronting the Marine Corps in the immediate post-war period. Equally challenging were the questions being raised concerning the effect of nuclear weapons on the conduct of future amphibious operations. Could the Navy and Marine Corps henceforth concentrate amphibious forces off a landing area without presenting an exceptionally attractive target for nuclear weapons; if not, how then should the amphibious assault be organized? Indeed, was it still possible to conduct amphibious operations in a nuclear age? These and related questions were complex and troubling issues. But the ultimate challenge came from the political machinations associated with the Unification Act of 1947, in which the very survival of the Marine Corps was threatened.

The study of these issues occupied the years near the mid-century. The restructuring of the Marine Corps following demobilization had left it with much reduced Fleet Marine Forces on both coasts. Equally serious, the validity of the amphibious operation continued to be questioned even though the corps' use of helicopters to complement that of boats and amtracs appeared to offer much promise and was being actively studied. Meanwhile, pending the availability of adequate numbers of helicopters, the amphibian tractor itself was modernized and prepared for operations on a nuclear battlefield.

The impetus for this latter development had been given at Camp Pendleton in 1948 where a number of cargo LVTs were overturned in the surf and a Marine drowned during a training exercise. In the investigation that followed, it was recorded that the armored amtracs had less difficulty landing through a high surf because the turret kept the vehicle from shipping excessive water. Note was also taken of the practice used in World War II of rigging tarpaulins over the open cargo wells of the amtracs to help keep seas from breaking into the vehicles and swamping them. The outcome of these observations was a recommendation to fit cargo LVTs with armored overhead covers. These would reduce the likelihood of swamping in high seas. They would also offer protection to embarked personnel from overhead fire and air burst weapons, and shield personnel from the effects of nuclear explosions. The Test and Experimental Unit at Camp Pendleton acted on the recommendations and worked with Navy representatives and contractor personnel to design the armored cover. A program to modify all the LVT(3)s in the Marine Corps was undertaken at the Naval Shipyard in Long Beach, California at the end of 1948.

Fortunately these efforts to retain and even modestly improve on its amphibious warfare capabilities were not in vain. The National Security Act of 1947 included statutory protection of the Marine Corps[1] and formalized its amphibious mission. That accomplishment represented the culmination of an extensive effort to enlist public support. Perhaps the best sense of the issue and how it was addressed is conveyed in the declaration made by General Vandegrift before the Senate Naval Committee in May 1946 in these words:

> "... we do not rest our case on any presumed ground of gratitude owing us from the nation. The bended knee is not a tradition of the Corps. If the Marine as a fighting man has not made a case for himself after 170 years of service, he must go. But, ... he has earned the right to depart with dignity and honor, not by subjugation to the status of servility planned for him by the War Department .."[2]

By 1950 the Marine Corps had survived. But, like all of the armed forces of the country it was at the nadir of its fortunes. The influence of nuclear weapons on the roles of the military services remained uncertain and austere appropriations were doing little to lessen inter-service rivalries. Then, in mid-year, a new war intruded and America found reason to restore its military power so that it could better champion the cause of free and open societies.

One of the more consequential disillusions to befall the United States after World War II occurred in Korea in June 1950. The sequence of events leading to that fateful month had begun five years earlier when Russia declared war on Japan, a brief six days before Japan collapsed. The vanguard of 250,000 Soviet troops entered Korea on 12 August 1945. Soon after, the terms imposed on Japan prescribed that Russian troops would receive the surrender of Japanese forces north of the 38th Parallel in Korea. Although considered by the Americans as only an administrative convenience, the 38th Parallel was promptly transformed by the Russians into a barrier behind which they went on to create a separate Communist state.[3]

The American XXIV Corps entered South Korea on 8 September 1945; the last Americans forces, except for 500 military advisors, were withdrawn in June 1949. Six months later the American Secretary of State made a public reference to America's strategic frontiers as extending from Japan through the Ryukyus to the Philippines; i.e., excluding Korea and Formosa. The Communists lost no time in exploiting this American expression of apparent disinterest. Before daybreak on Saturday, 25 June 1950, eight North Korean divisions crashed through the 38th Parallel in a bid to reunite Korea under the hammer and sickle. The day after, President Truman ordered the evacuation of American nationals from Korea and the immediate delivery of ammunition and military supplies to the lightly armed forces of the Republic of Korea. On the Monday, General MacArthur was authorized to use American Air and Navy forces to assist South Korean forces below the 38th Parallel. On the Tuesday, the United Nations, fortuitously being boycotted by the USSR, called upon member nations to help repel the attack on South Korea. Seoul fell the next day. That same Wednesday U.S. fighters shot down seven North Korean aircraft, and the next morning American warships began to bombard targets along the Korean coasts. On Friday, General MacArthur flew back to Korea, found the South Koreans badly hurt and reduced to 25,000 men. He immediately urged President Truman to allow him to intervene with U.S. ground forces. The President agreed, and by Friday night a regimental combat team drawn from the four understrength U.S. Army divisions in Japan was on its way. The Korean War had begun!

The first phase of the war was a race in which the Americans were forced to throw units into Korea in piecemeal fashion to hold what they could against the determined aggressors. By 13 July, when Lieutenant General Walton H. Walker was named commander of the U.S. Eighth Army, there were 18,000 American troops in Korea. But even as reinforcements continued to arrive, the Americans and remaining South Korean units found themselves compressed into a perimeter some 100 by 50 miles in southeast Korea, centered on the port of Pusan. On 29 July, the Eighth Army reached its final defensive positions. The delaying action had cost the Americans more than 6,000 casualties and the South Koreans 70,000. But there were now 47,000 U.S. ground troops in the country, not enough for a major offensive but sufficient to restore confidence. Included among these fresh troops was Brigadier General Edward A. Craig's 1st Provisional Marine Brigade which had landed at Pusan on 2 August, a scant thirty days after General MacArthur had requested Marine Corps assistance.

The Brigade, an air-ground team built around the 5th Marine Regiment and Marine Air Group 33, comprised 6,534 Marines, 255 of whom were in the 1st Amphibian Tractor Company, commanded by Major James P. Treadwell. The Brigade, which had been formed on 7 July, had sailed from San Diego only seven days later. It had been quickly built up by gutting the already austere Fleet Marine

Force units available on the west coast. Even so, the infantry battalions had only two rifle companies each and much of the Brigade's ground equipment had been hastily furnished by the huge desert depot at Barstow, California to which stocks from the Pacific had been transferred in 1946 and 1947. Fortunately, the Brigade was made up largely of veterans of World War II. It thus was able to live with the multitude of problems that accompanied it from Camp Pendleton to Pusan where, five days after arriving, it found itself engaged in the first American counter-offensive of the Korean War. The date was 7 August 1950 . . . eight years to the day when the same 5th Marines had established another first on a remote Pacific island called Guadalcanal!

While the Brigade was being assembled and readied for movement, Lieutenant General Shepherd, commanding the Fleet Marine Force, flew to Tokyo. There, on 10 July, he heard General MacArthur disclose his intention of making an amphibious assault on the enemy rear. In the discussion which followed, General Shepherd assured MacArthur that the 1st Marine Division could be made available for the mission. MacArthur agreed to request its services, thereby setting into motion events that led President Truman to call-up 33,000 men of the Organized Marine Corps Reserve on 19 July, followed on 7 August by the call-up of 50,000 Volunteer Reserves.

General MacArthur's plan to land a force at Inchon to seize Seoul less than three months after that capital had fallen to the Communists dismayed all the commands concerned, including his own. To land over a seawall directly on to the waterfront of a large city was difficult enough. But when the approach had to be made through a tortuous channel during the one three-day period of the month when a 30-foot tide provided enough water to float the ships and craft required, bordered on the impossible. The General listened to all objections, followed attentively all proposals for alternate landing sites and later dates, and remained adamant . . . the landing would be made at Inchon and it would begin on 15 September.[4]

The X Corps created for the Inchon landing was commanded by U.S. Army Major General Edward M. Almond and included the 1st Marine Division and the 7th Infantry Division. The Marines were to form the assault landing force which was to be augmented by the 1st Korean Marine Regiment and 2,750 U.S. Army specialists. The further difficulty to be added to the nightmare of natural hazards that characterized Inchon, was that the 1st Marine Division had been denuded to form the 1st Provisional Marine Brigade. It now became necessary to repeat the effort on a greater scale to build up the Division with assets remaining on the west coast plus those of the 2nd Marine Division on the east coast. Because of this, the 1st Marine Regiment did not arrive in Japan until 3 September and the 7th Marines did not reach Korea until a week after the landing. In short, of the two regiments that were to make the assault at Inchon, the 5th Marines would not be released from frontline duty in the Pusan area until 5 September. The other regiment, the 1st Marines, had been hastily assembled and given no opportunity to work as a unit, and would only reach the Far East twelve days before the landing was to begin. Neither of these units would have much time to prepare for a highly complex and risky operation.

Another problem was the scanty information of the enemy's dispositions.

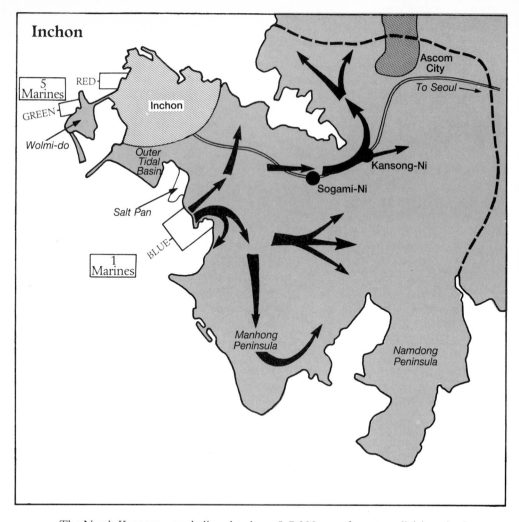

Inchon

5 Marines
RED
GREEN
Wolmi-do
Inchon
Outer Tidal Basin
Salt Pan
BLUE
1 Marines
Manhong Peninsula
Sogami-Ni
Kansong-Ni
Ascom City
To Seoul
Namdong Peninsula

The North Koreans were believed to have 5-7,000 men from two divisions in the Kimpo-Inchon area, but how these units were deployed was uncertain. Reliable information on the landing areas was equally limited even though American units had been in the locality for four years. Fortunately, Marine Major Donald Bush was able to fill many gaps with excellent aerial photos. Even so, plans had to be kept flexible so that they could be readily adjusted to meet the many unknowns that remained.

One comforting thought was that many of the Navy people, as well as the Marines, had participated in amphibious operations in World War II and would bring a high degree of professionalism to the operation. There was some added comfort in knowing that the 7th Infantry Division, which was to follow the Marines ashore, had received amphibious training from a Marine Mobile Training Team under Colonel Edward Forney, who had just been assigned to General Almond's headquarters as Deputy Chief of Staff.

The Inchon landing, Operation CHROMITE, hesitatingly approved by the Joint Chiefs of Staff on 28 August, had multiple objectives. The first was the landing of Marines to seize the port of Inchon. This was to be followed by the landing of the remainder of the X Corps which then would advance on Seoul by way of Kimpo, Sosa and Yongdungpo. After crossing the Han River and taking the South Korean capital, the X Corps was to take up positions to block the escape of North Korean forces withdrawing before the advance of Eighth Army units breaking out of the Pusan perimeter in the southeast.

The first step in this bold plan, the seizure of Inchon, would involve three separate assaults. The first, to seize the island of Wolmi-do controlling access to the port, would be launched at dawn on 15 September by Lieutenant Colonel Robert Taplett's 3rd Battalion, 5th Marines, landing from boats on Green Beach. Then, after a delay imposed by the tidal range, the main landings would be made late in the afternoon. The remainder of the 5th Marines, under Lieutenant Colonel Raymond L. Murray, would land at the seawall directly fronting the city, optimistically designated Red Beach. Because the seawall blocked access inland, the troops were to come ashore in boats equipped with scaling ladders to help them clear the obstacle.

Colonel Lewis B. Puller's 1st Marines would land three miles to the south on the slightly more accessible Blue Beaches to envelop the city from that direction and block the Inchon-Seoul highway. Because there appeared to be some usable exits from the the the Blue Beaches, the landings there were to be made in amtracs. The 1st Amphibian Tractor Battalion, under Lieutenant Colonel Erwin F. Wann, Jr., whose lead unit had sailed from San Diego on 12 July, now had 164 covered LVT(3)Cs available for the landing. The 1st Armored Amphibian Tractor Battalion, however, had not been reactivated until 5 August 1950 and had only sailed from San Diego on 18 August, under command of Lieutenant Colonel Francis H. Cooper. It would not be available for duty in Korea until the end of September. However, the Army had the 56th Amphibian Tank Battalion in the theater and would provide eighteen LVT(A)s from its "A" Company to lead the two battalions of the 1st Marines ashore on the Blue Beaches at Inchon.

From the start, General MacArthur attached great importance to regaining Seoul by 26 September, three months to the day after it had been lost to the North Koreans. The Marines were quite willing to try, but not by taking rash chances. For this reason, Major General O. P. Smith, the 1st Marine Division Commander, opposed the idea of landing a lightly equipped Special Operations Group from rubber boats before D-Day to make an unsupported dash to the Kimpo airfield. The General was equally opposed to forming a battalion of Marines embarked in amtracs into an armored column to punch out of the beachhead and make a run to Kimpo. He believed there were already enough problems associated with the Inchon landings to discourage any effort to complicate things further. His view prevailed.

The amphibious task force made up of more than 230 ships, 30 Japanese-manned LSTs and more than 70,000 embarked troops, arrived off Inchon in the early hours of 15 September. The landing areas and their vicinities had already been subjected to naval gunfire and aerial bombardment for two days. Additional preparatory and support fire was now to be provided by four cruisers, six destroyers and four rocket ships (LSMRs) together with two squadrons of Marine Corsairs and three squadrons of Navy Skyraiders. As this fire was being delivered,

Above: *5th Marine Units in landing boats approach Red Beach, Inchon, Korea. (USMC)*

Left: *The 5th Marines using scaling ladders to storm ashore at Red Beach, Inchon, in the late afternoon of D-Day. (USMC)*

Above right: *A supply LST and LCM beached at low tide during the Inchon landing; the tidal range of 30 feet required that landing be spaced in two phases during D-Day.*

Left: *A grounded LST unloads supplies at Inchon to support the drive inland towards Seoul. (USMC)*

Taplett's battalion finished loading into LCVPs by 0600. The ten tanks of Company "A", 1st Tank Battalion, scheduled to land in the third wave, were loaded in three LSUs. The final airstrike against Wolmi-do ended at 0615 and immediately after, three LSMRs saturated Green Beach with rocket fire. The thunder of impacting rockets was still echoing over the water when the lead wave came ashore; it was 0633. Only fifty yards of beach in the devastated area remained usable. However, the Marines were able to force a passage and rapidly fan out under the covering fire of F4Us overhead. By 0800, the Marines had overrun the island and gained control of the harbor; their losses in the entire effort consisted of only fourteen wounded.

Selective firing continued during the day while the remainder of the landing force awaited the next high tide. At 1430, H-Hour was set at 1730 and the bombardment ships opened up for a three-hour preparation in which all available aircraft actively joined. The pall of smoke which covered the city, mixed with heavy storm clouds, hastened the evening twilight in which the main landings were about to begin. The first wave of boats of the 5th Marines hit Red Beach at 1733 and the troops scrambled up their ladders. Heavy fire struck the 1st Battalion on the left, but the momentum of the 22 waves that followed carried both it and the 2nd Battalion inland to where, by midnight, all terrain dominating the landing area was in Marine hands.

The landings over the Blue Beaches were more confused, largely because many of the troop units and ships crews had only recently been assembled. Even so, the armored amtracs came ashore on Blue 1 on schedule and pushed inland without encountering any opposition. These were followed by the 2nd and 3rd waves, so that within a few minutes of H-Hour there were thirty amtracs and 600 troops of the 2nd Battalion, 1st Marines ashore. On Blue 2, the other nine armored amtracs approached the beach at 1730, but were discouraged from landing by mud flats. Ten minutes later, the 2nd wave arrived, passed through the armored amtracs and delivered its troops ashore. Soon other amtracs arrived to repeat the process. The troop-carrying amtracs had become intermingled in the gloom offshore, but after a quick reorganization the companies of the 3rd Battalion, 1st Marines began to drive inland. Like the 5th Marines, the 1st

Marines gained control of all assigned terrain objectives by the end of the day.

The build-up ashore was facilitated by the arrival of eight supply LSTs which beached late in the day and were unloaded during the night. By midnight, two battalions of the 11th Artillery Regiment had come ashore in 85 DUKWs and were in firing positions. Thus, when the day ended, there were 13,000 Marines in Inchon. It had been a long and violent day that had cost 22 dead and 188 wounded. But, once again, an amphibious assault had opened the way for what would prove to be a smashing victory. General MacArthur's prophetic vision had been fully vindicated.

The advance inland was resumed the next morning, Saturday the 16th. The two Marine Regiments established contact beyond the city and then continued towards the east, astride the Inchon-Seoul highway. That same morning, the Eighth Army, 180 miles to the south, launched its effort to break out of the enemy ring. In the north, the 5th Marines veered toward Kimpo, while the 1st Marines continued straight toward Sosa and Yongdungpo on the way to Seoul. The 5th Marines engaged in several firefights in their 16-mile advance to Kimpo, but were at the airfield by the morning of 19 September; patrols were pushed to the Han River immediately. The 1st Marines fought their way to Sosa the same day.

The 5th Marines had planned to cross the Han River on the night of the 19th and had sent a patrol from the Reconnaissance Company over to check out the opposite bank. The patrol swam across after dark, picked up two prisoners and returned to report all clear. The first group of nine amtracs with the remainder of the Reconnaissance Company promptly moved out, and suddenly found themselves blanketed by enemy fire. In the dark and confusion, four amtracs reached the far bank and got stuck in the mud. They worked their way free and returned; the other amtracs had turned back before reaching the enemy shore. The next morning the Marines tried again in strength. At 0630 on the 20th, amtracs with Marines of the 3rd Battalion started up and quickly ran into heavy fire. But this time the amtracs pressed on, their machine guns blazing. Four Corsairs appeared overhead and joined in the fight. Despite the welcome support, the enemy kept up such a brisk fire that the first six amtracs later counted 200 hits among them. Surprisingly, only four crewmen were wounded and the embarked troops were landed safely; some on the mudflats at the river bank, others, some distance inland. Notwithstanding their disorganized approach, the Marines took the enemy on and, in a vicious three-hour firefight, worked their way to the high ground overlooking the landing site. By 0940 the remainder of the Regiment was free to cross over and turn toward Seoul.

Meanwhile, the 1st Marines had been fighting their way to Yongdungpo, which they reached on 21 September. That same day, the 7th Marines landed at Inchon, just 35 days after they had been activated at Camp Pendleton. Forty-eight hours later, the fresh Regiment had crossed the Han River and was covering the northern flank of the 5th Marines as they drove toward the capital. By then, the 1st Marines, with the 32nd Infantry Regiment of the 7th Division, and the 17th South Korean Regiment all had reached the Han River. Once again the 1st Battalion's amtracs went into action and the 1st Marines with the U.S. Army and South Korean troops, stormed across the river.

Above: *A patrol from the 1st Marines flushes out a North Korean emplacement near Blue Beach, 16 September 1950. (USMC)*

The commanding general of the 7th Infantry Division commended the Marine amtrac unit stating, "So effectively did the unit (Company "C", 1st Amphibian Tractor Battalion) function that our troops were able to reach the far shore with minimum casualties."[5] The amtracs continued to provide ferry services across the Han until, beginning in early October, the 1st Amtrac Battalion returned to Inchon. There, it serviced its vehicles and prepared for a new deployment. On 14 October the battalion embarked in 22 LSTs. The next day it departed for Wonsan, on the east coast of Korea, where it arrived on the 26th. The 1st Armored Amtrac Battalion, with Companies "A" and "B", had joined the Division at Inchon on 30 September and been assigned support missions in the vicinity. On 14 October, it had detached part of Company "B", which had sailed with the cargo amtracs. The remainder of the armored battalion remained in the Inchon area until the end of November, when it was sent back to Japan.[6]

The crossing of the Han by the 1st Marines on 24 September put all three infantry regiments of the 1st Marine Division north of the river and on the approaches to Seoul. Even so, General Almond's determination to satisfy General MacArthur's public relations requirement to retake Seoul by the 26th made him impatient with the Marines' progress. The X Corps commander might better have directed his dissatisfaction to the south where the tempo of advance had been truly slow. There, General Walker with 140,000 men, 60,000 of them U.S. troops, had jumped off against 70,000 North Koreans on 16 September. The enemy had stood firm for three days until the threat of X Corps on his communications could no longer be denied. He had then fought a tenacious delaying action which kept the Eighth Army from breaking free until the 23rd. After that, it had still taken until 26 September for 7th Division patrols to meet advance elements of the 1st Cavalry Division. That same day, the Marines and other X Corps units entered Seoul, where the enemy was putting up a fierce resistance. General MacArthur had declared the city taken the day before, but had prudently waited until the 29th before holding the ceremony in which he restored it to President Syngman Rhee.

Only one year earlier, in October 1949, General of the Army Omar N. Bradley, Chairman of the Joint Chiefs of Staff, appearing before the House Armed Services Committee, admitted to "wondering whether we shall ever have another large-scale amphibious operation." Now, twelve months later,[4] a single such operation had made it possible to clear South Korea of an invading army and return its government to the nation's captital city in the space of two weeks. The Korean War could well have ended then. But North Korea's aggression was considered too blatant to go unpunished and the conflict was continued.

Washington had been divided on the question of carrying the fight beyond thte 38th Parallel. The issue was settled when President Truman approved a Joint Chiefs of Staff directive of 27 September which authorized General MacArthur to send forces to the north if neither the Russians nor the Chinese had entered North Korea . . . or threatened to do so. Further, no non-Korean forces were to operate in the provinces bordering the USSR and China. Even as these instructions were being prepared, the offensive unleashed by the landings at Inchon on 15 September was gaining momentum. By 1 October, South Korean units were across the 38th Parallel. The Chinese Government warned that if U.S. forces followed, it would enter the war. But little credence was given to that warning, and on 7 October, the United Nations lent support to the idea of a unified democratic Korea. On that encouraging note, the U.S. Army's 1st Cavalry Division crossed the 38th Parallel. The Chinese quietly carried out their threat and on 26 October, the Fourth Chinese Army struck at Republic of Korea forces below the borders of Manchuria.

Coincident with the Eighth Army's move north, the 1st Marine Division had been ordered back to Inchon, embarked and sailed for Wonsan, a port 110 miles north of the 38th Parallel on the east coast of Korea. The port was captured by the Republic of Korea I Corps on 10 October. Thus, by the time the Marines arrived, the only dangerous work remaining was to clear the 2,000 mines in the harbor and on the beaches. By the time that was done and the Marines were able to land, it was 26 October and new orders had been received. These required the Marines to relieve the ROK I Corps at the Chosin and Fusen reservoirs and

assume responsibility for a corridor fifty miles wide and three hundred miles long reaching to the Manchurian border. The Division proceeded north as ordered leaving the 1st Marine Regiment at Wonsan. On 4 November the Division opened its command post at Hungnam and on 10 November X Corps ordered an advance to the northern border with the ROK I Corps on the right, the 7th Infantry Division in the center and the 1st Marine Division on the left. These columns were not mutually supporting and, with the Eighth Army in the west already thrown back by Chinese forces, General Smith was worried over the situation facing his Marine Division.

The epic story of the Marines' advance in November against North Korean and Chinese Communist forces is only surpassed by their superlative performance when they "attacked in the opposite direction" beginning on 29 November.[5] By that time, the brutal Korean winter and seemingly inexhaustible flow of Chinese troops had combined to deny the numbed Marines any respite. However severe the test, the Marines remained resolute and by 11 December the last elements of the 1st Marine Division closed on Hungnam. To reach there they had to beat off seven Chinese divisions and drive the enemy IX Corps away from Hungnam. Four days later, 22,215 Marines, including the armored amtracs, were aboard ship heading for Pusan. The embarkation and departure of the Division had been covered by a security force which included Companies "A" and "B" of the 1st Amtrac Battalion, which was withdrawn shortly before Christmas. This whole venture, whose only virtue was to add lustre to an already illustrious Corps, cost the Marines 342 dead and 1,683 wounded. The Inchon-Seoul operation had cost 421 dead and 2,029 wounded . . . a somewhat higher cost but for a far more important result.

While the Marines at Masan, near Pusan, recovered from their ordeal in the north, the inconclusive war continued. On New Year's Eve the Communists launched a major offensive. Seoul and Inchon were again taken by the enemy, and the Marines were brought in to fight Communist guerrillas operating behind friendly lines. Then, in February 1951, the Marines were assigned to IX Corps in the middle of the peninsula, where they participated in a limited counter-

Left: *It is December 1950 and Marine units leave the Chosin Reservoir area and advance towards Hungnau for re-embarkation and re-deployment southwards. The Operation, carried out in bitterly cold weather, was contested by seven Chinese divisions. (USMC)*

Far left: *The Marines drive north beyond Wonsan towards the Manchurian border, Korea, November 1950. (USMC)*

offensive dubbed Operation KILLER. The operation went through several phases, during which Seoul changed hands again, and ended when the Eighth Army was again at the 38th Parallel. Finally on 11 April, as the Army prepared to strike north, President Truman relieved General MacArthur, and the fighting paused.

Four days earlier, the British Royal Marine Commando under Lieutenant-Colonel Douglas Drysdale had landed in a dense fog on a stretch of enemy-held coast where a major rail line was destroyed. The nine-hour operation, supported by a composite amtrac force formed in Japan under Major G. M. Warnke with ten LVT(3)Cs and five LVT(A)5s, went off without incident. Two North Korean soldiers, surprised by the lumbering machines emerging from the sea, quickly withdrew; no other enemy appeared. Beyond such rare diversions, operational activity for the Marines' amtrac units was routine. The armored battalion, now based in Japan, began rotating one company into Korea on a regular basis. Thus, for the first four months of 1951, Captain Lewis E. Bolt's "B" Company from the armored amtrac battalion worked with the 1st Amtrac Battalion, initially in the Masan-Pusan area and later, between Inchon and the Han River. The LVT(A)5s were most often used as artillery for the support of Allied units such as the British, Belgians or others who lacked this capability.

On 22 April 1951, a Chinese offensive struck South Korea's 6th Infantry Division on the 1st Marine Division's left. The South Korean unit collapsed and the Marines found themselves in trouble. Once the American positions were restored and the fighting died down, the Marines were returned to the X Corps for a quiet spell. The lull in the fighting was brief, however, for the Chinese hit again on 16 May. A violent and combat-filled two months followed until, on 25 June, Peiping agreed to hold truce talks. These began on 10 July but were interrupted on 22 August when the Communists walked out. The war, which had quietened down just as it entered its second year, flared up again. The Marines spent the month that followed in a succession of serious engagements, which were finally halted on 20 September as too costly and unproductive. The conclusion of this bloody episode, unknown to the Marines at the time, was also the end of the war of movement.

The remaining 22 months of the Korean War were static, but no less bloody. The Marines suffered some 40 per cent of their 30,000 casualties during these endless months. The frustrating and costly period was characterized by trench warfare in which artillery duels, night patrols and hand-to-hand struggles for outpost positions were intermingled with routine training reminiscent of peacetime activities at home. The Marines made much of the opportunity to experiment with helicopters during this period. As the numbers of these machines increased, it became possible to use them for troop lift in addition to their normal role of rescue and medical evacuations. Several battalion lifts were made. These clearly demonstrated the feasibility and value of the technique which was to become a standard feature in the Vietnam War more than a decade later. The services of helicopters were particularly prized in the difficult terrain of central Korea where the 1st Marine Division spent most of 1951.

In March 1952, the Eighth Army command brought additional South Korean units into the line and shifted the Marines to the extreme west flank. There they were deployed in positions on the left of I Corps to help safeguard the approaches to Seoul. These positions were held until the war ended. The 1st Amphibian Tractor Battalion, which had remained in the Masan-Pusan area in 1951, sailed to Inchon where it soon found itself, less its Company "A", holding a section of the 32-mile front assigned to the 1st Division. This was the so-called Jamestown Line which ran across the Kimpo Peninsula, over the Han River, thence along the Imjin River to where it joined the positions of the Commonwealth Division. The amtracs were dug-in behind the main-line-of-resistance, with their crews deployed in defensive positions. Sergeant Eugene Alvarez recalls that he commanded one such position made up of a personnel bunker and three machine gun bunkers, all interconnected by trenches and occupied by only twelve men. This was a very thin front line indeed, and, in the Sergeant's words, "Had the Chinese crossed the Imjin we would have been in a hell of a fix."[9]

Because of the tactical importance and the physical separation of the Kimpo Peninsula, the 1st Marine Division commander brought all units involved in its defense under a single command, the Kimpo Provisional Regiment. This Regiment included the 1st Armored Amphibian Tractor Battalion which had recently arrived from Japan, less one platoon that had been assigned to the 1st Amphibian Tractor Battalion located across the Han River. The 1st Armored, under Lieutenant Colonel John T. O'Neill, provided artillery support for the infantry.[10] The battalion had a tank platoon attached for direct fire missions against enemy positions across the Han. It also had two searchlights which were used to discourage enemy swimmers from coming over during the night. Later, the 1st Armored Amtrac Battalion was further reinforced with a three 90mm gun battery to extend the range of its support capabilities. Meanwhile, Company "A" of the 1st Amtrac Battalion had been assigned to the west side of the Kimpo Peninsula where its main duties were to screen traffic on the Yom River. In this fashion, the amtrac units, both cargo and armored, were used to help the 1st Marine Division cover the extensive water areas within its defense sector and hold its unusually wide front.[7]

The Korean War ended officially on 27 July 1953. But, unlike the homeward rush that followed the Japanese capitulation in 1945, the Marines remained in Korea until February 1955, when the 1st Marine Division embarked at Inchon for its return to San Diego and Camp Pendleton. The 1st Armored Amphibian Tractor Battalion, less its Company "B", also returned home at the time. The 1st Amphibian Tractor Battalion, with Company "B" of the 1st Armored, remained in Korea until March 1956, when it moved to Japan to join the 3rd Marine Division deployed there the previous August. In this manner, the Marine Corps established a Division-Wing ready force in the Far East that, in the years that followed, participated in contingencies, served in the Vietnam War, and remains to this day a major support of American foreign policy in that world area.

The Korean War lasted three years and one month, caused over four million casualties and destroyed one-third of the housing and 40 per cent of the industrial base of South Korea. Yet, it was initially acclaimed as welcome evidence of America's determination to resist Communist aggression. Unfortunately, the decision to carry the war above the 38th Parallel proved disastrous and led to prolonged inconclusive actions and a frustrating stalemate. Still, the prompt creation by the United Nations of a unified command headed by General MacArthur, to which sixteen member nations sent armed contingents, was a convincing manifestation of Free World solidarity. The international support given to the Korean War was evidently sincere and came in equal measure from the French who were already engaged in a bitter struggle in Indochina. The day that President Truman announced the commitment of United States forces to repel the invader in Korea a large crowd of former French military personnel blocked traffic in Rue la Boetie in Paris seeking entry to the offices of the U.S. military attachés to volunteer their services in Korea.[11] This was at the same time that Communist activists in Marseilles were interfering with the loading of supplies and equipment destined for the French Expeditionary Corps in Indochina![8]

The Indochina War, which began on 19 December 1946 and endured for seven years and eight months, never enjoyed the popular support given to the struggle in Korea. In France, the public took little notice of the conflict in far off Vietnam, and few found merit in the effort. In the United States, the public was even less aware of Indochina, although there were a few who remembered that it was the Japanese entry into Indochina in 1940 that had led the Americans to embargo shipments of metal scrap and oil to Japan . . . which, in turn, had been a critical factor in the Japanese decision to attack Pearl Harbor. Now, the French were struggling to hold that strategic area and were using resources needed in Europe by the newly established North Atlantic Treaty Organization. But, even so, what the French had available to commit to the war in Indochina was inadequate and, in 1950, the United States began a military assistance program headquartered in Saigon to assist the French.

What at first had appeared as a French effort to regain part of its colonial empire, soon came to be accepted as an anti-Communist struggle, not unlike that waged in Korea. The American commitment to support the French in Indochina, made on this latter premise, increased to the point where, by 1953, the United States was carrying three-quarters of the cost of the war. This still did not enable the French to overcome the consequences of their defeat at Dien Bien Phu and avoid the Geneva Accords of 1954 which brought an end to the Indochina War.

The austerity imposed upon the French forces in Indochina had stimulated their innovativeness. This was most strikingly evident in the specialized forces they created to wage the war in the deltas of the great rivers where most of the populace was concentrated. Best known among these forces were the French Naval Assault Divisions, the *Dinassaut*, made up of modified World War II landing craft. These units were widely used to gain control over the inland waterways of the Red River delta in North Vietnam and of the Mekong River delta in South Vietnam. After the Indochina War, the *Dinassaut*, became the River Assault Groups (RAGs) of the South Vietnamese Navy. The organizational and operational concept of the *Dinassaut* also passed to the Americans, who adapted it to the mobile riverine force which they used in the Mekong delta from 1967 to 1969.

Less known among the specialized forces developed by the French in Indochina were the amphibious combat commands. These were created by the French Army to conduct mobile surface operations in deltaic areas using the light tracked vehicle, the M29C, and the heavier LVT(4), both introduced in the

Right: An M29C (Crab) operated by a French Foreign Legion Reconnaissance squadron climbs a dike bordering a rice field during action in Indochina, 1952. (E.C.P. Armées, France)

Pacific War in 1944. The parent of the amphibious combat commands was the 1st Cavalry Regiment of the Foreign Legion which had arrived at Tourane, as Danang was then called, in early January 1947.[12]

The poorly equipped and understrength Regiment soon found itself involved in a vicious little war in central Vietnam which kept it busy performing such traditional cavalry missions as reconnaissance patrolling, raiding, and the conduct of wide envelopments and pursuits in conjunction with other forces. Towards the end of 1947, the 1st and 2nd Squadrons of the Regiment were sent south to the Mekong delta country, where their light wheeled vehicles proved unsuited to the environment. At that same time, some artillery units in the area were using M29Cs, which the Americans had called "weasels" and the French nicknamed "crabs". The Legion unit was able to acquire several of the "crabs" and put them to work in the Plain of Reeds. This vast swamp area astride the Vietnam-Cambodia border was used as a transit area for supplies being provided for the Viet Minh units in the south by their cousins in the north . . . an arrangement that was repeated later in the Vietnam War. The Legion, charged with sanitizing the Plain of Reeds, found the "crab" ideally suited to the purpose.

The organization that evolved from this experience was a squadron made up of a headquarters and three platoons, each with ten "crabs". Two such units were organized by the Legion in the south and another was created in the north by an Army cavalry unit. These proved highly effective in rice-growing areas and marshlands where they were able to maneuver rapidly and encircle fleeing enemy units to ensure their destruction. This versatility was negated often enough by imprudent use when "crabs" were sent far beyond the support of the infantry units with which they were working. The Viet Minh, predecessors of the Viet Cong, soon discovered that a "crab" with only two men aboard was a highly vulnerable vehicle when operating alone. As a result, the Plain of Reeds was soon dotted with hulks of "crabs" that had ventured too far alone.

By 1949, it had become standard practice to use "crabs" for long-range operations in groups of two or more vehicles. Equally important was the practice of assigning an infantry platoon to each "crab" squadron. The infantry was embarked on the "crabs" and fought from the vehicles or as dismounted troops. But, the Viet Minh's battle experience was evolving as was that of the French. The result was that a platoon of infantry, already large enough to tax the lift capacity of the "crab" squadron, was becoming too small to furnish the support now needed when the enemy was encountered. The solution was found in the amphibian tractor.

On 25 October 1950, the first LVT(4)s arrived in Indochina. These vehicles had been used for training at the French amphibious base at Arzew, Algeria and had been requested by Admiral Ortoli, then commanding French Naval Forces, Far East. The vehicles were put through their paces soon after their arrival and, after they had demonstrated considerable promise in the difficult delta environment, they were made available to the Army. The 1st Squadron of the 1st Cavalry Regiment of the Legion undertook trial operations with LVTs in the southern delta in 1951. In that same year the number of squadrons of the 1st Cavalry Regiment were increased to allow for the support of the Army's three area commands in north, central and south Vietnam. Then, on 1 September 1951, the three "crab"-equipped squadrons in the south were each augmented by one rifle company embarked in eight LVT(4)s and the whole was formed into the 1st Independent Group.

In the year that followed, the organization of the 1st Independent Group continued to evolve as field experience was acquired. Thus, by April 1953, when the unit was redesignated the 1st Amphibious Group, it had become a hard-hitting autonomous force not unlike the combat commands of armored divisions. The new amphibious group included two squadrons of "crabs" each with three tactical platoons of ten "crabs". These units were conceptually identified as reconnaissance and rapid maneuver elements. A second, shock element, comprised three squadrons each with eight LVT(4)s embarking a 130-man rifle

Left: An LVT(4), carrying troops of the French Foreign Legion's 1st Amphibious Group, emerges from a waterway in the Mekong delta area during 1953. (E.C.P. Armées, France)

Right: An LVT(4) loaded with Legionnaires of the 1st Amphibious Group in the Plain of Reeds, Mekong delta area of South Vietnam, 1953. (E.C.P. Armées, France)

company, plus three LVT(A)4s to provide the squadron with its own artillery fire support. Finally, a platoon of six LVT(A)4s was available to the Amphibious Group commander for general support of the whole command. Later, a 2nd Amphibious Group of similar composition was organized for service in North Vietnam.

These amphibious groups with highly mobile maneuver units had a substantial array of supporting weapons. The "crabs" and amtracs carried .30 and .50 caliber machine guns. In addition, each "crab" squadron had six 57mm recoilless rifles and three 60mm mortars. Beyond those were the fifteen LVT(A)4s each mounting a 75mm howitzer. The powerful force normally carried three days' supplies in an operation. It was capable of independent sustained combat and, because it had sufficient headquarters personnel and communications, it could fragment itself into two sub-groups each retaining balanced combat capabilities.

But the qualities of these groups were not all positive. Both the "crabs" and amtracs had to be transported to assembly areas near the intended zone of operations by land or water transport. Once there, the "crab" could move readily over swamp areas because of its low track pressure. The amtracs, on the contrary, could easily be stuck in the mud and were not always able to crawl out of waterways when the banks were of soft earth. Amtrac transmissions suffered accordingly. The "crab" in turn, had track problems, a weakness certainly aggravated by the usual practice of overloading them. Because of these and related problems, the French were careful to balance strengths and weaknesses when planning their combat operations. When this was done, the Legion's amphibious groups rendered exceptional service.

The general effectiveness of the amphibious groups did not lessen the need for Dinassauts and riverine operations, but rather served to complement them. In both cases, it was a question of making do with World War II equipment. The French were well aware that the helicopter offered much potential for operations in the deltas and elsewhere, but there were never enough of these aircraft. In

1952, the French had only ten helicopters in Indochina; two years later the number had quadrupled, but they were still committed to medical evacuation and liaison missions. Plans for 1955 envisaged a substantial increase in the number of helicopters to allow the beginning of tactical operations. When the war ended in Indochina in 1954, these helicopters were diverted to Algeria where the war just beginning would enable these machines to demonstrate their full potential. Meanwhile, sufficient amtracs were retained by the French so that they could land units of the 1st Foreign Legion Parachute Regiment and the 3rd Navy Commando at Port Fuad during the Suez crisis of 1956.

In the decade that followed the Indochina War, the French withdrew from southeast Asia. However, the Americans became increasingly involved and on 8 March 1965, the 9th Marine Expeditionary Brigade was landed near Danang. Thenceforth, the American military assistance effort that had already brought 20,000 American troops into the country became the Vietnam War.

The French conducted few amphibious operations during the Indochina War. Until 1952, operations along the 1,500-mile long coast of Vietnam were usually part of the coastal surveillance effort. Landings were most often made by ship's companies to investigate activity ashore; on occasion an embarked Navy commando or a small Army unit carried out a raid. Beginning in 1952, LSTs were used for more ambitious operations in which troops were landed from LCVPs and LCMs. Three landings were made that year in support of ground operations, but none of them proved a great success. The underlying problem was that the French had few resources. The landing craft that had been heavily armored and armed for riverine warfare had lost their seakeeping qualities, and there were insufficient numbers of unmodified craft to conduct meaningful landing operations. Further, the focus on inland warfare and the need to commit all ground forces to conventional ground combat allowed few opportunities for amphibious training. It was not until 1953, the same year that an LSD was deployed to Indochina, that the French organized an amphibious training center at Cam Ranh Bay. The regimental force that featured in the major landing made in early 1954 as part of Operation ATLANTE was trained there. Other units were also to train there for operations that year, but the Geneva Accords brought an end to the war and the Cam Ranh Bay facility closed down.

The Americans, in sharp contrast, would be able to take full advantage of the flexibility granted by amphibious operations in a country with limited land communications but readily accessible from the sea. From 1965 to 1969, the peak years of U.S. military involvement in the Vietnam War, the Marines conducted 62 landings, most of them with the Special Landing Force/ Amphibious Ready Group (SLF/ARG) of the Seventh Fleet. Other participants in several of the landings included Vietnamese and Korean units. These frequent operations left no doubt in the enemy's mind that no coastal area of Vietnam was immune from attack from the sea.

American military personnel had been present in Vietnam for fourteen years before these amphibious operations had begun. During the Indochina War this presence had been modest and concerned mainly with supply support for the French. But, once that War ended, Americans began to replace the French in

Above: An LVT(P)5 of the 2nd Amphibian Tractor Battalion on the Beirut waterfront following Marine deployment there in 1956. (USMC)

advisory duties and slowly grew in numbers. At the beginning of this process, in the latter part of 1954, an energetic French officer, Captain Jean Louis Delayen, had gathered the Vietnamese commando and river force units, whose survival was threatened by the post-Indochina War force reductions, and assembled them at Nha Trang. There, three U.S. Marines had formed the units into the 1st Vietnamese Marine Corps Battalion and ensured that it was integrated within the U.S.-supported Vietnamese Armed Forces. The Battalion subsequently grew to Brigade strength under a succession of U.S. Marine advisors. Then, in 1962, the American Marines took on a new function when they brought in a helicopter task unit to provide combat support for South Vietnamese forces in the Mekong delta area. This was followed in time by the rotational deployment of various ground defense and support elements, culminating in the arrival on 8 March 1965 of the 9th Marine Expeditionary Brigade whose lead units came ashore below Danang in eleven LVTP5s of the 4th Platoon, "B" Company, of the 1st Amphibian Tractor Battalion.[13] At that time there were already more than 1,000 Marines in Vietnam in tactical units; by the end of the year, their number would be just short of 40,000. The U.S. Military Assistance Command in Vietnam, the senior American headquarters in South Vietnam, would by then have an additional 145,000 men under its command made up of Army units, a lesser number of Air Force personnel and several hundred U.S. Navy advisors, of whom at least 300 were serving with Vietnamese units afloat.

The major ready force in the western Pacific since the end of the Korean War was the air-ground team made up of the 3rd Marine Division and the 1st Marine Air Wing. These two units could take the field as the III Marine Expeditionary Force (III MEF) or could form subordinate air-ground teams such as the 9th Marine Expeditionary Brigade which had landed near Danang in March 1965 to defend the nearby airbase. Soon after landing, the Brigade's mission had been expanded to permit "aggressive" patrolling and offensive "reaction force" operations.[14] Meanwhile, the Marines continued to build up their forces in the country. By 6 May 1965, the III MEF headquarters was established near Danang to control all Marine units in the Vietnamese I Corps Area and the headquarters of the 9th MEB had been deactivated. The next day the Marine Expeditionary Force was redesignated the Marine Amphibious Force. This was done on the recommendation of General Westmoreland, the commander of U.S. forces in Vietnam to whom the Vietnamese had mentioned that the use of the term "Expeditionary" in the Marine unit designation was disliked because it was too close to that of the French Expeditionary Corps and hence reminiscent of their recent colonial status.

The 4th Marine Regiment had arrived at Chu Lai in the spring of 1965 at the same time that the III MAF was becoming operational. The Regiment had brought with it Company "A" of the 1st Amphibian Tractor Battalion, equipped with 34 LVT(P)5s, plus one command LVT, one recovery LVT, and two engineer LVTs. The remainder of "B" Company at that time had already come ashore in the Danang area where its fourth platoon had landed earlier. Finally, the battalion headquarters with Lieutenant Colonel Jack Glenn arrived in Danang on 21 July bringing the total of amtracs in that area to 66 LVT(P)5s, seven command LVTs and two recovery LVTs. In addition, the 1st Provisional Armored Amphibian Platoon with six LVT(H)6s arrived with the amtrac battalion headquarters.

To reconstitute the ready forces in the western Pacific deployed to Vietnam, the Marine Corps progressively moved units of the 1st Marine Division to Okinawa; these all would soon go on to Vietnam. The 7th Marine Regiment, however, deployed to Vietnam directly from Camp Pendleton. It landed in Chu Lai in August 1965, bringing with it Company "A" of the 3rd Amphibian Tractor Battalion with 42 amtracs to be added to the 115 already present with the 1st Amtrac Battalion.

The LVT(P)5 was already an ageing vehicle in 1965. It had been developed during the Korean War to replace the LVT(3)C whose numbers were rapidly declining as that war dragged on. The LVT(P)5 had improved track efficiency and better personnel protection than the LVT(3)C, but it was twice as heavy and somewhat larger without any added carrying capacity. A number of variants of this vehicle were produced. First was the LVT(H)6 which featured a fully covered turret mounting a 105mm howitzer. The other variants included a recovery vehicle, a command vehicle and an engineer vehicle equipped with a dozer blade and a device to fire a 350-foot line charge to clear a path through a minefield. The LVT(P)5 and its variants had entered the Marine Corps inventory in 1953–1954.

The first major action for the Marines in Vietnam took place in mid-August 1965. Until July, III MAF had been limited to reaction-type operations in support of South Vietnamese forces. Then, on 6 August, General Westmoreland authorized Major General Lewis W. Walt to undertake offensive operations. The timing was good, for the Viet Cong had been building up their strength and threatening the Marine base at Chu Lai, some thirty miles below Danang. The decision was made to remove the threat by landing a battalion by sea and maneuvering it in co-ordination with another battalion brought in by helicopter

Right: The LVT(H)6 was the last amphibian tractor model to mount a major gun. The vehicle, with its 105mm weapon in an enclosed turret, was last used in Vietnam. (USMC)

Right: An LVT(P)5 landing supplies on a South Vietnamese beach in October 1967. (USMC)

Below: An LVT(P)5 carries its patrol atop the overhead cover in order to minimize any loss should a mine ignite the fuel cells in the bottom of the amtrac. (USMC)

to encircle the enemy. The Special Landing Force (SLF) with the Seventh Fleet would serve as the operational reserve afloat.

Operation STARLITE began at noon on 17 August, when Company "M" of the 3rd Battalion, 3rd Marines embarked in amtracs at Chu Lai for a four-mile run to blocking positions along the coast. The remainder of the battalion embarked on ships and landed at 0630 the next morning in amtracs against light resistance. At 0645 the helicopter-borne battalion began to arrive in its landing zones. Forty-five minutes later the helo-lifted battalion was in position while tanks and other support elements had landed from the sea. All units then maneuvered to close the trap. The situation was evolving as planned when, shortly before noon, a supply column of five LVT(P)5s escorted by three flame tanks ran into an ambush. Attempts to extricate the column led to a general engagement of sufficient violence to require commitment of the Special Landing Force. The area of operations was finally cleared late the next day after hard fighting. General Walt then directed the Marines to sweep through the area again to uncover any enemy that might have gone underground. This took another four days. When Operation STARLITE ended on 24 August, 57 Marines were dead and 203 were wounded; the Viet Cong had left 614 dead on the field.

A similar operation, named PIRANHA, was launched on 7 September to complete the destruction of the 1st Viet Cong Regiment, which had been badly hurt during STARLITE. The landing of the amphibious battalion was preceded by two engineer LVTEs which did a good job of clearing mines off the beach; it was the first such use of these specialized vehicles. The amphibious battalion was ashore in twenty minutes. The helicopter-borne force which began landing four miles inland took three hours to complete its assembly. The subsequent encirclement went off as planned except that the Marines were unable to find an

Left: *The Marine Amphibious Cargo Carrier M76 was used in 1966 by III MAF in delta area of I Corps in Vietnam where it could carry cargoes of up to 3,000 pounds over marshlands. (V. J. Croizat)*

effective means of flushing the Viet Cong out of caves and tunnels. The normal solution to such a problem would have been to use tear gas, but this had been ruled out by Secretary of Defense McNamara earlier in the year. That intedict had not been known to Lieutenant Colonel Leon Utter when he allowed his 2nd Battalion, 7th Marines to use tear gas in an operation near Qui Nhon launched just before PIRANHA. Utter's innocent act had touched off a flood of Communist propaganda and comment in the American press, with the result that the prohibition had been made known to all units in Vietnam. Fortunately, the matter was straightened out by the end of the month when Washington authorized the use of "riot-control munitions" for clearing the enemy out of subterranean areas. But, by then, Operation PIRANHA was over.

The Marine Corps' 190th birthday on 10 November was marked by the start of Operation BLUE MARLIN. This, the first combined U.S. Marine and Vietnamese Marine operation, was launched fifteen miles north of Chu Lai. It was followed by an amphibious raid conducted by the Special Landing Force near Phan Thiet at the end of November. The year ended with a large combined operation near Tam Ky code-named HARVEST MOON. For this operation, III MAF grouped three Marine battalions into Task Force Delta to operate in conjunction with three battalions of the 5th South Vietnam Army Regiment. The Vietnamese began the operation on 8 December by an overland advance which soon ran into trouble. The U.S. Marines were then brought in by helicopter and the sweep continued until 20 December, when all units returned to their bases. The enemy lost 407 dead in that period, but American casualties totaling 51 dead and 256 wounded were unexpectedly high. It is significant that much of the success of the operation, modest as it was, was due to the active participation of Marine Air Groups 11 and 12, which faithfully flew support missions despite poor weather.

In this manner, the pattern of Marine operations was set. Once the authority to engage in offensive action had been received, the Marines had set about sanitizing areas to bring them under friendly control. The Marines had engaged in fifteen battalion-level operations in the second half of 1965, most of them involving encirclements seeking to trap the elusive enemy. In such action, full use had been made of helicopters, amphibian tractors and tanks to position friendly troop units and support their maneuvers. Marine air had played a key role in all these operations. A further welcome contribution had been made by 72 Navy ships providing gunfire support; 70,000 rounds had been fired against 2,411 targets in that year. After BLUE MARLIN and HARVEST MOON, many U.S. Marine operations were carried out in co-ordination with Vietnamese Army and Marine Corps units, and with Korean units, when these began arriving later in the year.

In 1966, the remainder of the 1st Division was deployed to South Vietnam, where its headquarters was established at Chu Lai on 29 March. In that same period, Lieutenant Colonel Richard E. Harris brought the remainder of the 3rd Amphibian Tractor Battalion, comprising Company "B" and the Headquarters and Service Company, to Vietnam. This made the support of one amphibian tractor battalion available to each of the two Marine Divisions in that country. Both of these amtrac battalions were organized with two tractor companies each with fifty LVTs. This gave the battalions the same lift capacity as the three company battalions used in World War II.

In contrast, the numbers of armored amphibians, the LVT(H)6 with 105mm howitzer, were kept below the levels of World War II and Korea. The 1st Amphibian Tractor Battalion had arrived in South Vietnam in 1965 with a platoon of six LVT(H)6s attached. Later, in October 1966, the 1st Armored Amphibian Tractor Company sailed from California with twelve more LVT(H)6s. The company arrived in Vietnam in November where one of its platoons was retained in Danang and the other assigned to duty with the Special Landing Force; the platoon deployed the preceding year was already supporting the 3rd Marine Division near the Demilitarized Zone. In this manner, each Marine Division had the support of one platoon of six LVT(H)6s and the third platoon was afloat ready to support the Special Landing Force in its frequent landings.

The continuing build-up of American forces in South Vietnam in 1966 responded to the imbalance created by the inability of the South Vietnamese to counter the steady increase of Communist strength in their half of the country. The presence of North Vietnamese regulars had been confirmed in October 1965 when soldiers of the 1st U.S. Cavalry Division defeated elements of the 32nd and 33rd North Vietnamese Army Regiments in the Ia Drang Valley. The appearance of these regular forces in the highlands and in areas peripheral to the I Corps Area was troubling, but for the Marines the immediate concern remained the Viet Cong. By 1966 the Viet Cong controlled one-third of the population in the five provinces making up the I Corps Area, and influenced another third through terror.

In recognition of this widespread Communist infection, the Marines had devoted much of their energies in 1965 to small unit actions aimed at eliminating Communist control of villages and hamlets. The large-scale, battalion or larger unit, operations using ships, landing craft, amtrac and helicopters had been useful and newsworthy, but the tedious, unspectacular pacification effort also received much of General Walt's attention as well as the support of Lieutenant General Krulak, then in command of the Fleet Marine Force, Pacific. These views, however, were not fully shared by the Saigon command, which favored the larger-scale mobile operations to seek out and destroy main enemy forces in the field.

The increase in strength of the III MAF in 1966 enabled it to organize three enclaves within which the pacification effort could be pursued effectively. These three Tactical Areas of Responsibility (TAORs), which centered on Danang, Chu Lai and Phu Bai, extended over 800 square miles and contained a large part of the population in the I Corps Area. In addition, the Marines retained the capability for the large-scale search and destroy operations which the Saigon command encouraged. The demands of the latter were substantial, as is evident from the requirements of Operation DOUBLE EAGLE.

On 7 December 1965, General Westmoreland ordered III MAF to initiate a co-ordinated offensive against enemy forces in the border zone between the I and II Corps. Task Force Delta headquarters, originally activated for Operation HARVEST MOON, was given the task of planning the new operation. The concept for DOUBLE EAGLE I, called for a two-week reconnaissance of the beaches and

Above: An Assault Support Boat covering US Army helo operations in the Mekong delta. (USN)

intended area of operations. This was to be followed by the landing of two Marine battalions on 28 January 1966 to engage in the clearing of a 500 square-mile area below Quang Ngai in co-ordination with other American and South Vietnamese forces. The area of operations was cut by many streams and interspersed with swamps which placed a premium on amtracs and helicopters for the maneuver of the units ashore. Because of this, a company of LVT(P)5s and a platoon of LVT(H)6s were made available.

The reconnaissance phase began on 7 January when elements of the 1st Force Reconnaissance Company were airlifted to the Ba To Special Forces Camp. The extensive patrol effort which followed built up an excellent picture of enemy activity in the area the Marines would shortly enter. On the 24th, the South Vietnamese command in I Corps launched five infantry battalions overland to seize blocking positions against which the Marines were to drive the enemy. The Marines' landing phase began on schedule on 28 January, in dismal weather. The first assault battalion got ashore in the morning with little trouble; the LVT(H)6s followed and went into position to provide artillery support. However, the landing of the follow-on units was slowed by heavy surf. The bad weather continued throughout the next day, further delaying the assembly of the Marine force ashore. Finally, on the 30th, the weather cleared and the remainder of Task Force Delta was landed. The Special Landing Force, serving as the force reserve, was brought in by helicopter to a landing zone eight miles inland. By the 31st, Brigadier General Jonas M. Platt had gathered and positioned his 5,000-man task force and was ready to begin an orderly advance inland. Opposition was light and, by the end of the first week ashore, it became evident that the enemy main force units had withdrawn. Nevertheless, the search continued until 17 February, when the operation ended. The Marines had accounted for 312 enemy killed at a cost of 24 dead Marines and 156 wounded. The 1st U.S. Cavalry Division, which had launched a brigade in the northern part of the II Corps Area in coordination with a twelve-battalion South Vietnamese Army force on 24 January, had encountered much stronger resistance. In a single five-day period they had killed 600 of the enemy at a cost of 75 of their own dead and 240 wounded. Even so, the action in II Corps proved no more conclusive than that in I Corps.

No sooner had the Marines ended their foray below Quang Ngai than a large enemy force was reported in the Que Song Valley west of Tam Ky. General Platt was ordered to redeploy his Task Force Delta to meet this new threat. Using a combination of trucks and helicopters, Platt quickly moved his force and launched Operation DOUBLE EAGLE II. The search was pursued for ten days, but again, the enemy main force units had disappeared. Fifteen enemy were captured and 125 killed for a loss of six Marines dead and 125 wounded. In these operations, the results were modest when compared to the magnitude of the forces engaged and the resources expended. General Krulak found little to commend DOUBLE EAGLE and decried the weakening of the enclaves that resulted whenever TAOR security forces had to be withdrawn for other purposes.

While the Marines were centering their efforts in the southern part of I Corps, the North Vietnamese began to infiltrate forces directly across the Demilitarized Zone (DMZ) just below the 17th Parallel. The Marines, with a promising pacification campaign moving ahead favorably in the south, were not alarmed by the yet unconfirmed reports of unusual enemy activity. They did, however, send a battalion in April to clear the area near Khe Sanh, and another in May to remove the threat to the air facility at Dong Ha. Other similar operations followed until, in July, the presence of large North Vietnamese Army formations was confirmed in Quang Tri, South Vietnam's northernmost province. The Marines responded by again activating Task Force Delta and engaging four infantry battalions to sweep the area west of Dong Ha and north of Cam Lo. Operation HASTINGS was launched on 15 July. When it ended on 3 August, it had used 8,000 Marines and 3,000 South Vietnamese in a successful effort to defeat an invasion attempt by a North Vietnamese division. Not only were the resources committed in HASTINGS the largest yet used in a single operation, but the casualties suffered attested to the violence of the action. The Marines had 126 dead and 448 wounded; the South Vietnamese lost 21 dead and 40 wounded. Enemy losses were counted at 700 dead and seventeen prisoners.

No sooner had HASTINGS ended than a new operation was launched to ascertain what additional North Vietnamese forces were infiltrating through the DMZ. Operation PRAIRIE, soon confronted by elements of two North Vietnamese divisions, absorbed more and more Marine resources until General Westmoreland, concerned that the North Vietnamese might end-run the Marine units in the Dong Ha/Cam Lo area, urged General Walt to occupy Khe Sanh. This was reluctantly done on 29 September, when the 1st Battalion, 3rd Marines was airlifted into the area. One week later, General Walt ordered the 3rd Marine Division to move north; its headquarters was established at Phu Bai on 10 October. The 1st Marine Division thenceforth assumed responsibility for both the Danang and the Chu Lai TAORs, while the 3rd Division, less one regiment retained at Danang, became wholly engaged in the northern province of I Corps.

The amtracs, during these action-filled months continued to participate in over-the-beach operations and provide a variety of additional services. In February 1966, for example, the month in which the 9th Marines suffered 70 per cent of their casualties to mines and booby-traps, an LVTE from the 1st Amtrac Battalion was used to demine a hilltop. The LVTE fired 31 line charges which set off 99 explosive devices. In another incident on 21 April, a detachment of "B" Company, 1st Amtrac Battalion, moved two infantry companies of the 3rd Battalion, 9th Marines in an overland displacement near Tam Ky. LVT(H)6s were used to support this move as they would be for the attack against Phu Long on 3 May. During this same period, the Special Landing Force began to conduct landing operations outside the I Corps. Notable among these was Operation JACKSTAY in which the Marines joined the Vietnamese Navy and Marine Corps in a sweep of the Rung Sat. This operation, which lasted from 26 March to 16 April, was the first introduction of the Marines to the riverine environment near Saigon. Subsequently, a series of other landings, identified as DECKHOUSE I to IV, were carried out by the Special Landing Force in the I, II, and III Corps Areas. The second and fourth were co-ordinated with Operation HASTINGS and PRAIRIE, to provide the Marine commander with an amphibious maneuver element.

At the beginning of 1967, the III MAF, even though 65,000-men strong, was stretched thin over the I Corps Area. The tempo of operations in the north had intensified to a point where the 3rd Marine Division was fully engaged in fighting a conventional type of war against regular enemy forces. In the south, the 1st Marine Division was attempting to carry on the offensive and pacification missions it had formerly shared with the 3rd Division. In February, General Westmoreland, concerned with the situation in the north, directed the preparation of a plan to organize a division-size task force to take over the southern part of I Corps and release Marine units for duty in the north. This plan was implented on 9 April with the assignment of an Army brigade at Chu Lai. By 20 April, Major General William Rosson, U.S. Army had moved the headquarters of Task Force Oregon into the Chu Lai TAOR and, on 26 April, he assumed

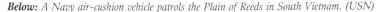

Below: A Navy air-cushion vehicle patrols the Plain of Reeds in South Vietnam. (USN)

responsibility for that area. The 1st Division was thus freed to concentrate on the Danang TAOR while the 3rd Division was fully engaged north of Hai Van Pass.

In parallel with these developments, the amtrac units, other than the one assigned to the Special Landing Force, found themselves increasingly involved in operations inland, both ashore and on the waterways over which large quantities of American military supplies were being moved. The performance of all the units under these demanding circumstances was of sufficient note to earn a number of awards. The 1st Amphibian Tractor Battalion (Reinforced), received the Meritorious Unit Commendation for services rendered between 5 November 1967 and 27 January 1968, when Lieutenant Colonel Edward R. Toner commanded, for "fulfilling the mission of an infantry battalion while simultaneously performing the inherent mission of an amphibian tractor battalion".[12] Later, when the battalion command had passed to Lieutenant Colonel George F. Myers, a second Meritorious Unit Commandation was given:

> "For . . . service . . . in Quang Tri Province . . . from 26 August to 9 December 1968 . . . when the Napoleon/Saline II Tactical Area of Responsibility . . . was assigned to the 1st Amphibian Tractor Battalion . . . This . . . area . . . of approximately 32 square miles encompassed some 14 miles of . . . waterways, eighteen miles of desert, and . . . land ideally suited . . . for enemy ambush. By conducting 543 day patrols and 675 night patrols, the battalion was instrumental in killing 3476 of the enemy and capturing 613 individual [and] 19 crew served weapons . . ."[16]

Less rewarding were the routine operations which, none the less, were costly. An excellent example is found in the daily log of the 1st Amtrac Battalion for the first part of March 1967 which includes the following entries:[17]

> "1 March . . . LVT(A-18) detonated a pressure type mine; No casualties
> 3 March . . . LVT(A-19) detonated a pressure type mine; three wounded
> 5 March . . . LVTE-1 detonated an anti-personnel mine; one wounded
>   . . . LVT(A-12) detonated a pressure type mine; five wounded
> 6 March . . . LVT(A-28) hit by an anti-tank rocket; two killed, five wounded
> 9 March . . . LVT(A-48) detonated pressure type mine; No casualties
> 14 March . . . LVTE-1 detonated a pressure type mine; three wounded

Above left: *A 5-ton Navy air-cushion vehicle was capable of carrying 20 troops. (USN)*

Above: *A Navy river patrol boat prepares to land a small patrol in a delta area of South Vietnam. (USN)*

> . . . LVT(A-35) detonated a pressure type mine; one wounded
> 15 March . . . Danang base hit by rocket attack. River patrol dispatched to Song Dau
> Co."[14]

The year 1967 also witnessed the last Special Landing Force landing outside of I Corps, Operation Deckhouse IV, which introduced the Marines to the Mekong delta proper. Unfortunately, information on the landing site in Kien Hoa Province, leaked and the operation had little value. But by this time, the value of the SLF had been well established. Thus, when the 26th Infantry Regiment of the 5th Marine Division was formed and deployed with Company "A" of the 5th Amtrac Battalion, to Okinawa in early 1967, it was possible to form a second SLF. This ensured that the Pacific Command had a force immediately available for contingencies outside of Vietnam as well as for the continued support of III MAF, without charge against its in-country personnel allowances.

The pattern of operations set in 1966 and 1967 continued as the war intensified in 1968 and 1969. Then, as the Vietnamization program was implemented, the 1st Amphibian Tractor Battalion with the armored amphibian company was returned to Okinawa in July 1969. The 3rd Amphibian Tractor Battalion remained until January 1970, when it too was withdrawn and sent back to Camp Pendleton. Both units and the armored amphibian company had well earned their way in the four hard years of a most demanding war. In addition to the two Meritorious Unit Commendations previously noted, the 1st Amtrac Battalion with its attached LVT(H)6s had also earned the Vietnam Cross of Gallantry with Palm. The same award was also given to the 3rd Amtrac Battalion, reinforced, which, because of its extended involvement in the pacification program, also earned the Vietnam Meritorious Unit Citation for Civil Action. These citations provide a fitting conclusion to the combat service of the amphibian tractor that had begun over a quarter of a century before on the strange and far-away beaches of Guadalcanal.

Above: *An Air-Cushion Landing Craft (LCAC); this has a cargo capacity of 60–75 tons, speed of 40 plus knots, and can be carried by any number of current amphibious ships fitted with well decks such as the LSD, LPD, LHA and LHD. These LCAC are currently assigned to the West Coast unit ACU–5. (USN)*

Left: *A modern AAVP7A1 in the Caribbean area. (USMC)*

8. Fifty Years and Still Running

The amphibious operation in modern times

FIFTY years have passed since that meeting in October 1937 when the amphibian tractor first came to the attention of the Marine Corps. During these five decades, the Marine Corps evolved from a small, relatively unknown military organization into a unique component of American naval power recognized throughout the world for its mastery of amphibious warfare. The amphibian tractor shared in this evolution from the beginning and appears destined to continue to do so.

The amphibian tractor captured the imagination of all who witnessed its appearance and early trials at Quantico in 1940. Even before the Marine Corps had received its first production cargo LVT(1) in July 1941, the Commandant was proposing an armored version mounting a 37mm gun. At the same time, newspapers were carrying cartoons of amtracs with machine guns blazing, thundering on to enemy-held beaches. The vision of a combat vehicle, however, had yet to come. First, the amtrac would enter service in a logistic role.

The Guadalcanal campaign did nothing to change this status, although the firefight that one amtrac of the 2nd Battalion got into on Gavutu revealed the combat potential of the vehicle. This was again demonstrated in 1943 at Bougainville, New Britain and elsewhere. But it was not until the Tarawa operation in November of that year that the amtrac was actually assigned a combat role. The 75 LVT(1)s and fifty LVT(2)s were armored for the occasion with slabs of ⅜in boilerplate or ¼in armor fitted over the cab. When contrasted with the concern over the vulnerability of the amphibious operation which influenced much post-war thinking, the "armoring" of the vehicles that were to lead the way to Betio's heavily defended beaches appears to have been a very modest precaution indeed.

After Tarawa conclusively demonstrated that the amphibian tractor, with open well and insignificant armor, could brave surf and violent enemy fire to land troops across wide reefs, it became the Marines' assault vehicle. Strangely enough, it was not until 1977, some 34 years later, that the amphibian tractor was formally designated an assault amphibian. Long before that name change, 1944 provided ample opportunity for the amtrac to justify the eminence they had gained in the Gilberts. The appearance of the LVT(A)1 with its 37mm gun in the landings in the Marshalls in January of that year magnified the image of the amtrac as a fighting vehicle. Meanwhile, the cargo-carrying LVT(2) continued to show its logistic value, even though it remained difficult to embark troops and manually load and unload ammunition, rations and other priority supplies over its high sides. The Marshalls also confirmed the importance of avoiding the transfer of troops and supplies from boats to amtracs at sea; after the Marshalls, assault troops came to the ships carrying the amtracs they were to land in, and the loading of the vehicles was done while they were aboard ship.

The LVT(4) with stern ramp was first used in the Marianas campaign in mid-1944. The stern ramp made it possible for infantry to step ashore rather than roll over the side and drop heavily to the ground. It also greatly facilitated cargo handling and permitted the landing of small vehicles and heavy weapons, which further expanded the amtracs' logistic value. In addition, the Marianas provided islands of large size which encouraged the Marines to consider having assault amtracs carry troops some distance inland before unloading. This was attempted at Saipan with little success, not because the concept was invalid, but because the debris and congestion on the beaches and the difficult terrain beyond the few exits made an orderly movement inland impossible. Thereafter, the practice of unloading troops on or near the beach continued throughout the remainder of the war. Still, the idea of the amtrac as an armored personnel-carrier had been sown. That role was exploited in Korea, and even more widely in Vietnam.

In parallel fashion, the initial inclination to use the LVT(A)1 as a light tank ashore proved unwise. The vehicle was too high, too slow and far too vulnerable to enemy infantry weapons to survive in such a role. The LVT(A)4 with 75mm howitzer, which first came ashore at Saipan, demonstrated that it was an assault gun rather than a tank. Later, when the armored amtrac battalions had been trained in indirect fire techniques they rendered excellent service as self-propelled artillery. This was confirmed during the final campaign of World War II on Okinawa, which also witnessed the introduction of the LVT(3). That cargo vehicle closely resembled the LVT(4) in having a stern ramp. But, where the LVT(4) had resulted from moving the engine on the LVT(2) from the rear of the vehicle to a position just behind the driver, the LVT(3) had been originally designed as a ramp-vehicle with two engines, one in each flotation pontoon. As a result, it had a larger cargo compartment, somewhat improved performance, and the added security of a dual power plant.

Although the combat role of the amtrac was firmly established in 1944, its logistic services, particularly after it was fitted with a ramp, continued to be highly prized. The historians, Jeter A. Isely and Philip A. Crowl, who detailed the story of the Marines in amphibious war, wrote in their analysis of the battle of Iwo Jima:

> ". . . without the cargo amphibian tractor . . . and especially the later model equipped with a ramp, it is impossible to see how any advance could have been sustained for these almost alone supplied the fighting forces in the first several days of the assault . . . ."[1]

By 1945, the Marine Corps had three armored amphibian battalions equipped with the LVT(A)4s and nine cargo amtrac battalions equipped with LVT(3)s or LVT(4)s. These were being brought together under two Groups corresponding to the two Marine Amphibious Corps in the Pacific when the war ended. The surrender of Japan brought a quick end to LVT production, which over the preceding four years had delivered 18,816 amphibian tractors of all models. After the shock waves of the rapid demobilization had dissipated, it was found that enough LVT(3)s amd LVT(A)5s were on hand to meet the foreseeable needs of the Marine Corps. All other amtracs were declared surplus and disposed of; the Chinese Nationalists acquired all ordnance stocks at the 5th Field Depot on Guam which included more than 300 LVTs that had been processed for storage by the 1st Amphibian Tractor Battalion in 1946.

During that same immediate post-war period, the Tracked Vehicle Test and Experimental Unit, was established at the Boat Basin in Camp Pendleton. The Unit undertook a number of modest programs to improve existing amtracs and design new ones. Of particular significance among these efforts was the conversion of 1,200 LVT(3)s beginning in 1948. This involved raising the deck of the vehicle to accommodate an armor overhead cover for the cargo compartment, and mounting a cupola with machine gun forward. The resulting vehicle became the LVT(3)C, destined to serve in the Korean War.

The success of the amphibian tractor in World War II was assured when it proved able to cross reefs and land troops on beaches otherwise inaccessible from the sea. But beyond this fortunate conjunction of requirement and capability, was the presence of Marines prepared to accept the hazards of sea, surf and reef, in addition to those of enemy fire. Amphibian tractor units were without precedent and provided opportunities for early command and rapid promotion. Further, because their operations were unfettered by established operational procedures, the way was open for innovative Marines to exploit the full capability of the amtrac in the amphibious assault. There were indeed many attractive opportunities open to young Marine leaders, but these were offset by the exceptional difficulties arising from the need to create new battalions. In the U.S. Army, the requirement was met simply by changing the designation of an existing battalion, usually a tank unit, to form an amphibian tractor or amphibian tank battalion. The Marines had no such assets in existence and had to form new units by fragmentation of existing organizations which then were completed by fresh arrivals from whatever manpower sources could be tapped. Since the requirement for new units did not always appear until after a new mission had been assigned, the formation of amtrac units was often a last-minute affair. Such was the case in the 4th Marine Division authorized to form the 10th Amtrac Battalion reinforced by Company "A" of the 11th Battalion in December 1943, with a sailing date for the Marshalls operation thirty days away. It was also the case when the 1st Marine Division was directed to fragment its 1st Amtrac Battalion to form two amtrac battalions, the 3rd Armored and the 6th Cargo in July 1944, to participate in the landings on Peleliu scheduled to begin on 15 September.

Thus, young captains and majors found themselves commanding amphibian tractor companies and battalions engaged in complex operations with few guidelines beyond the immediate landing plan. In like fashion, teen-age privates were required to land 30-man infantry platoons in tractors they had to drive through treacherous surf and over hidden reefs in full view of enemy gunners determined to keep their beaches inviolate. No less trying were the demands imposed on the non-commissioned officers and lieutenants to lead their tractor sections and platoons through the intricacies of the ship-to-shore operation, which required reaching hard-to-find rendezvous points, transfer areas and the line of departure, all several miles out at sea. Then, there were the seemingly endless shuttle trips to bring in additional troops, heavy weapons and priority supplies, stopping each time at aid stations on the beach to pick up a load of wounded. It was a hard school for all concerned. For the men manning the thin-skinned LVT(A)s, which carried the initial burden of fire support ashore, to the cargo amtracs, which played the key role in building up the fragile beachhead, the challenges were endless; the problem was to find the ways and means of responding to them. Major General Roy S. Geiger recognized these values when, as commanding general of the III Marine Amphibious Corps, he wrote in a letter dated 27 April 1945:

> ". . . Except for the 'amtracs' it would have been impossible to get ashore on Tarawa, Saipan, Guam or Peleliu without taking severe if not prohibitive losses. But, their use is by no means limited to the assault waves; after landing troops and equipment, they play an indispensable part in the movement of supplies, ammunition, et cetera, ashore. In fact, the whole ship-to-shore movement in the normal amphibious operation is to a considerable extent dependent on one or more of the 'amtrac' family . . ."[2]

Throughout its pre-World War II history, the United States had maintained a modest peacetime military establishment. Thus, when World War II ended, the country had quickly reduced its forces and returned those remaining to routine peacetime duties. The violent and unprovoked attack of Communist forces across the 38th Parallel in June 1950 forced the United States to re-arm and accept, once again, the heavy military burden it continues to bear to safeguard the political freedom of the West.

Five years after the Japanese surrender, the Marine Corps was down to 75,000 men of whom less than 28,000 were in the Fleet Marine Forces at their east and west coast bases. Even though modest, this strength represented a substantial victory, for the Marine Corps had just been through a difficult period when its very existence had been challenged, as had the retention of any amphibious warfare capability. Yet, despite its recent trials, the Marine Corps was able to field a powerful brigade within weeks of President Truman's decision to help repel the North Korean invaders. Soon after, the 1st Marine Division led the assault at Inchon where it vindicated its readiness to conduct amphibious operations. Inchon thus assured the future for the Corps. The 1st Amphibian Tractor Battalion shared in this historic event as it did in the crossing of the Han River and the liberation of Seoul. The amtracs were subsequently used as armored personnel-carriers, for the movement of supplies and on various defensive missions to include holding a front on the Kimpo Peninsula. The 1st Armored Amphibian Tractor Battalion arrived in Korea after the Inchon landing and went on to serve primarily as self-propelled artillery. At home, meanwhile, added impetus was given to developing a new family of amphibian tractors.

The Marines had been working with the Navy and defense contractors for some time on an improved amphibian. The effort culminated in 1953 with the introduction of the LVT(P)5 as the replacement for the LVT(3)C. The LVT(P)5 was twice as heavy and somewhat larger than its predecessor, but carried no more cargo. However, it had improved performance and, most important, was accompanied by several variants. These included the basic LVT(P)5 hull modified for recovery, command, engineer support and fire support. The latter, LVT(H)6, mounted a 105mm howitzer in a turret, a weapon fully compatible with divisional artillery at the time.

The appearance of the LVT(P)5 and its variants was followed by continuing research in the design of light-weight amphibians. But by then the Marine Corps was enthusiastically building on the experience it had gained in Korea with helicopters. The French, too, were acquiring a vertical assault capability, which they developed and refined during the Algerian War. The Marines, greatly interested in the use of helicopters for over-the-horizon amphibious assault operations, followed activities in Algeria and added those findings to their own studies at home. As a result, there was lessening interest and fewer funds for the further development of the amphibian tractor. This situation continued for more than a decade, although work was pursued on an LVT(P)X12.

The rearming of the United States for the Korean War and the retention of substantial military power after the Korean Armistice, resulted in a strengthened Marine Corps with three divisions and three aircraft Wings.

The 2nd Amphibian Tractor Battalion continued to serve with the 2nd Marine Division at Camp LeJeune. The 3rd Amphibian Tractor Battalion, reactivated for the Korean War in 1952, did not go overseas but remained at Camp Pendleton where it joined the 1st Marine Division when that unit returned from duty in the Far East. The 1st Amphibian Tractor Battalion, which had served throughout the Korean War, remained in the Far East where it joined the 3rd Marine Division when that unit was deployed first to Japan and later to Okinawa. These assignments remained valid until the Vietnam War, by which time the cargo units had long since been re-equipped with the LVT(P)5 and the armored units had been deactivated and their LVT(H)6s placed in storage.

The Vietnam War was fought with the LVT(P)5 and its variants. The 1st and 3rd Amphibian Tractor Battalions, each with two fifty-tractor companies, supported the 3rd and 1st Marine Divisions respectively. In addition, the 1st Armored Amphibian Tractor Company with three platoons of six LVT(H)6s each was activated, deployed, and its platoons assigned one each to support the two Marine Divisions ashore in Vietnam and one to serve afloat with the Special Landing Force. The amtracs in Vietnam were engaged in prolonged and highly varied service. They were used in most of the 62 landings made by the Marines along the southern coast of that country. They also served as armored personnel carriers ashore, ferried troops and supplies across inland waterways, conducted patrols both afloat and ashore, and even gained fame as infantry when assigned a tactical area of responsibility near the Demilitarized Zone below the 17th Parallel. While the helicopters engaged in vertical assaults and envelopments, and handled emergency resupply and evacuation missions, the amtracs were never at a loss for useful tasks to perform. Thus, while the helicopter gained well-deserved eminence in Vietnam, the amtrac lost none of the utility and versatility it had been displaying for a quarter of a century. This is attested by the citations and awards accorded to both the 1st and 3rd Amphibian Tractor Battalions with their armored amtrac platoons attached.[3]

In 1970, by which time the Marine units in Vietnam had been withdrawn and returned to their original bases, the Marine Corps decided to go into production with the LVT(P)X12.[3] This vehicle tested, modified and redesignated

the LVT(P)7 . . . first reached the Fleet Marine Force in 1972 in its cargo version. Soon after, recovery and command variants were available. However, no engineer or artillery successors to the LVT(E) or the LVT(H)6 were produced.

The AAV(P)7, as the amtrac is now named, is the first water-jet propelled amphibian vehicle produced. It is 30,000 pounds lighter than the LVT(P)5. It also has a hull designed to improve water propulsion and exploit its novel propulsion system. But while this has increased water speed to about six knots, its troop-carrying capacity is only 25 troops or 10,000 pounds of cargo. Despite this drawback, the vehicle performed well in the eleven years it remained in service. In 1983, a modernization and life extension program was instituted wherein a total of 853 cargo, 77 command and 54 recovery AAV(P)7 were converted to AAV 7A1. In addition, 333 new AAV(P)7A1 have been procured. These vehicles represent the current inventory, which will probably remain valid until the end of the century.

The helicopter has added a new dimension to the ship-to-shore operation, without lessening the role of the assault amphibian (AAV). In addition, the helicopter has stimulated the development of specialized amphibious ships needed as launch platforms. Among the first of these were the Amphibious Assault Helicopter Carrier (LPH) and the Amphibious Transport Dock (LPD). These were followed by Amphibious Assault Ships (LHAs) which combine the features of the earlier two types. The Dock Landing Ship (LSD) and the Tank Landing Ship (LST) have also been redesigned and their configurations, particularly that of the LST, are far different from their World War II predecessors. Even the venerable cargo ship, now identified as the LKA, has taken on a new look. And, most recently, the first of a new class of LHD has been launched.

With the helicopter, the Marine Corps acquired the long-sought capability of launching an amphibious assault from ships lying twenty or more miles offshore. But the helicopter has limitations and vulnerabilities that preclude its exclusive use for such purpose. Thus, the Marine Corps envisages the landing

Above left: *A column of AAVP7A1 launched at high speed, now making their way to the beach. (USMC)*

Above: *The LHA1 Tarawa, multi-purpose assault transport, which can carry nineteen CH–53 or 30 CH–46 helicopters plus various landing craft, with up to four LCUs in the well deck. The ship accommodates 1,700 troops and 170 officers with a 10,000 mile range at 20 knots. (USN)*

Right: *The LPH–10 Tripoli is an amphibious assault helicopter carrier able to embark 1,900 troops and 190 officers together with 20–24 CH–46, four CH–53 and four utility helicopters. It can sustain a 20-knot speed and is equipped with excellent medical facilities. (USN)*

Left: The LPD 12 Shreveport *is a 10,000-ton amphibious transport dock ship able to embark 900 troops and various landing craft types in a large well deck including up 28 LVTs. It has a helicopter platform but only a small hangar and thus while it can accommodate up to six CH–46s in the deck, it can only be for brief periods.* (USN)

Left: The dock landing ship (LSD 38) Pensacola *is an 8,600-ton vessel, capable of 20 knots, which can carry 300 troops and up to four new LCACs. Helicopters up to the CH–53 size can use the flight deck, but there are no on-board support facilites.* (USN)

Left: The Tank Landing Ship (LST 1185) Schenectady *is a 4,000-ton vessel which can sustain 20 knots and carry up to 400 troops as well as 500 tons of cargo. It uses a mobile aluminium ramp forward to offload vehicles onto a beach and can also carry four pontoon sections on its sides.* (USN)

assault as a co-ordinated action, where the vertical assault is complemented by an over-the-beach assault with troops carried in AAVs. The nature of the latter has not changed greatly from what it was during World War II. However, the technique of the high-speed underway launch of the AAV has reduced the need for concentrating ships close inshore, as well as positioning control ships off the landing beaches. This high-speed launch is accomplished by having the ships carrying the AAVs steam past the landing beach at maximum speed and as close as the hydrography permits, to drop off the AAVs at five-second intervals from the stern. The AAVs then make a quick run to the beach, vectored by the Remote Magnetic Heading System (RMHS).

Currently, yet another vehicle is being made available to the amphibious force commander for the execution of an assault landing. This is the Landing Craft, Air Cushion (LCAC), which can lift a rifle company, or 75 tons of cargo, and move it ashore at fifty knots through three-foot waves. The new LCAC, which can be accommodated aboard the LHA, LPD and LSD, improve the over-the-horizon assault landing capability now confined to the helicopter. The Navy plans to procure 90 of these vehicles by 1992, but this goal may well take longer to attain because of funding. Then, beyond the issue of numbers is the limited LCAC lift capability of amphibious shipping. Further, although a versatile vehicle, the LCAC remains sensitive to sea conditions and to terrain inland; it also offers a highly lucrative target to enemy guns and missiles. This suggests that the LCAC will complement rather than replace the other transport means currently used in ship-to-shore operations. In any event, the LCAC promises much added flexibility for the landing force, particularly in the ability to bring in heavy equipment with little delay. What this means in terms of the tactics and techniques to integrate current ship-to-shore capabilities with the added attributes of the air-cushion vehicle will have to await field experience. To that end, the Navy has recently organized two Assault Craft Units, ACU-4 on the Atlantic coast and ACU-5 on the Pacific coast, both of which are in the process of receiving their new machines.

Among other continuing efforts to facilitate the task of the amphibious force commander by providing him with more numerous and effective options for getting his landing force ashore, is the work being done to develop an advanced assault amphibian vehicle (AAAV).[4] The most serious limitation of the amtrac and AAV has always been its slow speed afloat. Even the AAV(P)7A1 is less than two knots faster than the LVT(3)s that went ashore on Okinawa in April 1945. The difficulty has always been that an amphibian vehicle is a compromise between the conflicting characteristics of land vehicles and boats, most often resulting in a degradation of the amphibian's performance afloat. The leap needed to put the AAV in the over-the-horizon landing is currently being addressed both as a modification of the existing AAV and as an entirely new hull. Several planing hull designs appear promising and there is every prospect for an early success. This will further ensure that the assault amphibian vehicle will continue to serve in the 21st century.

Yet another new amphibious vehicle intended to add mobility to the Marine Corps is the Light Armored Vehicle (LAV). This wheeled infantry fighting machine, armed with the 25mm gun and 40mm grenade-launcher or TOW, can

Left: This Marine Corps Light Armored Vehicle (LAV) is amphibious and was designed as a light reconnaissance vehicle for the transport of an infantry squad in a combat environment. The main armament is a 25mm gun. (USMC)

Left: An LCAC entering the well deck of an amphibious ship. (USN)

Left: AAVs dropping out of the well deck at five-second intervals while the ship maintains full speed. (USMC)

carry an infantry squad or can be modified as a mortar-carrier, a recovery vehicle, a command post or an anti-tank weapons platform. The LAV is amphibious, but is limited to calm water and cannot come ashore in any surf. It can, however, be slung under a CH-53 helicopter, or as many as four LAV can be embarked in an LCAC. The Marine Corps is organizing three battalions of LAVs, each equipped with 56 LAV-25s and sixteen LAV-Ls, the logistics variant. Each battalion is intended for the support of one Marine Division. The LAV have no more armor than an AAV and hence are probably better suited to reconnaissance and screening missions than to accompanying tanks in a mechanized advance. However, as is the case of the LCAC, it will require field experience to determine how best to integrate the LAV with the air cushion and assault amphibian vehicles and the helicopter in the dispersed landing operations of tomorrow.

In the domain of organization, the assault amphibian battalion has two or four companies each with 43 cargo AAV(P)7A1s, plus three command and one recovery AAV(R)7A1. This approximates the 50-vehicle company first adopted when the LVT(P)5 was introduced, and recalls the task-organized companies of World War II which were made up of about 50 amtracs, the number needed to land an assault infantry battalion. In like fashion, the present AAV company is intended to meet the landing requirements of an infantry battalion. It should be noted that with the advent of the helicopter, the convenience of having the AAV organization parallel that of the infantry is not as great as it was during World War II, since the current practice is to land two-thirds of the assault units by helicopter and one-third by AAV whenever this is feasible.

The Marine Corps now has the 1st Tracked Vehicle Battalion on Okinawa with two AAV and two tank companies for the support of the 3rd Marine Division. The 2nd AAV Battalion with four AAV companies supports the 2nd Marine Division at Camp LeJeune, North Carolina, while the 3rd AAV, similarly organized, provides the same support to the 1st Marine Division at Camp Pendleton, California. Finally, in the Reserve, the 4th AAV Battalion with two companies supports the 4th Marine Division. These, plus the assets in the Maritime Prepositioning Ships (MPS), make it evident that assault amphibian vehicles are available and ready to support a broad range of contingency operations.

The current capability of executing an amphibious assault from ships beyond the visual range of an enemy ashore depends upon the helicopter. This will soon be complemented by the air cushion vehicle. Then, it may be expected that the capability will be further increased by high-speed advanced assault amphibian vehicles (AAAV). Such vehicles, most likely using a planing hull design, will provide an amphibious force commander with multiple options for striking from over-the-horizon. This will permit a dispersal of ships that should reduce the vulnerability of an amphibious task force. But, whatever the situation, an amphibious operation, like all military operations, entails an element of risk. This was accepted by the Marines at Tarawa who crawled over fire-swept reefs in open amtracs protected only by a single piece of boilerplate; it will not be questioned by Marines today who stand prepared to make for other shores in helicopters, new air cushion landing craft or in the soon-to-be advanced assault amphibians that will carry on the legacy of the past half-century.

Appendix 1

Marine Corps Divisions

1st Marine Division
1st Marine Infantry Regiment (1st Marines)
5th Marine Infantry Regiment (5th Marines)
7th Marine Infantry Regiment (7th Marines)
11th Marine Artillery Regiment (11th Marines)
Combat and Service Support units

2nd Marine Division
2nd Marine Infantry Regiment (2nd Marines)
6th Marine Infantry Regiment (6th Marines)
8th Marine Infantry Regiment (8th Marines)
10th Marine Artillery Regiment (10th Marines)
Combat and Service Support units

3rd Marine Division
3rd Marine Infantry Regiment (3rd Marines)
9th Marine Infantry Regiment (9th Marines)
21st Marine Infantry Regiment (21st Marines)
12th Marine Artillery Regiment (12th Marines)
Combat and Service Support units

4th Marine Division
23rd Marine Infantry Regiment (23rd Marines)
24th Marine Infantry Regiment (24th Marines)
25th Marine Infantry Regiment (25th Marines)
14th Marine Artillery Regiment (14th Marines)
Combat and Service Support units

5th Marine Division
26th Marine Infantry Regiment (26th Marines)
27th Marine Infantry Regiment (27th Marines)
28th Marine Infantry Regiment (28th Marines)
13th Marine Artillery Regiment (13th Marines)
Combat and Service Support units

6th Marine Division
4th Marine Infantry Regiment (4th Marines)
22nd Marine Infantry Regiment (22nd Marines)
29th Marine Infantry Regiment (29th Marines)
15th Marine Artillery Regiment (15th Marines)
Combat and Service Support units

NOTES

(a) A Marine Infantry Regiment has three infantry battalions numbered 1st, 2nd and 3rd Battalions.

(b) A Marine Infantry Battalion under the World War II Tables of Organization had four lettered companies. Thus, Companies "A", "B" and "C" were the rifle companies of the 1st Battalion while Company "D" was the machine gun or weapons company of the same battalion. In like fashion, Companies "E", "F", "G", and "H" were in the 2nd Battalion while Companies "I", "K", "L", and "M" were in the 3rd Battalion. In the later part of WWII, the machine gun companies were broken up and the weapons assigned to the rifle companies. At that time the designations of "D", "H", and "M" companies disappeared.

(c) A Marine Artillery Regiment has four numbered artillery battalions each with three lettered artillery batteries.

Appendix 2

Amphibian Tractors in the Major Marine Corps Landings of World War II

	Number	Model
GUADALCANAL D-Day, 7 August 1942		
1st Amphibian Tractor Battalion	100	LVT(1)
Company "A", 2nd Amphibian Tractor Battalion	30	LVT(1)
(Note Only the 3rd Platoon landed and was re-embarked and withdrawn on 9 August)		
BOUGAINVILLE D-DAY, 1 November 1943		
3rd Amphibian Tractor Battalion	124	LVT(1)
TARAWA D-Day, 20 November 1943		
2nd Amphibian Tractor Battalion	75	LVT(1)
	50	LVT(2)
CAPE GLOUCESTER D-Day, 26 December 1943		
1st Amphibian Tractor Battalion	100	LVT(1)
	21	LVT(2)
ROI-NAMUR, NORTHERN KWAJALEIN ATOLL D-Day, 31 January 1944		
1st Armored Amphibian Tractor Battalion	75	LVT(A)1
4th Amphibian Tractor Battalion	100	LVT(2)
10th Amphibian Tractor Battalion	144	LVT(2)
SAIPAN D-Day, 15 June 1944		
2nd Armored Amphibian Tractor Battalion	70	LVT(A)4
	2	LVT(4)
708th Amphibian Tank Battalion, U.S. Army	16	LVT(A)4
	52	LVT(A)1
	3	LVT(2)
	1	LVT(4)
2nd Amphibian Tractor Battalion	85	LVT(2)
	33	LVT(4)
5th Amphibian Tractor Battalion	72	LVT(4)
10th Amphibian Tractor Battalion	91	LVT(2)
	9	LVT(4)
534th Amphibian Tractor Battalion, U.S. Army	35	LVT(2)
	64	LVT(4)
715th Amphibian Tractor Battalion, U.S. Army	67	LVT(2)
	33	LVT(4)
773rd Amphibian Tractor Battalion, U.S. Army	98	LVT(2)
	1	LVT(4)
GUAM W-Day, 21 July 1944		
1st Armoured Amphibian Tractor Battalion	75	LVT(A)1
	8	LVT(2)/(4)
3rd Amphibian Tractor Battalion, reinforced	193	LVT(2)/(4)
4th Amphibian Tractor Battalion, reinforced	180	LVT(2)/(4)

TINIAN J-Day, 24 July 1944

2nd Armored Amphibian Tractor Battalion	34	LVT(A)4
708th Amphibian Tank Battalion, U.S. Army	18	LVT(A)1
	14	LVT(A)4
2nd Amphibian Tractor Battalion, reinforced	96	LVT(2)
	40	LVT(4)
10th Amphibian Tractor Battalion, reinforced	104	LVT(2)
	32	LVT(4)
773rd Amphibian Tractor Battalion, reinforced, U.S. Army	92	LVT(2)
	44	LVT(4)
534th Amphibian Tractor Battalion, reinforced, U.S. Army	22	LVT(2)
	23	LVT(4)

PELELIU D-Day, 15 September 1944

3rd Armored Amphibian Tractor Battalion	24	LVT(A)1
	48	LVT(A)4
	2	LVT(2)/(4)
1st Amphibian Tractor Battalion	120	LVT(2)/(4)
6th Amphibian Tractor Battalion	80	LVT(2)/(4)
8th Amphibian Tractor Battalion	21	LVT(2)

IWO JIMA D-Day, 19 February 1945

2nd Armored Amphibian Tractor Battalion	68	LVT(A)4
	9	LVT(4)
3rd Amphibian Tractor Battalion	90	LVT(2)/(4)
5rd Amphibian Tractor Battalion	94	LVT(2)/(4)
10th Amphibian Tractor Battalion	94	LVT(2)/(4)
11th Amphibian Tractor Battalion	93	LVT(2)/(4)

OKINAWA L-Day, 1 April 1945

1st Armored Amphibian Tractor Battalion	70	LVT(A)4
	11	LVT(2)/(4)
3rd Armored Amphibian Tractor Battalion	75	LVT(A)4
	6	LVT(4)
1st Amphibian Tractor Battalion	108	LVT(3)
4th Amphibian Tractor Battalion	102	LVT(3)
8th Amphibian Tractor Battalion	106	LVT(4)
9th Amphibian Tractor Battalion	103	LVT(4)

(Note The two U.S. Army divisions landing over the southern Hagushi beaches had an equal number of amphibian tractor units.)

NOTE
Numbers of amtracs per battalion sometimes include maintenance and command vehicles and at other times only the troop-carrying or direct fire support amtracs are shown.

Notes and References

Preface
1. Smith, *Amphibious Tactics*, p .22.
2. Fuller, *The Second World War*, (1949), p. 207.

Chapter 1
1. Representative of those airmen were James Norman Hall and Charles Nordhoff who, after WWI, "yielded to a long suppressed desire to sail for the South Pacific Ocean". They settled in Tahiti in 1920 where, in the years that followed, they collaborated on many books set in the Pacific. The most famous of these comprised the Bounty Trilogy published from 1932 to 1934.
2. An excellent sampling of the writings on the Pacific are to be found among the 100 selections from 86 authors in Stroven and Day, *The Spell of the Pacific*, (1949)
3. Dilts, The *Pageant of Japanese History*, (1938) p. 258
4. Maki, *Japanese Militarism* (1945) Chapter VII p. 182–225 provides a highly useful background to the Pacific War.
5. This summary of Marine Corps history from the opening of Japan to the eve of WWII is elaborated upon in Moskin, *The U.S. Marine Corps Story*, (1977) pp. 281–467
6. Added details on American war planning prior to WWII are included in Spector, *Eagle Against the Sun*, (1985) pp 54–69.
7. Reber, *Huntington's Battalion, Forerunner of Today's FMF*, p. 73
8. Reber, *Pete Ellis, Amphibious Warfare Prophet*, p. 54
9. USMC OPlan 712H, p. 2. (War Portfolio)
10. Ibid. p. 5 (War Portfolio)
11. Ibid. p. 20, (OPlan)
12. Ibid, p. 22 (OPlan)
13. Ibid. p. 27 (OPlan)
14. Moskin, *The U.S Marine Corps Story*, (1977) p. 461
15. Hough, *Pearl Harbor to Guadalcanal*, (1958) p. 11

16. U.S. Navy General Order 241, 7 December 1933
17. Isely and Crowl, *The U.S. Marines and Amphibious War*, (1951) p. 34
18. U.S. Government, Joint Board of the Army and Navy, *Joint Overseas Expeditions*, (1933)
19. U.S.M.C. *Tentative Landing Operations Manual*, (1935) Chap I, p. 13
20. Ibid. Chapter II, p. 9.
21. Dyer, *The Amphibians Came to Conquer*, (1969) p. 203
22. Krulak, *First to Fight*, (1984) p. 89
23. Isely and Crowl, *The U.S. Marines and Amphibious War*, (1951) p. 68
24. Krulak, *First to Fight*, (1984) p. 90
25. Isely and Crowl, *The U.S. Marines and Amphibious War*, (1951) p. 68
26. Clifford, *Amphibious Warfare Development*, (1983) p. 116
27. Ibid. p. 118
28. Croizat, *The Marines' Amphibian*, (1953) p. 43
29. Krulak letter to author dated 10 October 1952
30. Krulak, *First to Fight* (1984) p. 104. The reference addresses the performance of the amphibian tractor and concludes that nothing among the deficiencies encountered "condems the basic idea"
31. Bailey, *Alligators, Buffaloes and Bushmasters*, (1986) p. 41

Chapter 2
1. Morison, *The Two Ocean War*, (1963) p. 86. See also Churchill, *The Second World War, Vol.III*, (1950) p. 118
2. Hough, *Pearl Harbor to Guadalcanal*, (1958) p. 86
3. Ibid. p. 207
4. Toland, *But Not in Shame*, (1961) p. 401
5. Zimmerman, *The Guadalcanal Campaign*, (1949) p. 2
6. Morison, *The Two Ocean War*, (1963) p. 140

7. Hough, Pearl Harbor to Guadalcanal (1958) p. 210. See also Agawa, *The Reluctant Admiral*, (1982) p. 304

8. Frank and Harrington, *Rendezvous at Midway*, (1968) p. 164

9. A summation of Japan's basic war plans are included in Dupuy and Dupuy, *Military Heritage of America*, (1956) p. 569–571

10. Hough, *Pearl Harbor to Guadalcanal*, (1958) p. 230

11. Ibid. pg. 64

12. Ibid. pg. 68

13. Ibid. pps. 35–46

14. U.S. Army, *Strategic Planning in Coalition Warfare*, p. 2

15. Dyer, *The Amphibians Came to Conquer*, (1969) footnote on p. 244 lists U.S. ground force deployments in the Pacific by mid-1942.

16. Hough, *Pearl Harbor to Guadalcanal*, (1958) p. 235

17. Ibid. p. 236 quotes JCS Joint Directive

18. Ibid. p. 239

19. Letter from Colonel John I. Fitzgerald USMC(ret) dated 10 November 1986

20. McMillan, *The Old Breed*, (1949) p. 18

21. The author, present as commander Co.A, 1st Amtrac Battalion attached to the 5th Marines recalls the event as intensely dramatic.

22. Zimmerman, *The Guadalcanal Campaign*, (1949) p. 14

23. Ibid. p. 27. The map referred to is in the Marine Corps archives

24. Interview with Ralph J. Fletcher and William Price incident to the reunion of the 1st Amtrac Battalion held at Annapolis, Maryland 22 August 1987

25. Hough, *Pearl Harbor to Guadalcanal*, (1958) p. 252

26. Unsigned memorandum to Co.A, 2nd Amtrac Battalion dated 3 Oct. 1945 entitled *Historical Data*

27. Hough, *Pearl Harbor to Guadalcanal*, (1958) p. 259 and Zimmerman, *The Guadalcanal Campaign*, (1949) p. 50

28. Zimmerman, *The Guadalcanal Campaign*, (1949) p. 62 provides details on the Brush patrol.

29. Griffith, *The Battle for Guadalcanal*, (1963) p. 78 provides excellent narrative of the Battle of the Tenaru.

30. The author had become friends with Ringer and Cory on the long trip to New Zealand on the WAKEFIELD and from Wellington to Guadalcanal when they all were aboard the AMERICAN LEGION. Further, Goettge had been a senior instructor at the Basic School when attended by the author. Finally, Kaempfer, who took the patrol out to locate Goettge was a college classmate. The disaster was thus a highly personal incident. Details are contained in Hough beginning on p. 281 and in McMillan starting on p. 52 which includes a verbatim interview with one of the three survivors of the ill-fated Goettge patrol.

31. By September, many of the 1st Battalion's amtracs were no longer serviceable. As a consequence, the author was transferred and assigned command of Co. M, the weapons company of the 3rd Battalion, 5th Marines where he met Lieutenant Barret, one of the more innovative of his platoon leaders.

32. Spector, *Eagle Against the Sun*, (1985) p. 214

33. Zimmerman, *The Guadalcanal Campaign*, (1949) The Vandegrift letter dated 5 December 1947 in the Preface.

Chapter 3

1. Letter from the Commandant of the Marine Corps to the Chief of Naval Operations dated 27 June 1941 and CNO endorsement to the Chief of the Bureau of Ships dated 15 July 1941 as cited in Hough (1958), p. 33.

2. The author was directed to report to the Division headquarters on the evening of 5 December where Colonel W. W. Wensinger, the G–3, showed him the activation order and stated he would assume command of the new 10th Amphibian Tractor Battalion (reinforced). For details on the tasks involved see battalion after-action report addresses to the Commanding General, 4th Marines Division dated 17 March 1944 in headquarters, Marine Corps archives.

3. Isely & Crowl, *The Marines and Amphibious War*, (1951) p. 166. Specific reference to the conduct of operations in the "middle Solomons" by South Pacific (Navy) forces under "general directives" of CINCSWPA (MacArthur) is found in Dyer, *The Amphibians Came to Conquer*, (1969) p. 448.

4. Kane and Shaw, *The Isolation of Rabaul*, (1958) p. 229, 252, 253, and 292.

5. Hough and Crown, *The Campaign of New Britain*, (1952) p. 18.

6. Ibid., p. 51

7. Ibid., p. 71

8. Stockman, *The Battle of Tarawa*, (1947), p. 2.

9. Letters from John F. Sullivan, former member of Co. "A", 2nd Amphibian Tractor Battalion, to author dated 9 and 10 October 1986.

10. Headquarters, 2nd Amphibian Tractor Battalion, *Special Action Report* addressed to the Commanding General, 2nd Marine Division, dated 23 December 1943.

11. Incidental details of the Tarawa operation were provided by Colonel Eugene A. Siegel, U.S. Marine Corps (ret) who received the Silver Star for his participation in the operation; interview, 29 July 1986.

12. The official history of the landing contained in Stockman (1947), is supplemented by much incidental detail in a lecture delivered by Brigadier General Merrit Edson to the staff officers at the Marine Corps Schools on 6 January 1944. A transcript of the general's remarks is available in the archives of the Marine Corps Historical Center, Washington, D.C. General Edson, who gained the Congressional Medal of Honor during the Battle of the Ridge of Guadalcanal, served as Chief of Staff, 2nd Marine Division at Tarawa.

13. Siegel Interview

14. Shaw, *Central Pacific Drive*, (1966) p. 97

Chapter 4

1. Initial planning considerations and decisions for the assult of the Marshall islands can be found in Shaw, Nalty and Turnbladh, *Central Pacific Drive*, (1966) pp. 117–123.

2. Crowl and Love, *Seizure of the Gilberts and Marshalls*, (1955) p. 219.

3. *Report on Operations of the 10th Amphibian Tractor Battalion During the FLINTLOCK Operation*, with four enclosures, dated 17 March 1944.

4. Quoted from *Medical Problems Incident to the Operation of Amphibian Tractors*, by Perry R. Ayres, Lieutenant (jg) Medical Corps,

U.S. Navy Reserve, Annex "B" to the Tenth Amphibian Tractor Battalion *Report on LVT–2 Activities in the Kwajalein Operation*, dated 17 February 1944.

5. Dod, *The War Against Japan*, (1966) p. 227.

6. Shaw, *Central Pacific Drive*, (1966) p. 234–236 and 239–42.

7. Ibid., p. 255–62.

8. Johnson, *The West Loch Story*, (1986)

9. Tenth Amphibian Tractor Battalion, *Report on Amphibian Tractors During FORAGER Operation to Date*, dated 3 July 1944.

10. Data on all amphibian tractor battalions participating in the invasion of Saipan are contained in a 21-page report prepared by Colonel W. W. Davies as Amphibian Tractor Officer, Northern Troops and Landing Force, *Report on Amphibian Tractors and Amphibian Tanks in FORAGER to Date*, 26 July 1944.

11. The concept of landing troops directly on the 0–1 line some 1,500 yards inland was unsuccessful for reasons detailed in Isely and Crowl (1951) p. 336

12. Carl W. Hoffman *Saipan* (1950) p. 58.

13. Shaw, *Central Pacific Drive*, (1966) p. 292.

14. G–2 Translation of Japanese document captured on Saipan dated 6 July 1944. In author's personal files.

15. Letter from Lieutenant Colonel Jack F. Tracy dated 5 September 1986 recalled details of the "volunteer detachment" that had been organized under Tracy's command by the author.

16. Eighth Amphibian Tractor Battalion, *State of Readiness Report on*, dated 31 May 1944.

17. Details on the organization of amphibian tractor units for the Peleliu operations are contained in multiple letters from Colonels Jack Fitzgerald and Albert Reutlinger addressed to the author in late 1986 and early 1987.

18. Letter from Colonel J. I. Fitzgerald dated 19 April 1986 in author files. Added information is contained on Garand and Strobridge, (1971) p. 270.

19. Morison, *The Two Ocean War*, (1963) p. 474.

20. Letter from Thomas F. Edwards to author dated 25 July 1987 enclosing *A Brief Historical Overview of the 727th Amphibian Tractor Battalion, U.S. Army Amphibious*

Forces, 1944–1945. An earlier letter from Edward L. Kitchens furnishes additional historical material on the 727th Battalion and includes a copy of a letter from General Walter Krueger, Commanding the Sixth Army dated 12 May 1945 on the *Service of the 727th Amphibian Tractor Battalion* which commends "the outstanding manner in which your organization has discharged its duties during its lengthy service with the Sixth Army."
21. Interview with Colonel Victor J. Harwick, August 1987. Colonel Harwich later landed on Okinawa as executive officer of the 1st Amphibian Tractor Battalion and later assumed command of the 2nd Amphibian Tractor Battalion on that island.
22. Louis Metzger, "Getting the Job Done with Un-artillery", p. 64.
22. RCT 23, 4th Mar Div (Rein), OPN PLAN NO 4–44, p. 4, paras X(2) and X(8).

Chapter 5
1. Bartley, *Iwo Jima, Amphibious Epic*, (1954) p. 5.
2. Ibid., p. 64.
3. 10th AmphTracBN, 4th MARDIV (Reinf) *Special Action Report, Iwo Jima Campaign* Enclosure A *Report of Medical Officer*, 1 April 1945.
4. Morison, *The Two Ocean War*, (1963) p. 521.
5. Frank and Shaw, *Victory and Occupation*, (1968) p. 103.
6. Third Armored Amphibian Battalion (Prov), Special Action Report, *The Nansei Shoto Operation* 1 July 1945 p. 13.
7. Ninth Amphibian Tractor Battalion, Special Action Report, *Okinawa Operation Phase II*, 1 July 1945, p. 1.

Chapter 6
1. Churchill, *The Grand Alliance,* Vol III, (1950), p. 579.
2. Dyer, *The Amphibians Came to Conquer*, (1969), p. 214.
3. Morison, *The Two Ocean War*, (1963), p. 354.
4. Colonel A. J. Harvey, OBE, RM, of the Royal Marines' Amphibious Warfare Centre at Fremington, provided the author with a summary of operations in Europe in which amphibian tractors were used. Colonel Harvey's letter of 5 January 1953 identified

the 79th Armoured Division as the unit "which initiated and operated all types of specialized armour in N.W. Europe". The history of that division provides amplifying details.
5. Churchill, *The Second World War, Vol. IV* (1950), p. 790
6. Fletcher, *Vanguard of Victory*, (1984), p. 177.

Chapter 7
1. The behind-the-scenes struggle to ensure wording in the National Security Act of 1947 to safeguard the existence of a Marine Corps "organized, trained and equipped to provide fleet marine forces of combined arms, together with supporting air components, for service with the fleet in the seizure or defence of advanced naval bases and for the conduct of such land operations as may be essential to the prosecution of a naval campaign" is detailed in Krulak (1984), pp. 17–51.
2. U.S. Government, Senate Committee on Naval Affairs, *Unification of the Armed Forces*, Hearings on S.2044, statement of General A. A. Vandegrift 79th Congress, 2nd session, 10 May 1946.
3. Montross and Canzona, *The Pusan Perimeter*, (1954) p. 9
4. Heinl, *Inchon*, (1967)
5. Headquarters, 7th Infantry Division, *Commendation* 5 October 1950, letter addressed to the Commanding Officer, 1st Amphibian Tractor Battalion through the Commanding General, X Corps. Author files.
6. The 1st and 7th Marines each were reinforced with a platoon of armored amphibians during the Chosin Reservoir operation. The cargo amtracs were retained under division control.
7. Testimony of General Omar Bradley before the House Armed Services Committee, 17 October 1949 as quoted in Krulak (1984) p. 71.
8. Moskin (1977) p. 750. The statement that the Marines were only attacking in another direction is attributed to Major General O. P. Smith who commanded the 1st Marine Division.
9. Letter from Eugene Alvarez to the author dated 7 March 1987 citing his experiences as an amtrac section leader whose unit was

assigned machine gun duties on the Imjin River defenses; author files.

10. Letter from Colonel John T. O'Neill to author dated 14 May 1987; author files.

11. The author was present on the occasion, having just returned to Paris from Marseilles where equal support for President Truman's commitment was manifest.

12. Hubert Ivanoff, "Le ler Escadron du ler Regiment Etranger de Cavalerie en Indochina 1947–1955" p. 243–261.

13. Letter from Hollis J. Dunn to author dated 1 July 1987 detailing initial deployments of amtracs to South Vietnam in March 1965 when he commanded Company "B" of the 1st Amphibian Tractor Battalion; author files.

14. Shulimson and Johnson *U.S. Marines in Vietnam*, (1978) p. 27.

15. Secretary of the Navy, Meritorious Unit Commendation to First Amphibian Tractor Battalion, Third Marine Division (Reinforced) for exceptionaly meritorious service from 5 November 1967 to 27 January 1968.

16. Secretary of the Navy, Meritorious Unit Commendation to First Amphibian Tractor Battalion Third Marine Division (Reinforced) for exceptionally meritorious service from 26 August to 9 December 1968.

17. First Amphibian Tractor Battalion, Part III *Sequential Listing of Significant Events*, March 1967.

Chapter 8

1. Isely and Crowl, *U.S. Marines and Amphibious War*, (1951) p. 521.

2. Secretary of the Navy, *History of the Landing Vehicle, Tracked*, Vol 1 Supplement, (1 December 1945). General Geiger's letter, addressed to Mr. S. L. Hanscom of the Food Machinery Corporation, is reproduced in full on p. IV of the report.

3. Donald A. Gressly, "A LVT for the Battlefield" November 1979, p. 66.

4. Interview with Lieutenant Colonel Richard E. Dietmeier, Officer-in-Charge, Amphibious Vehicle Test Unit, Camp Pendleton, California, July 1987.

Bibliography

Books

AGAWA, Hiroyuki. *The Reluctant Admiral: Yamamoto and the Imperial Navy*. Tokyo, 1982

BARTLEY, Whiteman S. *Iwo Jima, Amphibious Epic*. Washington, 1954

BENIS, Frank M. and SHAW, Henry I. *Victory and Occupation, Volume V: History of U.S. Marine Corps Operations in World War II*. Washington, 1968

BROWNE, Courtney. *Tojo, The Last Banzai*. London, 1967

CHURCHILL, Winston S. *The Second World War, Volume III: The Grand Alliance*, London, 1950; *Volume IV: The Hinge of Fate*. London, 1950

CLIFFORD, Kenneth J. *Amphibious Warfare Delelopment in Britain and America, 1920–1940*. New York, 1983

CROIZAT, Victor J. *The Brown Water Navy, The River and Coastal War in Indo-China and Vietnam, 1948–1972*. Poole, 1984.

CROWL, Philip A., and LOVE, Edmund G. *Seizure of the Gilberts and Marshalls: United States Army in World War II, The War in the Pacific*. Washington, 1955

DILTS, Marion M., *The Pageant of Japanese History*, (New York, Longmans Green and Co., 1949.)

DOD, Karl C. *The Corps of Engineers, The War Against Japan.* Washington, 1966

DUPUY, R. Ernest and DUPUY, Trevor. N. *Military Heritage of America*, (New York McGraw-Hill Book Company, Inc., 1956)

DYER, George C. *The Amphibians Came to Conquer: The Story of Admiral Richard Kelly Turner.* Washington, 1969

FLETCHER, David. *Vanguard of Victory: 79th Armoured Division.* London, 1984

FRANK, Pat, and HARRINGTON, Joseph D. *Rendezvous at Midway.* New York, 1968

FULLER, J. F. C. *The Second World War.* New York, 1949

GARAND, George W., and STROBRIDGE, Truman R. *Western Pacific Operations, Vol IV, History of U.S. Marine Corps Operations in WWII.* Washington, 1971

GRIFFITH, Samuel B. *The Battle for Guadalcanal.* New York, 1963

HOFFMAN, Carl W. *Saipan: The Beginning of the End.* Washington, 1950

HOUGH, Frank O., and CROWN, John A. *The Campaign on New Britain*, Washington, 1952 *Pearl Harbor to Guadalcanal, Volume 1 of The History of U.S. Marine Corps Operations in World War II.* Washington, 1958

ISELY, Jeter A., and CROWL, Philip A. *The U.S. Marines in Amphibious War.* Princeton, 1951

JOHNSON, William L. C. *The West Loch Story.* Seattle, 1986

KANE, Douglas T. and SHAW, Henry I. *The Isolation of Rabaul.* Washington, 1958

KRULAK, Victor H. *First to Fight.* Annapolis, 1984

MAKI, John M. *Japanese Militarism*, (New York, Alfred A. Knopf, 1945)

McMILLAN, George. *The Old Breed: A History of the First Marine Division in World War Two.* Washington, 1949

MONTROSS, Lynn, and CANZONA, Nicholas. *The Pusan Perimeter: U.S. Marine Operations in Korea, Volume I.* Washington 1954

MORISON, Samuel E. *The Two-Ocean War: A Short History of the United States Navy in the Second World War.* Boston, 1963

MOSKIN, J. Robert. *The U.S. Marine Corps Story.* New York, 1977

PROEHL, Carl W. (ed). *The Fourth Marine Division in World War II.* Washington 1946

RENTZ, John N. *Marines in the Central Solomons.* Washington, 1952

SHAW, Henry I. *et al. Central Pacific Drive: History of Marine Corps Operations in World War II, Volume III.* Washington, 1966

SHULIMSON, Jack., and JOHNSON, Charles M. *U.S. Marines in Vietnam, the Landing and Build Up, 1965.* Washington, 1978

SPECTOR, Ronald H. *Eagle Against the Sun.* New York, 1985

STOCKMAN, James R. *The Battle for Tarawa*, Washington, 1947

STROVEN Carl and DAY Grove A, *The Spell of the Pacific*, An Anthology of its Literature, (New York, The MacMillan Company, 1949)

TOLAND, John. *But Not in Shame: The Six Months After Pearl Harbor.* New York, 1961

VANDEGRIFT, A. A., and ASPREY, Robert. *Once a Marine.* New York, 1964

ZIMMERMAN, John L. *The Guadalcanal Campaign.* Washington, 1949

Documents

AYRES, Perry R. *Annex B: Medical Problems Incident to the Operation of Amphibious Tractors* in *Report on LVT–2 Activities in the Kwajalein Operation.* Washington, 17 Feb 1944

BAILEY, Alfred D. *Alligators, Buffaloes and Bushmasters*, Occasional Paper. Washington, 1986

DAVIES, W. W. *Report on Amphibian Tractors and Amphibious Tanks in FORAGER to Date.* Washington, U.S. Marine Archives, 26 July 1944

EIGHTH AMTRAC BATTALION. *State of Readiness Report.* Washington, US Marine Archives, 31 May 1944

FIRST AMTRAC BATTALION. Monthly Activities Report for March 1967, Part III, *Sequential Listing of Significant Events*, Washington, Us Marine Archives

NINTH AMTRAC BATTALION. Fleet Marine Force, Pacific. *Special Action Report Okinawa Operation, Phase III.* US Marine Archives, Washington, 1 July 1945

RCT 23, 4TH MARINE DIVISION. *OPN PLAN No 4–44*, In the Field. Washington, US Marine Archives, 16 May 1944

SECOND AMTRAC BATTALION. *Special Action Report*, Washington, US Marine Archives, 23 December 1943 – *Historical Data*. 3 October 1945

SECRETARY OF NAVY, Continuing Board for the Delevopment of the Landing Vehicle, Tracked, *History of the Landing Vehicle Tracked*, Vol. 1 Supplement. Washington, US Marine Archives, 1 December 1945

TENTH AMTRAC BATTALION. *Report on Operations During the FLINTLOCK Operation*. Washington, US Marine Archives, 17 March 1944 *Report on Amphibian Tractors During FORAGER Operation to Date*, Washington, US Marine Archives, 3 July 1944 *Special Action Report, Iwo Jima Campaign*, Enclosure A, *Report of Medical Officer*. Washington, US Marine Archives, 1 April 1945

THIRD ARMORED AMPHIBIAN BATTALION (Prov). Amphibian Tractor Group, Fleet Marine Force Pacific, *Special Action Report – The Nansei Shoto Operation*. Washington, US Marine Archives 1 July 1945

U.S. ARMY. *Landing Operations, Field Manual 31–5*, Washington, 1941

U.S ARMY, *Strategic Planning for Coalition Warfare*, (Department of the Army, Washington D.C., 1950)

U.S. GOVT, Joint Board of the Army and Navy. *Joint Overseas Expeditions*. Washington, US Marine Archives, 12 January 1933

Senate Committee on Naval Affairs, *Unification of the Armed Forces*, Hearings on S.2044, statement of General A. A. Vandegrift, 79th Congress, 2nd Session, 10 May 1946

U.S. JOINT CHIEFS OF SAFF. *Joint Directive for Offensive Operations in the Southwest Pacific Area*. Washington, US Marine Archives, 2 July 1942

U.S. MARINE CORPS. *Advanced Base Operations in Micronesia, Operations Plan 712H*. Washington, US Marine Archives, 1921; *War Portfolio*, Washington, US Marine Archives, 1921; *Tentative Landing Operations Manual*, Washington, US Marine Archives, 9 July 1935

U.S. NAVY, *Navy Department General Order 241*, Washington, 7 Dec 1933; *Fleet Training Publication – 167, Change No 1*, Washington, 1941

Articles

CROIZAT, Victor J. "The Marines' Amphibian", *Marine Corps Gazette*. June 1953

GRESSLY, Donald A. "An LVT for the Battlefield", *U.S. Naval Institute Proceedings*. November 1979

HEINL, Robert/D. "Inchon", *Marine Corps Gazette*, parts One and Two, Sept/Oct 1967

IVANOFF, Hubert, "Le ler Escadron du ler Régiment Etranger de Cavalerie en Indochine, 1947–1955", *Revue Historique des Armées, No Special 1981, Légion, Etrangère*, Paris

METZGER, Louis. "Getting the Job Done with Un-artillery", *Marine Corps Gazette*. November 1978

REBER, John J. "Huntington's Battalion was The Forerunner of Today's FMF", *Marine Corps Gazette*, (Nov. 1979).

REBER, John J., "Pete Ellis, Amphibious Warfare Prophet, *Marine Corps Gazette*, (Nov. 1977)

SMITH, Holland M. "Amphibious Tactics", *Marine Corps Gazette*. October 1946

Index